Student Research and Report Writing

Student Research and Report Writing

From Topic Selection to the Complete Paper

Gabe T. Wang and Keumjae Park

WILEY Blackwell

This edition first published 2016
© 2016 John Wiley & Sons Ltd

Registered Office
John Wiley & Sons Ltd, The Atrium, Southern Gate, Chichester, West Sussex, PO19 8SQ, UK

Editorial Offices
350 Main Street, Malden, MA 02148-5020, USA
9600 Garsington Road, Oxford, OX4 2DQ, UK
The Atrium, Southern Gate, Chichester, West Sussex, PO19 8SQ, UK

For details of our global editorial offices, for customer services, and for information about how to apply for permission to reuse the copyright material in this book please see our website at www.wiley.com/wiley-blackwell.

The right of Gabe T. Wang and Keumjae Park to be identified as the authors of this work has been asserted in accordance with the UK Copyright, Designs and Patents Act 1988.

Library of Congress Cataloging-in-Publication Data applied for.

Hardback   9781118963906
Paperback   9781118963913

A catalogue record for this book is available from the British Library.

Cover image: © Stuart Dee / Getty

Set in 11/13 Dante MT Std by Aptara

Printed in Singapore by C.O.S. Printers Pte Ltd

1   2016

Contents

Chapter 4: Reviewing the Literature   58

Chapter 5: Research Questions and Methods   81

Chapter 6: Steps of Quantitative and Qualitative Research Designs   105

Chapter 7: Writing a Research Proposal   133

Chapter 8: Practical Issues While Carrying Out Research   150

Chapter 9: Quantitative Data Analysis   173

Acknowledgments

During the process of writing this book, many people have helped us in various ways. We deeply appreciate their help. First, we would like to thank the anonymous reviewers who have provided us with many insightful comments and constructive suggestions. These comments have inspired us in various ways and we have incorporated many of their suggestions in our writing. It is these comments and suggestions that have improved the quality of this book.

Second, we are indebted to several colleagues at William Paterson University of New Jersey, who provide feedback on our manuscript at various stages while we were writing the book. Professor Peter Chen at the Department of Mathematics provided good comments and suggestions for Chapter 9. Anthony Joachim at the Cheng Library offered many valuable suggestions for Chapter 3. We thank Professor Carol Frierson-Campbell of Music Department for her constructive comments on Chapter 1. Special thanks are also extended to Professor Mary Chayko of Rutgers University, and Professor Janet Ruane of Montclair State University. Their reviews of multiple chapters of our manuscript were instrumental in shaping the book the way it is now.

Finally, we would like to thank the wonderful staff at Wiley. Our editor Justin Vaughan has been most supportive and patient throughout the entire process. Our project editor Ben Thatcher has guided us through the final stages of manuscript preparation and the production process. Lisa Sharp has provided help with many administrative issues.

Our deepest gratitude goes to our families for their love and support.

List of Boxes

Box 1.1 What Is Research?
Box 1.2 Basic Terms in Social Science Research.
Box 2.1 Ways to Narrow Down a Topic Idea.
Box 2.2 A Feasible Topic.
Box 3.1 Popular Article Databases for Social Science Research.
Box 4.1 A Sample Reference List in Various Citation Styles.
Box 5.1 Quantitative and Qualitative Data.
Box 5.2 Summary on Data Collection Strategies.
Box 8.1 Sample Time Management Planner.
Box 10.1 Web Resources for Qualitative Software Programs.
Box 10.2 Open Coding: An Example.
Box 10.3 Second-Level Coding: Merging Codes.

List of Figures and Tables

Figures

Tables

About the Website

The companion website for Student Research and Report Writing: From Topic Selection to the Complete Paper includes a number of resources created by the author that you will find helpful.

Please go to:
www.wiley.com\go\wang\researchreportwriting

For students:
- Links to online video resources

For instructors:
- PowerPoint lecture slides

Chapter 1

Introduction: Start Your Research Journey

If you have picked up this book, you are likely to be a student of the social sciences, business, or education. You may be thinking about original research for a major paper, for an undergraduate seminar class, or for a bachelor's or master's thesis. Or you may be in a practicum course in social science research and writing (often called "Senior Seminars" in many U.S. universities). You probably have already learned about different theories and have taken research methods courses in your discipline. Perhaps, you feel that you know a fair amount about research terminology, but you might not have had practice designing and carrying out original research of your own. Or you may be simply overwhelmed by the magnitude of the work ahead and do not know exactly where to start. You know what you need to produce in the end but are anxious about how to get it done. If this is the case, this book is for you.

Conducting social science research is a journey that requires a step-by-step blueprint and a time-management plan. Most people today rely on a GPS (Global Positioning System) device or internet map services when they drive to unfamiliar locations. We hope this book works as your GPS research guide, a one-stop shop of practical help for you in each step of your research project, from coming up with a research topic to completing the report. Most chapters provide you with exercises corresponding to each research phase, which will help you complete the work effectively, and work out solutions to problems you may have.

What Is Research?

Before you get on the road, let's first talk about the definition of the term which we will use throughout the book. What is research? These days "research" has become

Student Research and Report Writing: From Topic Selection to the Complete Paper, First Edition. Gabe T. Wang and Keumjae Park. © and Published 2016 by John Wiley & Sons, Ltd.

a part of our everyday life. For example, when you ask someone in business about a new product or a new service, he/she may reply, "let me research that for you." As a consumer, you do research on a daily basis, whether it is the price of a car, which tablet device to purchase, or opportunities in the job market. In these cases, research refers to gathering available information so that you may make informed choices. The use of the internet has made this practice so common and routine that even children search for toys on the internet and compare various gadgets they can find before asking their parents to buy them.

On other occasions, you may be asked to do "formal" research that involves more systematic and conscious processes of gathering information, careful evaluation of evidence, and a methodical synthesis of the information gathered. Examples include doing research for term papers in undergraduate and postgraduate courses, writing a thesis to satisfy a requirement of a bachelor's or master's degree, or writing scholarly papers for publication or conference presentations. Or at work you may be asked for a market analysis or a needs assessment. The main difference between the casual everyday research you do as a consumer and the more formal research is the extent of the information to be considered and the methods to be employed in analyzing the information. For the everyday research, you may look up a few pieces of information you can easily find on the internet or from a few people around you; but more formal research will require you to examine issues thoroughly and draw careful conclusions. Formal research requires systematic methods of investigation and a critical analysis of evidence to discern credible and not-so-credible knowledge.

We will use the term "research" with specific meanings in this book and we want to clarify it here. When we refer to "research," it will involve: 1) questions that are academic in nature and advance a scientific understanding of human society or human behavior; 2) systematic and evaluative screening and collection of information on a topic; and 3) tasks of systematic and careful data analysis and report-writing. It is the type of research that students conduct for educational purposes and to gain and produce knowledge in academic settings.

Box 1.1   What Is Research?

In this book, we will focus on the following type of research:

- Asking questions that are academic in nature and advance a scientific understanding of society and human behaviors;
- Requiring systematic and evaluative screening and collection of information;
- Involving systematic and careful data analysis and report-writing.

Today, there is a growing expectation for student research. Students like you are often trained and required, as part of the university curricula, to conduct research and write papers or theses that meet the professional standards of the discipline. A good reason behind this trend is that research skills are increasingly expected in the workplace worldwide. Doing empirical research enables you to acquire many valuable skills. It requires you to raise appropriate questions; assess existing information; set goals and make plans to meet the goals; collect, analyze, and interpret data; and use data in a meaningful and appropriate way. The process requires systematic project management skills to allocate time, resources, and handle unexpected problems. Your research experiences will provide you with rich, in-depth learning, which many of your future employers will highly value. With advances in technology you have greater access to the tools of field research and to a broader population whom you can engage in your research. The continuing efforts of colleges and universities to establish networks with professional and local communities are increasing opportunities for your learning experiences in the real world.

What Type of Research Project Do You Have?

We have designed this book to guide a journey of an empirical research, mostly involving observations and analysis of empirical data. Empirical research is an effective way of doing research and it is widely employed by social scientists, especially in North America. Empirical research is often based on the principle of positivism, or the pinning down of social world into tangible data and reasoning with them to explain social phenomena. But other empirical research is rooted in different traditions; for example, anthropologists often analyze their empirical data through interpretation of qualitative (narrative) data, instead of quantitative data. Your particular research will be guided by requirements of different research methods, depending on the nature of your assignment/project; some will involve empirical research of various types, and others may be mostly based on bibliographical research. Though not an exhaustive list, some possible types of assignment you may have are the following:

Empirical Research Project with Original Data Collection
Your project may require a collection of original empirical data. Empirical research projects can vary in their scope and magnitude. They range in lengths, from thirty-page journal article style papers to book lengths projects such as doctoral dissertations. Regardless of the scope and lengths, empirical research projects follow a similar process. There is a truly wide range of different kinds of empirical research project as we will discuss in chapters of this book. They may use numerical data or text data. They may use large or small sized samples. They may focus on one group or setting, or on the general population. Regardless of the styles, a successful empirical project will depend on clearly defined topics or problems, thorough and careful reviews of the literature, well-planned research methods to ensure validity and reliability of the data, proper applications of analytic techniques, and careful interpretation of the results of the analysis.

Empirical Research Project with Secondary Data

Everything mentioned above is also applicable to empirical research projects using secondary data, except that this latter uses data already collected by someone else. Thus, your task will include locating and extracting most suitable data sets for your project, instead of designing original sampling and data collection strategies. Using secondary data has its advantages and disadvantages. When you use secondary data collected by government agencies or large institutes, you are likely to work with data obtained from large representative samples; this will increase your ability to generalize the findings from your study to a larger population. One of the main disadvantages of using secondary data is that the variables in the data set may not be the perfect measures for the themes and concepts you wish to investigate. Whether you can use secondary data for your project depends on the requirement of the assignment given to you. You should consult your project supervisor or faculty mentor before you make your decision.

Synthesized Literature Reviews or Review Essays

Some of you may work on an assignment based on bibliographical research without a requirement for empirical data collection. If it is the case, your assignment may be literature reviews. Many undergraduate course assignments are different versions of literature reviews. Synthesized literature reviews provide a comprehensive and organized overview of the studies focusing on a topic area in social sciences. For this type of assignment, you need to identify the relevant literature, review the studies carefully, and produce a synthesized assessment of the field of study. A successful execution of this type of assignment depends on 1) the quality of information search which successfully identifies the right range of relevant literature and produces a near-exhaustive list of the literature on the topic, 2) your ability to evaluate the studies' validity, relevance, and significance in the subfield, and 3) your ability to create an organized report, or synthesis which delineates agreements and contradictions, well-explored themes and overlooked ones, over-studied population and under-studied ones, and tested and un-tested theories. A good literature review project can also suggest research directions and questions to explore further, based on the "gaps and voids" identified in the existing literature.

Theoretical Essays

Theoretical essays are somewhat different from literature reviews, as they aim to do more than synthesize what is known, but to extend theoretical ideas further. Theoretical projects are primarily based on bibliographical research, just like literature review assignments, but they will focus on theories and theoretical concepts in the literature. For successful theoretical projects, you will not only need to have a comprehensive understanding of related theoretical traditions, but also be able to reflect and evaluate clarity and usefulness of theoretical concepts, internal logic of theoretical claims, and the applicability of a theory in light of social reality. Theoretical essays typically do not require empirical data but they use examples from empirical reality or cite results from empirical studies to support and illustrate particular theoretical points.

Not only may your projects be of different kinds of assignments, but also they may ask fundamentally different kinds of questions. Today, social science research is guided by a multitude of different perspectives and philosophical traditions, and increasingly becomes diverse and inter-disciplinary. This means that the research methods and the process of deciphering meanings and uncovering theories have become more malleable and creative. There is still a common emphasis on systematic exploration and investigation into the inquiry. Consider the two major paradigms or perspectives below, which have influenced social sciences, and find out which approximately approach your own project ideas.

Positivism

Social sciences have come a long way since the earlier days of Auguste Comte (1798–1857) who was committed to the enterprise of discovering "scientific laws" to explain human history, or Max Weber's idea of excluding emotions or value-judgments (except for when choosing problems to investigate) in social science investigations, which some people call "instrumental positivism" (Bryant 1985: 137). But the influence of positivism is clear in many research projects, in their assumption that observations using tangible and measurable measures are the foundation of knowledge and that they can accurately reflect social reality. The importance of measures, or the emphasis on validity and reliability of measures, as a way to uncover "objective" knowledge, is implied in a lot of investigative traditions in social sciences, especially in quantitative studies. In this tradition, research projects are likely to assume that there are pieces of social reality that are "out there" to be discovered, attempt to develop measures to capture those pieces, and examine what parts of social reality cause another.

Constructionism

The constructionist view is very different from the positivist view in that it views social reality and human conditions as something produced, created, and "constructed" by members of society. Rooted in epistemology, or the study of knowledge formation, constructionism in social sciences focuses on uncovering meanings in human activities and social reality. According to this tradition, social reality is always in motion, and it is experienced differently by different individuals. Therefore, research in this tradition strives to describe what people experience from their own perspectives, while carefully focusing on the meaning people give to their experiences and observations. Constructionist views are found in several different methodological traditions, including hermeneutics, phenomenology, and anthropological "thick descriptions" (Bernard 2002).

It is impossible to produce all-encompassing guides for the variety of assignments you have; we believe this speaks for the diversity within social science research and the potential of creative and yet systematic research. What we attempt to lay out in this book is a guided road map, focusing on the *principles of systematic and organized investigation*, which you can use creatively and flexibly to suit the purpose of your unique research project. Furthermore, this book will focus on the practical problems of your research.

What Are the Procedures for Scientific Research?

The premise of social sciences is that a systematic investigation ensures our chance of obtaining accurate knowledge about social reality. Formal research using scientific methods usually follows common step-by-step procedures. These procedures ensure high quality research and valid and reliable findings. The flow chart below illustrates the common procedures of social science research.

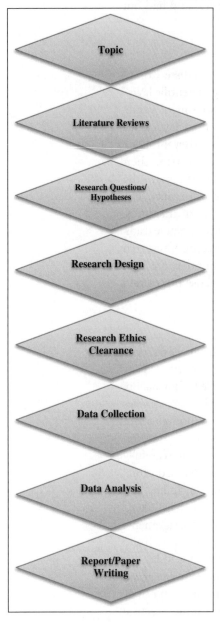

Figure 1.1   Process of Scientific Research.

As you can see in the diagram, the systematic research process begins with a carefully selected topic followed by a thorough and critical review of existing knowledge on the topic, a process we call "literature reviews." At the end of the literature review, you will be able to find a "niche" or some themes and questions about your topic that you feel you need to investigate further. These will become a set of specific hypotheses or research questions for your study. Then, you may design your research, a process which includes careful planning of the sample size and sampling methods, decisions on data collection methods (e.g., questionnaire surveys, experiments, in-depth interviews, or participant observations), construction of measures for the concepts, and ethical concerns for safeguarding your participants. You will then put all of these plans together into a research proposal. If your research involves human subjects or animals, it should be approved by the committee in charge of reviewing research ethics. Of course, your research proposal should also be approved by the professor, tutor, or supervisor with whom you are working. You will then collect data according to your research design. After collecting data, you will analyze and summarize them and write a report or thesis to share your findings. *Student Research and Report Writing: From Topic selection to the Complete Paper* will follow these steps and guide you to complete a quality research project and finish writing your report or thesis.

Will There Be Bends and Detours in the Research Process?

As it is often the case with real life travels, research journey is not neatly streamlined like the above diagram. The diagram is meant to illustrate *what it is like to take a systematic approach to a query*, if you wish to pursue valid and reliable answers to your questions. But, even in this systematic approach, your research journey in reality will be bumpy and messy. Just like a real life journey with roadblocks and traffic jams, you will encounter difficulties, problems with no clear answers, and changes and dead ends in your thinking. You may begin with an idea but as you read and investigate more, you may find yourself steering toward new directions. Consider that there are many different alternative routes to reach a destination; some of the detours may actually bring you back to where you started! Don't feel defeated if this happens; we assure you that these are frequently and naturally occurring aspects of social science research. Remember that, even if you are at the starting point again, you now have many more insights which you gained during your detour. This is why people consider research as an "iterative," or repeating, process. It is also reflexive, as you will constantly make adjustments to your research plans in light of new issues you learn in the process of research. In fact, research you do as a student will look more like Figure 1.2.

How to Embark on Your Research Journey

When you engage in a research project, you set out to explore a curious social phenomenon, start getting information to answer the questions you have, or verify a theory that you have learned. Here we compare research to a journey; it is a path to the unknown and an exciting process of discovery. Like a journey, you will need some background information to decide on a destination (i.e., select a topic), prepare a road map and a plan (i.e., write a proposal of your research designs), and make observations during your journey (i.e., collect data). You are likely to have some type of log or chronicle when you travel, such as photographing, blogging, or writing in a journal, and in the end, you will probably want to share with other people what you discover and experience. Likewise, you may write research journals to keep records of your study, and are most likely to write a report at the end of your research to share your findings with other students, colleagues, or your faculty mentors. Just as you need to pack your suitcases for a journey, there are a few things you may want to have before embarking on a research journey.

Curiosity
Research starts with a desire to learn about something new or to better understand a complicated problem or social issue. Your research will typically start with a question or set of questions. Questions in social sciences frequently involve the causes and consequences of a social issue or a pattern of human behavior. For example, what causes some students to drop out of high school? What programs are effective in helping children eat more fruits and vegetables? Why does random violence occur? What factors allow some people to feel happier than others? How can we better counsel people with suicidal thoughts? How can we bring clean water into remote villages in sub-Saharan Africa? Are there

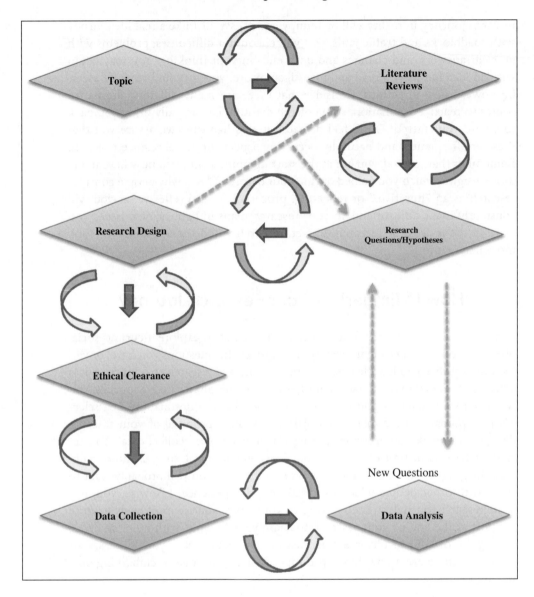

Figure 1.2   Iterative Process of Social Science Research.

effects of the "digital" gap between children of higher income families and lower income families? What programs will help girls to stay in school in rural areas of Pakistan? Why are public opinions on the death penalty different in different countries?

Questions like these are rooted in your interests in patterns of human behavior, social phenomena, and the relationship between different aspects of society. Other questions concern ways to improve people's experiences or the effectiveness of social programs and institutions. Other times, you may be curious about new patterns of activities and trends in society. All these issues are fine research topics. An inquisitive mind and an interest in exploring the unknown are probably what will trigger your research. Your personal interests and passion for a question is very important prerequisite for the research journey. Keep in mind research requires constant questioning and probing along the way. Curiosity is something you will carry with you throughout your research journey.

Research Skills

We assume that you have already received some training in social science research skills and have learned the procedures for conducting research, including reviewing the literature, constructing research questions or hypotheses, designing ethical and methodical research plans, collecting and analyzing data. You may have taken research methods or data analysis courses but may have forgotten some of what you learned. You will need to dust off your knowledge and research skills and be ready to apply them to a real life research setting. In this book, we want to refresh your memory on the research methods, and help you further to navigate the process of research and resolve the practical problems you may encounter.

If you extend the metaphor of journey and think of the typical research methods and data analysis books as more comprehensive series on the different methods and destinations of world travels, this book will serve as your on-the-spot guide book. Like a travel guide that follows the different steps of your journey – how to get from the airport to downtown, which hotels are in your price range, or what sights are must-sees – this book will provide you with help when you come to a difficult point of your research journey or when you are likely to get lost. We hope that you will find in this book some specific information on practical problems, which you may not find in general methods and data analysis texts.

Since there are some basic terms we need to use throughout this research guide, we summarized in Box 1.2 a few "must-know" terms in social science research.

Box 1.2   Basic Terms in Social Science Research.

Here are some basic research terms which will be used throughout the book. These terms are explained in greater detail in the chapters in which they are discussed:

Variable: It refers to logical groupings of attributes. A quality or characteristic that varies across different cases. For example, suppose your research question is whether getting enough sleep affects academic performance/grades of teenagers. In this case, sleep hours per night, and academic performance are both variables.

Hypothesis: A testable expectation, or a prediction, about a relationship between two variables. The prediction is usually based on a theory. For example, a hypothesis for the above research question could be: Insufficient sleep time negatively affects academic performance of teenagers.

Independent variable: The cause in a predicted relationship between two variables. The variable that is logically prior to, and is expected to lead to a variation in the other variable in an expected relationship between two variables. In the above example, the independent variable is "sleep hours per night."

Dependent variable: The outcome or effect in a predicted relationship between two variables. The variable that is expected to be affected by the other variable in a paired relationship. In the above example, the dependent variable is "academic performance."

Conceptualization: The process whereby vague or imprecise ideas or notions develop into specific and precise concept. For example, your observations of treating people of other races differently or inappropriately gradually develop into the concept of "racial discrimination."

Operationalization: The identification of observable and measurable indicators that can be used in empirical research to measure abstract concepts. For example, you may ask and use the information about students' church attendance and their participation in church related activities to measure the concept, "religiosity."

Indicators: The specific observations that reflect an abstract concept or questions to be asked in order to observe and record an abstract concept. For example, you may ask students' grade point average, class attendance, and time spent on study to measure their academic performance.

Validity: The extent to which a measure accurately measures what it is intended to measure, or the extent to which findings of research reflect the social reality it intends to describe. For example, students' grade point average (GPA) is a more valid measurement of their academic achievement than students' study hours.

Reliability: Whether or not repeated use of a measure yields consistent outcomes. The degree to which you can trust that a measure will produce consistent answers or scores each time.

Levels of measurement: Different types of mathematical qualities of measures. Depending on whether the measure has only qualitative values or highly quantitative values, nominal level, ordinal level, interval level and ratio level are differentiated.

Unit of analysis: The units that are the focus of your research. This could be individuals, schools, business organizations, paragraphs in a text, stories, blog entries, cities, countries, and so on.

Data analysis: Systematic summary and examination of collected data in order to draw valid and reliable conclusions from empirical research.

How Will This Book Help You?

Student Research and Report Writing: From Topic Selection to the Complete Paper is a comprehensive, yet concise, all-in-one guide for carrying out research *and* writing an academic paper that reports on the findings from your research. Conducting research and writing reports are connected phases of one research process. Thus, you will find that we try to maintain a balance between research and the writing phases of the project. Now that you have already begun on your research road trip, you may be working away from your classroom settings and away from routine discussions with your professor, tutor, or supervisor. Even if you understand that you are in charge of this process, you may be feeling nervous, like a novice driver behind the wheel for the first time.

We hope to be a guiding voice on your dashboard in this adventure as an independent researcher. We want to tell you upfront that this book will not teach research methods in their various and encyclopedic details. But it will aid students like you, who already have project goals and questions in mind, to make progress. Our descriptions of each stage of the research process are geared toward providing ideas to resolve practical problems and challenges that you may encounter as a student researcher. Keep in mind that you may feel that you need to know more in-depth details about a particular research method at some point; in such case, you should still consult traditional research methods textbooks as supplementary sources.

The goal is to move forward with your own research project as you progress through the chapters in this book. We have included exercises or worksheets for most chapters, corresponding to the tasks you will need to complete at that stage of the research procedure. The exercises break down your project into smaller steps and help you make steady progress through the research and writing processes. You should not feel that you need to complete all exercises in each chapter. We offer a few different styles of exercise for different kinds of projects and thinking styles. We suggest that you choose the exercises that will work for you best.

If you are working closely with a project supervisor, you may select together what will work for your project. For example, Chapter 2 on selecting topics is followed by a series of exercises designed to help you with brainstorming. Exercises 2.1, 2.2, and 2.3 are all geared toward getting you started on some topic ideas. You may choose just one of these three to come up with a topic you are interested in. Then, you can develop your ideas further by doing Exercise 2.4 or 2.5. These exercises will assist you in developing a general idea into more specific set of key themes or questions. We designed the exercises and worksheets in later chapters to build on your work from earlier chapters. If you follow the cumulative nature of the exercises and add to and revise the work done in previous chapters, you are likely to have a completed project by the end of this book.

The format of each chapter is based on typical questions students have asked us over the many years of our teaching. You will find guidelines to address those questions in the chapter. We hope the book will provide a step-by-step road map toward a successful completion of your project.

How Is This Book Organized?

The 11 chapters of *Student Research and Report Writing: From Topic Selection to the Complete Paper* follow the process of your actual research project step-by-step, from topic selection to the complete research report. Most chapters are accompanied by some exercises or worksheets. Knowing and doing are sometimes two different things. You may find it challenging to apply what you know about the research process to the project you want to get done. The exercises in each chapter will help you to work through such challenges.

Chapter 1 helps you demystify research, which we believe will make you more confident to start your research. At the same time, this chapter provides you with a brief introduction to the content, structure, and features of the book.

Chapter 2 assists you in selecting your research topic. The chapter starts with the definition of a research paper, moves on to the problems in your topic selection, and finishes with a consideration about what would make a good topic. It also discusses how to make your topic manageable. The exercises of the chapter will assist you not only in selecting your topic but also help you finalize your decision on the selected topic.

Chapter 3 describes different methods of searching for available information. The internet has given you easy access to an abundance of information, but this comes with the challenge of distinguishing accurate and reliable sources of knowledge from dubious ones. The chapter discusses these issues and points out practical ways of searching for the information you need. We also show you how to search for information using journal article databases. Exercises for this chapter will enable you to conduct a more efficient and effective information search.

Chapter 4 walks you through the process of a literature review, a task many students find difficult and confusing. This chapter discusses the nature and purpose of literature reviews and tells you how to identify which literature to review. The chapter focuses on how to evaluate and synthesize your topic's literature. The last part of this chapter discusses how to use the literature you have reviewed to rationalize your research and develop specific research questions. Finally, we provide some practical guidance for writing effective literature reviews for your research proposal. The exercises for this chapter will help you accomplish these tasks.

Chapter 5 covers research questions and methods. It starts with a discussion of research questions and moves on to the research methods and the characteristics of quantitative and qualitative research. The chapter summarizes a variety of research methods and discusses the strengths and weaknesses of each method. These discussions should enable you to make informed decisions about how to select a method for your particular research project. After the discussion of methods, the chapter considers how to use theories in research, how to look into potential problems in your research, and how to work out remedies for the potential problems of your research. The chapter also discusses the ethical issues in research and informs you the principles that you should follow in dealing with the ethical problems. The exercises for this chapter will also help you identify the goals and orientation of your research project.

Chapter 6 has two sections that cover quantitative and qualitative research designs. The first section starts with a discussion of research questions, independent and dependent variables, and moves on to the selection of study population, unit of analysis, and sample size. Then, the section continues the discussion on operationalization of abstract concepts, level of measurement, the development of survey questionnaires, and quantitative data analysis. The second section describes the purpose of qualitative research and discusses several qualitative data collection strategies including interviews, observations, and focus-groups. The exercises for this chapter will also help you design your research project and develop survey questionnaires and interview schedules.

Chapter 7 discusses research proposal writing. A research proposal is often necessary to get approval for your research project from your supervisors and/ or university. Your research proposal can also create a clear road map for your data collection. The chapter tells you what you should include in your proposal. It also explains how to write a clear introduction, literature review, research method, schedule, potential problems and remedies. The chapter reviews citation and reference formats for your proposal. Standard styles for listing references typically used in social sciences are discussed (e.g., American Psychological Association (APA) style, Chicago Manual of Style (CMS), American Sociological Association (ASA) style). The exercises for this chapter will help you outline your proposal and provide a self-evaluation of your written proposal.

Chapter 8 discusses practical issues while carrying out your research. It focuses on practical issues normally ignored in research method textbooks. These issues include scheduling your research project and carrying it out on time, establishing and maintaining communication with your project supervisors, getting approval from your university to collect data, and handling relevant ethics issues related to your research. It also discusses common practical problems in qualitative and quantitative data collection and how to conduct your questionnaire surveys and field research effectively. Exercises for this chapter will show you how to construct a timeline for your research and how to keep research journal for your filed research.

Chapter 9 discusses quantitative data analyses. This chapter is designed to help you doing statistical data analysis, including how to select the appropriate data analysis procedures. The chapter starts with coding and data entry, moves onto data analyses, including simple descriptive analysis, cross tabulations and Chi-square tests, correlations, linear regression and multiple regression analyses. The chapter moves onto t-tests and one-way analysis of variance. We will discuss these data analyses using Statistical Package for Social Sciences (IBM SPSS 22) software since it is one of the most widely used computer tools in the social sciences. After the discussion of each computer data analysis procedure, we will show you how to do the actual data analysis, how to cite data analysis results, how to interpret the data, and what to present in your research report.

Chapter 10 discusses qualitative data analyses. It covers important issues in qualitative analysis, including the purpose of qualitative data analysis, where to start, the role of interpretation, the characteristics of qualitative data, the importance of transcribing, the integration of field research notes or records, how to code and analyze the qualitative data you have collected, what tools you can use in organizing and summarizing codes, and how to write about findings from your qualitative data analysis. Although qualitative data analyses are creative and diverse, we will provide some guidelines and tips for effective analysis of qualitative data in this chapter's exercises.

Chapter 11 focuses on how to write your final research report or thesis. It discusses the differences between a proposal and a final report. It shows you various ways of summarizing, writing, and presenting research findings in your final report. It clearly lists all the components you may need to write your final report and discusses different techniques you may use in presenting data effectively. Most important, it tells you how to write your findings and discussions in your final report or thesis. With the help of this chapter, you should be able to write your research report or thesis clearly, logically, and professionally. Your completed paper will be written with appropriate format and writing style. The exercises at the end of the chapter will help you write your final report appropriately and provide self-check mechanisms before you submit your paper to your professors.

Chapter 2

Topic Selection: Getting Started

Research is an exciting adventure when guided by genuine interest. Like a destination that you always wanted to visit, preparing for the journey provides lots of fun. Just as choosing the right destination for your journey is important; selecting a good topic is a critical process that will set the tone for your whole research project. A good topic will send you off in a right direction, keep you interested in the project, and lead to a successful research project. This chapter will discuss what topics are appropriate and interesting for your research and how to select such a topic. Finally, you will be provided with some exercises to help you get started with your research. Here are questions you may have about selecting a research topic.

- Where can I start to find a good topic?
- How do I narrow down my topic?
- What topic is appropriate for me?
- How do I know the topic I selected is a "good topic"?
- Can I change topics?

This chapter will respond to these frequently asked questions, discuss problems that students often encounter, and provide answers to questions you may have on your topic selection.

Where Can You Start to Find a Good Topic?

What is a good topic? The most obvious answer is that it is a topic *you are interested in*. What social issues or phenomena are you interested in? For what social problems you would like to find solutions? What kinds of news story in the media tend to grab your attention the most? As you read this, we invite you to stop for a

Student Research and Report Writing: From Topic Selection to the Complete Paper, First Edition. Gabe T. Wang and Keumjae Park. © and Published 2016 by John Wiley & Sons, Ltd.

moment, and list any topics, social issues, or problems that you want to learn more about. Are you concerned about health issues? Have you always been interested in children's behaviors? Or, are you curious about issues in the workplace? Chances are you will have some themes or questions you want to know more about, but the ideas may be somewhat unclear. A lack of clarity is normal at the beginning of your research. Your task is to crystalize and clarify your ideas and narrow them down to a manageable research topic. Any of these issues or problems you are interested in can be developed into your research topic.

If you have no idea what you are interested in at this time or have a few vague ideas but do not know exactly how to formulate them into more specific research questions, you can do some of the following. These are some initial resources for inspiration.

Talking to People

It is rare that you have absolutely no idea what your interests are. Often you have some ideas about a possible topic, but have difficulty elaborating what exactly you have in mind. If this is the case, talking to your project supervisor, teachers, classmates, or other professionals in the field may help you clarify your ideas. You may think about developing an idea from your direct observations of a community for a day, or talking to someone in your community. Such a dialogue will provide you with additional insights and resources and raise specific questions about your ideas and press you to clarify your initial thoughts.

Searching the Internet

This is probably what most of you are doing already. Internet search engines have become handy and useful tools for screening the vast landscape of potential topics. The advantage of an internet search is that it is very quick, and that it delivers to you a large amount and a wide variety of information, from media coverage, scholarly sources, images, and statistical information on a topic. You will probably be able to learn how much knowledge is already out there on the topic you searched, and begin to ask about what you want to know even more. In fact, the internet search could be a Litmus test for your interest; ask yourself what becomes easiest and most fun for you to gather and remember information about. What links do you tend to "click on" to dig deeper? Or, you may even look at your search histories to find out what topics you have been following, even without realizing yourself. These could be clues for your curiosity and passion. While you should carefully evaluate the information on the internet (see Chapter 3 for more discussions on this), you may find the internet helpful in inspiring informed curiosity on a topic.

Browsing Reference Books, Statistics, and Other Library Resources

While it is more traditional methods with admittedly fading popularity among today's students, references in bound book format can still be useful sources for inspiration. They lack the speed and the convenience of the internet search, but they allow you to make easy side-by-side comparisons for several topics in the same volume. If you happen to be in a library, look up some subject area encyclopedias in the references section (e.g., *The Encyclopedia of Social Work*, *Encyclopedia of Theoretical Criminology*, *Encyclopedia of School Psychology*, and *Encyclopedia of Social Problems*). Encyclopedias provide you with quick overviews and initial resources for a wide range of topics.

If you are interested in social issues, the recent *Annual Editions: Sociology* is a good series of books to search for research topics on current social issues. Topics discussed with different perspective in this publication include culture, social control, racial relations, social inequality, social institutions, social change, and globalization (Finsterbusch 2013). Such current and annual publications are also available in anthropology, psychology, criminal justice, and other social science disciplines.

Another type of reference book that may inspire you is a statistical abstract. As you look through statistics on different issues, you may develop questions about why certain things occur more frequently in certain areas or among certain groups. Most of these statistics are now available online. Statistics available online such as census data summaries, United Nations reports, and various research institutes' online resources can also be good sources of inspiration. Many countries conduct routine omnibus surveys on demographic characteristics, behaviors, and social attitudes using large representative samples. For example, British Social Attitudes Survey, European Social Survey, and General Social Survey in the U.S., all collect statistics on hundreds of different variables, including demographic characteristics, family patterns, opinions on controversial political issues, attitudes on sexuality, criminal justice system, and social inequality. There are interesting statistics which are likely to spark some curiosity in you.

Reading Some Scholarly Journal Articles
You may also want to search for scholarly journal articles on the topic area you are curious about. You will gain knowledge about the topic and see the sorts of research questions scholars ask. Journal articles offer good models of appropriate research questions. Their literature review sections usually give you an overview of the current debates on the topic. Another source of inspiration within journal articles is the theories cited. Theories are statements of the relationship between different concepts, and you can design a study to test whether the hypotheses derived from theories are supported by data in reality. Furthermore, in the conclusions section, journal articles typically include suggestions or directions for future study. Such suggestions or directions may provide you with a research question that you will explore. University libraries typically have bound collections of journals and subscriptions of many journals published online. Chapter 3 will provide more guidance on how to search for and use journal article databases.

Reading Current Events and Recent Policy Debates
Society itself is a rich repository of social science topics, whether they are heated policy debates on the economy, the healthcare system, adolescent depression, or a recurring social problem such as random violence, unemployment, drug trafficking, or alcoholism. What is happening in your country or around the world today may serve as a good step toward finding a research topic. If there is a topic in the news that you

want to learn more about, read through recent media coverage, government reports, and scholarly literature on the issue. As you gain additional knowledge, your interest is likely to be further sparked, and your questions will become clearer and more specific.

In short, two things are most helpful in furthering your thoughts on a topic: gaining other people's perspectives through discussions or interviews, and obtaining more in-depth knowledge and information on a topic. These practices help to kindle new interests, clarify vague ideas, and narrow down a general theme into specific research topics. When you consult other people on your research topic, you need to remember that it is your interests in the topic that matter the most. Seeking feedback from your supervisor, teachers, and fellow students is a great idea. Such a dialogue, however, also has its pitfalls, if you passively follow them without ideas of your own. As you listen to others' suggestions and advice, you may be led to areas or topics with which you are unfamiliar or not prepared to research. Therefore, you should take advice with some caution. The people you talk to may not know your interests, readiness to write on a suggested topic, career plans, or the feasibility of investigating a topic. Ultimately, you will have to decide whether the topic your professors or fellow students suggest is suitable.

How Can You Narrow Down Your Topic?

Whatever topic you select, it should be appropriately defined according to the requirements of the research project. You should define it specifically enough to conduct focused research but general enough to write as much as required. The most common problem with student research topics is that they are either too broad or too narrowly defined. On the one hand, you may select a grand topic which may be more appropriate for a book project. In fact, many students have a tendency to do so. When you select a topic which is so broad that you can write almost anything about it, you will end up writing only general and superficial overviews. You can discuss many aspects of the selected topic, but none is likely to reach in-depth understanding leading to more interesting discoveries.

For example, if you select "juvenile delinquency" as your research topic, you can immediately notice that it is too broad to be a topic for a research paper. There are a number of different focal points you can consider: the possible causes of youth crime, the effects of delinquent behaviors on their life chances, handling of youth crime in the juvenile courts, class and race inequalities and the juvenile justice system, and so on. Notice that each of these issues could be a topic for a paper. Without a clearly defined focus, you may touch upon the surface of a variety of issues without actually writing anything meaningful about them. Covering every aspect of a very broad issue like this would consume all your efforts and afford little time to complete the work. Eventually, you will have to scale down your research so that it can be done within a limited time frame.

What steps can you take to scale down the scope of your topic? If you are interested in juvenile delinquency, you may limit your research to its causes, its consequences, or an aspect of juvenile delinquency such as property damages, disorderly conducts, gang activities, or drug use. You can also limit your research to a type of deviant behavior, or narrow the investigation to particular factors; for example, the effects of the family relations and adolescent drug use, or the relationship between delinquent behaviors and school performance. Even more specifically, you may focus on how family support, communication, and conflict affect juveniles' cocaine and tobacco use. You can also choose to focus on a specific group of people, a specific geographic area, or a specific time period, as a way to zoom in to a narrower topic area. For example, you may focus your research on family and delinquent behaviors among minority youth, in rural areas, or during the 1990s.

Having a "just right" topic shapes the whole research journey. Johnson and his colleagues (1998) describe this succinctly:

> The task of narrowing your topic offers you a tremendous opportunity to establish a measure of control over the writing project. It is up to you to hone your topic to just the right shape and size to suit both your own interests and the requirements of the assignment. Do a good job of it, and you will go a long way toward guaranteeing yourself sufficient motivation and confidence for the tasks ahead of you. Do it wrong, and somewhere along the way you may find yourself directionless and out of energy. (Johnson, et al. 1998: 19–20)

On the other hand, your research topic should not be too narrow, either. Though less common, sometimes students define their research topic so narrowly that they have difficulty finding information sufficient enough to write a paper. For example, writing 30 pages on "the relationship between gender and cocaine use among university students in Canada" for a class project could prove difficult. The independent variable, gender has two variations, male and female. The dependent variable, cocaine use, is not a very popular substance among students. Therefore, it may not be easy for a student to find much information on this research topic to write a 30-page paper.

If a student came up with an idea like this, we would probably advise the student to include other factors such as race and ethnicity and family income, in addition to gender. Including more variables will broaden the scope of the project. If the data are still insufficient for a 30-page paper, the student can also change the dependent variable into a broader concept, "substance use," to include alcohol, marijuana, and LSD. By broadening the topic from "the relationship between gender and cocaine use" into "the relationships between race/ethnicity, gender, family income and substance use," the student will be able to study more variables and write a more extensive paper on the topic.

But, how broad or focused your topic should be is a question that also depends on whether you are planning a qualitative or a quantitative study. For instance, "how do university students use smartphones?" may be a somewhat broad topic for a statistical analysis and you may need to further define exactly what factors you want to investigate about smartphone related habits of university students.

However, if you plan to conduct an ethnographic study at a university by following closely a group of students in their behaviors using mobile phones in different aspects of their lives, this question may not be too broad.

Research process in general involves narrowing down to get to more specific issues or problems. This process of "zooming into" a focal area of study may occur earlier or later in the research process. By and large, quantitative studies require clarification process early on, as you need to construct specific hypotheses and determine measurements for the concepts even before you begin your data collection. On the other hand, more inductive and qualitative studies do not require very specific set of questions at the beginning. Rather, they start with somewhat broader questions to collect a wide range of data in the natural settings of social life; thematic focus tends to emerge during the analysis process, as you will try to make sense of the data collected without pre-set assumptions.

The bottom line is that how you define your topic depends on the objectives of your research, the requirements for your project, and how much you are going to write about for your research project. A rule of thumb is that the topic should be narrow enough for you to investigate within the given time (e.g., a semester, or a year), and broad enough to write a paper that meets the requirement of your professors or supervisors. Box 2.1 provides you with more suggestions.

Box 2.1   Ways to Narrow Down a Topic Idea.

You can also consider the following suggestions made by Neuman (2011) to develop and narrow down your research topic:

a. Replicate a previous research project exactly or with slight variations.
b. Explore unexpected findings discovered in previous research.
c. Follow suggestions an author gives for future research at the end of an article.
d. Extend an existing explanation or theory to a new topic or setting.
e. Challenge findings or attempt to refute a relationship.
f. Specify the intervening process and consider linking relations.

What Topic Is Appropriate for Your Research?

Selecting a research topic that you can handle and will be excited about is probably the most important step in the research process. Therefore, you should spend sufficient time collecting background information, discussing your ideas with others, and writing down your thoughts. If you do not think carefully, you may select a topic that you later discover is not really appropriate. While there are many good social science research topics, not all topics are necessarily right for *you*. What topics will you find appropriate? Consider the following factors.

A Topic Which You Are Excited About

In selecting your research topic, you should "Let your curiosity be your guide" (Johnson, et al. 1998). If you are interested in a topic and desire to understand it in its different aspects, it will be worth pursuing. In selecting your topic, you may simply jot down all the issues or topics in which you are interested; then take another look at the list. Are there recurring themes? Does your list relate to a social problem you feel passionate about, or something which has affected your life experience? Is there something you learned recently in a class that sparked your curiosity? When you are excited about a topic, you are likely to be motivated, and your writing can be joyful. Therefore, your research will become something you enjoy doing, not something you have to do. When you enjoy doing something, you will do a better job.

Sometimes, when students are working against a semester timeline, some students choose at the last minute a topic someone else suggests. Be careful. A haphazard decision on a topic can turn your whole research journey into a burden; you have to complete your research and hand in your paper on time, but you may not engage at all what you are studying. In such circumstances, you are less likely to do excellent research and write a quality paper. Instead of feeling energetic and rewarded, you may feel bored. This sounds like a cliché but it is a time-honored truth; a good topic is a topic *you are strongly interested in*.

A Topic for Which You Are Prepared

In general, a topic you are interested in is likely to be one you already know something about; a thirst for new knowledge usually starts from some background knowledge. If you select a topic you are familiar with from course work or have already read about, you will have a strong start. For example, if you have taken psychology classes and want to conduct a research project on bullying and school yard violence, focus on the psychological aspects of juvenile violence. Your interest and knowledge of psychology will motivate you to do a better job. Similarly, if you major in sociology, you may have advantages researching socioeconomic issues, or the institutional contexts of school yard violence. If you have taken a class related to your topic, the course textbooks should have provided you with a comprehensive overview and a list of suggested readings. Since textbooks give extensive reviews of the themes and relevant studies, they will take you to a good starting point. If you have worked on the topic before, it is always easier to build on your previous research than to start from scratch. Research that draws on what you already know is more likely to be high quality research.

If you select a topic that you have never covered in class or have never read much about, then it is a topic you are not really prepared to research. In such a case, you will have to make up for your lack of knowledge by investing more time in the most basic information. You may find that you cannot afford to do your research given the resources and time you have. Each paragraph or each page requires research or reading. If you press on, you may find that more time is needed and your deadline is drawing near. In this case, you may eventually have to hand in a paper that does not satisfy you. Taking up an unfamiliar research topic offers an opportunity to explore a new area, which is great. But be prepared to spend a lot of time on it. Keep in mind that you can go much further, if you tackle a topic for which you have already been prepared.

A Topic Related to Your Experience or Employment

When you select a topic related to past experience, your research and writing will be interesting not only to you but also to your readers because your past experiences make you better informed. For example, if you happen to have spent some time with troubled children, your past observations of these children may give you insights often unknown to outsiders. If you have volunteer work to help homeless people, your firsthand experience or observations may help you ask more meaningful questions about homelessness. If you have worked as an intern in an elected official's office, your experience will give you strong background knowledge of politics in your community. If you have participated in activism or in a social movement, such as anti-racism activism, or advocacy movement for refugees, you may find your network and connections useful for your research.

You should take advantage of your personal experiences and insider knowledge with a caveat. Social research requires you to reject biases and to make objective conclusions based on evidence. You should be aware that using personal experiences as an inspiration for research may also let your personal biases influence your perspectives on a topic. As you formulate a research project on a familiar topic, ask yourself if your understanding has been unnecessarily affected by your individual experiences. Once you choose a topic, you should try to rely on published research findings to inform you about the topic rather than rely on "instincts" from firsthand experiences. Published research helps you overcome your personal biases and develop an understanding based on evidence and data.

There are advantages to pursuing a research topic related to your current employment, if it provides an opportunity to collect primary data. Your work organization can be a site for your research, which can improve your understanding of your work and the functioning of your organization. In such cases, you may need permission and cooperation from people in authority positions in your organization before starting your field research.

A Feasible Topic

Sometimes, you select a topic that is interesting to you but cannot be done with the resources available to you. For example, we once had a criminology student interested in how prisoners interact with each other in prison. He reviewed the appropriate literature, designed a survey questionnaire, and planned to administer the survey in a prison. When he went to the intended prison, however, he found that the prison would not permit him to do the survey. Finally, he had to pick another topic and start a different research project. Before you make the final decision on your research topic, ask yourself: is it feasible? If you plan to conduct empirical research, such as conducting surveys, and use the data to write a research paper, you should make sure that you will have access to your study population. If your study population includes children, or people with limited power (such as prisoners), permission for research will be more difficult to obtain. If you are considering a participant observation or an ethnographic study, you should think ahead about how you may gain access to the site or the community. The point is that you must make sure that you can do what you are planning to do; otherwise, you will need to consider other options.

At the same time, you should remember not to bite off more than you can chew. There are two more things to consider in determining whether your research is feasible. First, is there enough existing information about your topic on which you can build your study? If you can find a lot of relevant information, it probably means that you can identify very specific issues to investigate and you are likely to have theoretical and methodological models to follow. This may increase the feasibility of your research. If you cannot find much information through library research on your topic, the topic may have not been adequately studied yet. If you are especially curious about the topic and want to conduct an exploratory study, you may still select the topic; but you need to be prepared to spend more time and effort on your research, for there may be little guidance.

Second, when you think of the feasibility of your research, you should ask if you can complete your proposed research within the given time frame and with available resources. You may be conducting this research for a semester course, or a year-long thesis course. If the available time and resources will not allow you to complete the selected research topic, you may have to revise your research questions, choose a different population, or consider different data collection methods. You do not have to abandon your project altogether; instead, you can modify your research plan to answer different questions within the topic area.

Box 2.2 A Feasible Topic.

Is your research project feasible? Can you answer the following questions with a "yes"? If not, you may have to modify your topic or even consider a different topic.

1 Do I have access to the study population?
2 Can I draw a robust sample of this population given my network and geographical mobility?
3 Can I complete my research within the given time frame?
4 Do I have the financial resources to carry out the field research necessary to answer my research questions?
5 Do I have sufficient research skills and knowledge to complete this project?

A Topic You Can Build Upon

If you have not done much research on a topic but have plans for future research related to it, it may be worthwhile doing it. For example, you may want to continue your education with graduate programs and pursue postgraduate studies in this topic area. Then, your current research will lay the foundation for your future academic pursuits or develop into your future thesis or dissertation. In this way, choosing a topic that you can build upon can work for you. Since your current research may also contribute to your future research, you may be more motivated in your current research.

A Topic with a Broader Audience
Your topic should have a social, practical, and academic value. Some topics are interesting to only a small number of people and have limited values. If you are an undergraduate student using this book to guide your term paper or your undergraduate thesis, you probably have not thought about the use of your paper beyond the submission to satisfy the required assignment. Still, it is advisable for you to select a topic which can be of intellectual value to scholars and students. What we mean by this is that you should work on a topic which has not been studied very often or on a newer aspect of a topic. If you choose a topic which has great social value, or a topic which has great practical values to the society, you may be stay more engaged with your topic. Research on an understudied population, on a new phenomenon, and on an issue of great policy relevance is likely to generate interests among those who read your report. Projects using innovative methods or robust data set have a greater potential to be presented to and welcomed by a larger academic audience.

A Topic Similar to Your Professor or Supervisor's Research
If your research topic is closely related or similar to your professor's or project supervisor's research, he or she can give you substantial help. Generally speaking, professors have great interest and expertise in their research fields. Sometimes, you may be able to use data collected by your professor. Because your professor has more experience doing research and better resources than you do, his or her data may have a better quality than the data you can collect. Usually, your professor will be happy to use his or her expertise to help you with your research.

How Do You Know the Topic You Selected Is a "Good Topic"?

Once you have selected your topic, do not fall in love with it quite yet. Ask yourself the following questions to evaluate your topic:

1 Am I really interested in the topic?
2 Am I familiar with the topic? If not, am I prepared to do extra research on it?
3 Is there adequate information available to me to research this topic?
4 Will I have access to my study population? Can I get permission to conduct this research?
5 Does this topic offer future opportunities for research?
6 Do I have personal experience related to this research topic?
7 Will my future employment benefit from this research?
8 Are there professors or tutors in my department who have expertise in this area? Will they be able to help me?

9   Is my research topic not too broad and not too narrow?

10   Will this research topic be valuable to society? And finally,

11   Is it feasible to do research on this topic within my time frame and with available resources?

If most of your answers to these questions are positive, you probably have selected a good research topic and are ready to move on. Otherwise, you may need to revise or find a different topic.

Can You Change Your Topic?

Although you have thought carefully about your topic, you may still want to change it after you have started writing your research proposal or reviewed more literature. Your literature review or actual research may allow you to see some aspects of the issue that you did not see before. This is unavoidable even among experienced researchers. In fact, some students change their topics more than once. All of these are a natural part of the interactive process of research, as illustrated in Chapter 1.

If you feel that you cannot complete your research with the topic you selected, either because you have no access to the study population or your literature review makes you feel another topic is much more appropriate, you should change it as early as possible. Before you change your topic, however, you need to make sure that the new topic is really a better choice than the old one. If both are equally interesting to you, why change your topic? If you change your topic more than once, completing your research within the limited time frame may not be easy. When you feel that you want to change your topic, you should consult your project supervisor, or your professor.

References

Finsterbusch, Kurt, ed. 2013. *Annual Editions: Sociology 12/13.* New York: McGraw-Hill.

Johnson, William A., Richard P. Rettig, Gregory M. Scott, and Stephen M. Garrison. 1998. *The Sociology Student Writer's Manual.* Upper Saddle River, NJ: Prentice Hall Inc.

Neuman, W. Lawrence. 2011. *Social Research Methods: Qualitative and Quantitative Approaches.* 7th ed. Upper Saddle River, NJ: Pearson.

Further Reading

Adler, Emily Stier, and Roger Clark. 2014. *An Invitation to Social Research: How It's Done.* Belmont, CA: Wadsworth Publishing Company.

Hult, Christine A. 2005. *Research and Writing across the Curriculum.* 3rd ed. Upper Saddle River, NJ: Pearson/Longman.

Roth, Audrey J. 1999. *The Research Paper: Process, Form, and Content,* 8th ed. Belmont, CA: Wadsworth Publishing Company.

Internet Resources

American Psychological Association suggests a list of popular psychology topics on their website: http://www.apa.org/topics/index.aspx

British Social Attitudes Survey: http://www.bsa-31.natcen.ac.uk/?_ga=1.232561622.871506555.1415022614

European Social Survey: http://www.europeansocialsurvey.org/

National Archives of Australia website makes suggestions on popular archival research topics. http://www.naa.gov.au/collection/explore/

Research America (a non-profit organization in the US) publishes public opinions and fact sheets on health related topics. http://www.researchamerica.org/public_opinion

Social Science Research Council (A New York based international non-profit organization for social science research) website has a social science essay collection on big cities, which could inspire ideas on urban research. http://citiespapers.ssrc.org/

United States General Social Survey: http://www3.norc.org/Gss+website/

Exercises for Chapter 2

These exercises are designed to help you select a research topic. Choose one or two of the following exercises that best suit your situation. Exercises 2.1, 2.2, 2.3, and 2.4 are designed to help you brainstorm. Exercise 2.1 is recommended if you wish to use the internet. Exercise 2.2 may be helpful if you want to use your own life experience in your research. Exercise 2.3 uses your own community as a source of inspiration. Exercise 2.4 is useful if you are curious about specific groups of people.

Exercise 2.5 and 2.6 are helpful for refining and evaluating your topic. Reading often assists in the topic selection process. A targeted literature search (Exercise 2.5) may help you refine your research topic. Exercise 2.6 intends to help those who have some ideas about their research topics to narrow them down to more clarified research topics.

2.1 Internet Search

The internet is arguably the first place we go to find information these days. Most of us search the internet to read stories we are interested in, to follow current issues or debates, and to learn new things. In fact, which website links we tend to "click" on may be an indication of what we are interested in. Internet search can also inspire new topic ideas and questions. Therefore, we suggest you brainstorm using the internet with a few potential topic ideas.

Have a list of two or three topic ideas you may have. Using the internet search engine you use the most, type in a topic; this could be a simple word, a string of words, or a question. As you already know, trying a few different words gives you an idea about what terms might lead you to the best results.

Browse the websites and the information which turn up on the search. There could be various types of information, including statistics, popular media stories, bookseller websites, teaching materials posted on university webpages, government documents, and blogs by individuals and non-profit organizations. Follow your interests and explore the various links as your intuitive interests guide you. Take notes as needed.

Do this for the list of two to three topic ideas you may have. After gaining more information on each of these from the internet, ask yourself which of the initial topics has made you feel most engaged, or which one you have had most fun with. Do you think you can develop this as a research topic? Try to construct some specific questions about this topic, which will be appropriate in your academic discipline.

2.2 Sociological Autobiography

In social sciences, students often find their own life to be rich sources for research ideas. Writing helps identify research themes in personal experiences. In writing an autobiographical essay, you will try to exercise what American sociologist C. W. Mills called "the sociological imagination," (1959) which is a practice of connecting "personal troubles" to "public issues" in society.

Directions

Think about a major event or aspect of your life that has shaped who you are: for example, immigration, economic hardship, victimization by violence, health issues, parental unemployment, friendship with a person from another culture, interracial dating, travel to a different country, religious life, work, or volunteer experiences.

First, write freely about what you remember from the experience. This writing is not for evaluation, so do not worry about writing a well-structured essay. You may just pour out whatever comes to mind. Do it over a few days. When you feel ready, read your unstructured essay and try to relate your personal experiences to the issues in the larger society. Ask yourself:

- Was my experience or thought something others also experienced at the time?
- Was it a general pattern among certain segments of the population (e.g., young people, women, new immigrants, lower socioeconomic classes, or minorities)? Who were they?
- Were my experiences affected by larger/broader societal events (e.g., economic changes, political changes, etc.)? Were they considered as social problems at the time?
- Were my experiences a part of a generational experience?
- Who else might have had similar experiences? Would someone else have had similar experiences but found their life affected differently? Why were we affected differently?
- Is there a theoretical concept that captures what I experienced?

The idea here is to extract from your personal life stories some commonly shared experiences which can be the subject of a social science inquiry. Try to identify concepts/theories in your discipline that explain how these experiences unfolded.

Alternatively, you can look for connections between your life experiences and social issues. Write notes on all of these connections. Are there questions that can be answered with empirical research? Based on what you have written, formulate a few questions you can investigate through research.

2.3 Community Observations

Have you ever wondered how communities change after a flood, hurricane, massive fire, or other natural disaster? Has your community/town faced recent controversies over an ordinance, a health hazard, or a budget issue? Free-writing can be combined with community observation to identify research topics. With some "leg work" you can conduct this exercise in your city/town/community, workplace, university, or the place you volunteer or worship. You should do a quick informal investigation of the demographics of the community using the internet (e.g., your country's census data, Google search), or read about the history of these places. If this is an organization, look up its website and its history and missions typically under the "About Us" menu.

A perusal of community sources – websites, local archives, books, newspaper stories, or town newsletters – may reveal recent debates or particular issues/social problems that have attracted media attention. Are there issues related to interpersonal relationships, education, politics, culture, the natural environment, social inequalities or diversity in your community? How are they manifested? What evidence did you find? Is there an issue unique to your community or is it part of a broader pattern in the society? This informal research may raise a set of questions about a community or organization and inspire you to look deeper into any number of social processes. Write a list of questions that come to mind.

Sometimes just sitting down in a public place (e.g., a park, busy thoroughfare, town hall, or a town court) for an hour or two may allow you to discover something interesting about your community. Who occupies this public space (e.g., what social groups)? What are they doing? How do they interact with one another? Why do they act in particular ways? Do your observations inspire you of any questions you would like to investigate?

2.4 Pilot Interviews

You may be interested in a particular group of people, but are unsure if you can do research on them or what research questions to ask. For example, you may wonder, "I don't know exactly what, but I would like to study something about how police officers feel about controlling protests when they agree with the protesters" or "I want to know something about couples living together for a long time with no intention to get married." If you have such an interest, but do not know enough to come up with specific questions to study, a pilot interview may give you more specific ideas on their perspectives.

Working mothers, minorities in your society, high school students, recent university graduates just starting to work, unemployed persons, members of a religious group, tourists, or bar goers are all a potential population of focus for your study. Interviewing a person from the population can give you many insights into their experiences and perspectives. Your interview can be an informal and unstructured conversation. In many cases, people are willing to talk to someone who is interested in them. As you listen to their stories, opinions, and even complaints, take good notes (make sure you get your interviewee's approval on note-taking).

After your interview, review the notes and ask yourself what would be interesting to investigate. At this point, look beyond the personal story and search for issues that may be common to people in this group. Are there any concepts or issues repeatedly appearing in your interview notes? Can you think of possible causes for these issues or their possible consequences? Do you think you can use concepts or issues as your independent or dependent variables? Jot down any thoughts and questions that come to mind. One or two days later, read your comments and see if you can formulate them into more specific research questions. You may use the same set of guiding questions listed in Exercise 2.1.

2.5 Making a List of Questions or Topics

Sometimes you simply cannot think of a word or a phrase that could be a topic, or you may be interested in various unrelated questions. Your thoughts may be vague or unclear. In these circumstances, writing is an effective tool to clarify ideas. You may simply jot down a list of research questions whenever they strike you and add to the list as new questions or new topics arise. Do not worry about whether the questions make sense or if they sound silly, but keep compiling the list. You can do this at least for a few days; list any questions you want to ask.

After a few days, review the questions or topics more carefully and identify those that are related. Can you merge similar questions? Are there recurring questions you have asked in different ways? Are you finding yourself asking questions about a group of people? Could this theme or group be your research topic? Delete any questions or topics you do not want to study.

Then, gradually, trim down your list to one or two questions or topics that you really want to ask or study. At this point, compare the remaining topics to decide which one is better for your research project. When you reach this stage, use Exercise 2.6 to finalize your research topic.

2.6 Key Words Search Using the Internet

We assume that you have *some* ideas about what your topic may be by doing one of the exercises on the previous pages. Next, existing literature is an excellent source to modify, refine, and even search for research topics. In this exercise, use your topic ideas or any terms you have in mind to identify specific and doable research questions.

Step 1: Write on a piece of paper the few topic ideas you have in mind. The ideas can be a word, a phrase, or a complete sentence. You can make your list as long as you like.

Step 2: Review your list and merge and combine related questions into one broader question, and delete any questions that are less interesting than the others. Reduce your list to two or three questions.

Step 3: What keywords could capture the questions you have? From your list in Step 2, decide on three to four terms to use as keywords for internet search.

Step 4: Using your library search engine or Google scholar, try a keyword search on one of the terms you have in Step 3. Read through the titles and abstracts of the books and articles you find and write down topics or terms that come up frequently in the list of articles. Is there a different term for what you had initially written down? Can you identify narrower aspects of these topics, which grab your attention? Is there a particular setting or population you are more interested? Is there a setting or population not studied in these articles? What theories do those articles use? Take notes on your thoughts on the above questions.

Step 5: Based on what you wrote in Step 4, develop more specific questions you would like to investigate in your study (i.e., research questions). In developing your own questions, use the suggestions by Neuman (2011, p.122) summarized in Box 2.1 of this chapter:

a. Replicate a previous research project exactly or with slight variations.
b. Explore unexpected findings discovered in previous research.
c. Follow suggestions an author gives for future research at the end of an article.
d. Extend an existing explanation or theory to a new topic or setting.
e. Challenge findings or attempt to refute a relationship.
f. Specify the intervening process and consider linking relations.

Your Project Outcome after Chapter 2

At this point:

- You have selected a topic in which you are *really interested*.
- You have a tentative list of research questions which are more specific questions about this topic you wish to investigate.
- You have consulted your project supervisor or faculty mentor and obtained the approval to pursue this project.
- You have confirmed that you would have an access to the population for this study.
- You have obtained some knowledge about doing research on the topic after your preliminary literature search.

Chapter 3

Searching for Information

Now that you have your topic, it is time to search for more scholarly information on this topic. By definition, research is about finding and analyzing information to answer your research questions. But it is not just finding any information but *valid and reliable* information on a topic. While technology today enables you to gather an overwhelming amount of information without leaving your computer, that proliferation of information makes determining which information is accurate a problem of its own. Being able to screen different types of sources and evaluate the scientific value of the information those sources reveal is a skill you will develop. This chapter will review various methods of bibliographical research and discuss how you may conduct a systematic search for information. We will address the following questions.

- What is valid and reliable information?
- What do I need to prepare before searching for information?
- Should I search in a library or on the internet?
- How do I go about doing library research?
- What sources are available?
- How do I keep organized records of the information I find?
- What do I do with the information I find?

This chapter addresses these frequently asked questions and provides you with essential and up-do-date information on the search process.

What Is Valid and Reliable Information?

If you have taken a research methods course in a social science discipline you must have learned about validity and reliability of data. Validity in social science

Student Research and Report Writing: From Topic Selection to the Complete Paper, First Edition. Gabe T. Wang and Keumjae Park. © and Published 2016 by John Wiley & Sons, Ltd.

research is about whether the measure accurately reflects the intended concept (Schutt 2011). To say it in another way then, valid information is information that addresses your question. Trustworthy sources are likely to provide you with valid information. But keep in mind that, even if the sources you found are credible, information unrelated to your topic is not valid information. For instance, if your research purpose is to investigate the relationship between family policy and the occupational achievement of women with children, information on growing number of childless couples and their marital satisfaction may not be valid information to address this topic. A good information search is one in which you are able to capture valid literature on your research topic.

Reliability is producing consistent, or even the same, results repeatedly over time (Schutt 2011). For instance, when the same findings are repeated in many different studies, you know that you can trust the data. This largely depends on whether the data are collected using systematic and scientific procedures that are replicable. For example, let's consider Wikipedia. It is a source students often look at to learn basic information about a topic. As you probably already know, Wikipedia entries can be freely written and edited by anyone. The contents, therefore, can be a mixture of reliable and unreliable information; some claims and "facts" may be based on a careful review of many references and supported by bibliographical evidence, while others may be haphazardly collected or even simply personal viewpoints. The information an entry provides can change at any time, as anyone may edit it at will. Would this be a reliable source? You guessed it! It may contain some reliable information but as a whole it is not a reliable source. You may be able to assess the reliability of the information only if you can check the statements in a Wikipedia entry against the information in the references cited and verify evidence yourself. When this is not possible, you know it is not a reliable source.

Validity and reliability are important criteria for the information you need to collect in order to ground your own study in this process. Validity and reliability of information will depend on whether the sources use evidence, whether the evidence is systematically collected and analyzed, and whether they are written and published by independent, non-partisan authors and organizations whose guiding principle is science and not economic interests or political agenda. Social science research projects like the work you are doing now require references based on scientific evidence to ensure validity and reliability. In the following sections, we will discuss steps and tools to obtain valid and reliable sources of information for your project.

What Do You Need to Prepare Before Searching for Information?

Before beginning your search, have a few things ready.

List Your Research Questions
Your topic idea should be appropriately defined at this point. We have already discussed how to define a clear topic in Chapter 2 and made the point that the topic

should neither be too broad nor too narrow. In general, if your topic idea is just one word or phrase, it is probably too broad. For example, "religious pluralism," "climate change," and "adolescent depression" are all too broad. If you search for information on these topics, you are likely to find thousands of articles on different sub-topics related to these themes. As a rule of thumb, your topic phrase should contain at least two concepts that are related to each other. It may include a term describing your target population, too. For instance, "use of social media" may be too broad. Instead, "use of social media in political mobilization" may be appropriately specific. Also, if until now you have only had a broad topic idea, you should think about more specific research questions you want to ask about this topic. Can social media be an effective method in political campaigns? Does government's active use of social media increase public support on government policies? In what ways do social media help social movements? And so on.

List Possible Keywords for Your Search

Once you have your topic and research questions, think about which terms in your topic and research questions you want to use for your keyword search. You should keep in mind that most search tools screen through the database and find articles that contain your search terms in the title, abstract, keyword list, or in the text. Your goal is to use the terms that will identify articles most relevant to your topic idea and find sources that are directly related to your questions.

To do this, you will probably have to cast your net several times. You may start with the concepts in your topic phrase (such as "social media" and "adolescent friendships"), but if the search results turn up too many sources or too few, try different terms. Since you do not know what terms are most commonly used in the published work, it is a good idea to prepare a list of several synonyms, or alternative terms, so that you can search using these different keywords (see the exercises in this chapter). For example, if your topic is the influence of friends on delinquent behaviors, your list of search terms may include "friends," "social relationship," or "peers," and "delinquent behaviors," "juvenile deviance," "youth crime," or "risk-taking." Obviously, these terms have slightly different connotations but they are close enough to try.

Select Available Search Tools

There are many available search tools today, thanks to the internet and computer technology. Because university libraries are now typically connected to indexes, databases, online catalogs of texts and multi-media materials, and other search tools, your university's library is likely to give you one-stop access to several search options. There are also highly popular internet-based search engines such as Google, Bing, and Yahoo, and many others which are popular in particular countries or particular segments of internet users. You should compare the pros and cons of each method before you decide to use these methods.

Once you have clarified topic phrases and a list of search terms and have identified what search options may be best for you, you are ready to begin your search for information. But where should you start?

Should You Search in Libraries or on the Internet?

Once upon a time, research required personal visits to the library. If we were writing this book about ten years ago, the answer to the question "what is the best place to start the search?" would have been simple and clear: a good university library. While we think that the answer is the same today, it is also true that the internet and your library are more inter-connected than ever. Online search technologies have improved and are more specialized. Library "visits" today often means logging on to your online library account and accessing different search tools from your home. You can view e-books and articles that are available as online texts. Many of you will also be able to use library resources from your home computers or tablets.

Just as our libraries have been transformed into online services, many popular internet search engines also have become more effective in recent years. It is difficult to dispute the popularity of Google these days. And there are many other popular search engines that are easily accessible from your home computer or mobile devices. Internet search engines can be effective in finding useful information, if you know how to discern reliable from unreliable information sources. But this is a skill-set which you need to develop.

Understanding the strengths and weaknesses of search tools devoted to mainly academic purposes and those popular internet search engines that deliver a wider field of information is therefore important. A well-tested internet search engine like Google can be effective in finding information, websites, and documents relevant to your keywords. The strength of internet search engines is their flexibility; you can type in the search box, a word, a phrase, or a whole sentence to find information. This is sometimes not the case with some library search tools; you can easily end up with no search results if you misspell a word or enter a long phrase.

On the other hand, evaluating search results can be a challenge when popular internet search engines list many different kinds of online documents and websites. For instance, if you type "environmental justice" in a Google search box, it lists everything from a Wikipedia entry, a political web blog, government and advocacy group websites to a college brochure on its environmental justice degree program; the list includes resources that are not very useful for your research. Without mechanisms for evaluation, the validity of some of these information sources is also questionable.

More specialized tools such as Google Scholar and Google Books will allow you to zoom into the kinds of academic literature you will need to write a research paper. When we searched "environmental justice" on Google Scholar, we obtained mostly books and peer-reviewed journal articles in our results. But keep in mind that even these targeted internet search engines have their limits. Journals often restrict the access to the text of the articles to paid subscribers. You may be prompted to pay for access to the full-text document when you get to it using popular internet search engines. But there is a good chance that your library will have free access to much of the material you locate, including a number of e-books, when you conduct a search through its databases.

Your university library typically subscribes to thousands of different journals. What you can find through Google Scholar or other specialized internet search engines for scholarly works is likely to be found in a search through your university library's indexes and databases. In fact, many university libraries now provide the Google Scholar search engine as an option within their library system. The bonus for using the university library is that you will have free and often instant access to the full texts of journal articles. We highly recommend you use your library resources as your main method for information searches. Library search tools present a different kind of challenge. Because they are less flexible in finding matching terms, you need to use the right search terms. We will discuss this issue further in the next section. Some journal databases now have "smart text search" options (for example, Academic Search Complete, ERIC or MEDLINE via EBSCOhost) to allow more flexible searches, but our librarian colleagues generally think that "smart text" option is still not as precise as a keyword search.

To summarize, popular internet search engines are useful for searching for topic ideas and skimming through basic information about your topic ideas. You may first try more flexible internet search engines o "test" your keywords to find out what terms are commonly used in the field. Make notes on those words, and use them when you search article databases through your library. Internet search engines may also help looking up some quick facts and statistical information. But since the bread and butter of academic research are scholarly books and articles, *your university library will be the best place* for your information search and retrieval.

With the widespread use of online library access, fewer students make physical visits to libraries these days, but a personal visit to the library for your research is often worthwhile. Even in the age of the internet there are resources, especially books and reference materials, available only in print. In addition, talking to the library staff in person can be invaluable for your research. It seems that the expertise of librarians is not being utilized as often as it should be because many students rely on self-guided online searches. Librarians in your university will be more than happy to offer you personalized help with your research. If you have difficulties locating books or journals, the reference librarians will also assist you in finding them.

What Different Sources Are Available?

Library databases have many kinds of documents, including journal articles, books, book chapters, conference presentations, government documents, magazines, newspapers, and trade publications. All can be valuable sources of information for your study, but there is a difference in the level of scrutiny with which each of these types of source is evaluated before being published. Therefore, carefully consider the validity of information before deciding to build your argument on it. To become a discerning researcher who can evaluate the quality of sources, you should understand the characteristics and publication processes of different sources. We would like to begin by explaining two terms you might have heard frequently: scholarly sources and peer-review.

Scholarly Sources

Scholarly sources are written by experts (usually with the highest academic credentials) in a field. You can expect that arguments in scholarly papers are based on evidence that has been collected using systematic methods. The goal of scholarly documents is to provide information and knowledge that are up-to-date and fit the scientific criteria for validity. Class instructors and librarians emphasize that you use scholarly sources for these reasons. In addition, scholarly sources tend to rely on the research of others to formulate questions and support arguments; thus, scholarly sources in the field are spaces for scholarly dialogues in which new ideas build on existing ideas and then become the foundation for even newer ideas.

Non-scholarly documents, on the other hand, may be written by experts on a topic or by people with little or no expertise. The audience for non-scholarly documents can be general public, particular professional communities, or people who share similar interests. The purpose of non-scholarly documents may be other than advancing scientific knowledge. Non-scholarly sources also transmit information, but some information may be haphazardly collected or unsubstantiated. Non-scholarly sources include trade publications, newsletters, popular magazines, newspapers, non-scholarly blogs, and various web documents.

Peer-review

You may have heard the term, "peer-review." Peer-review is the process of rigorous and critical evaluation of a scholarly document by fellow experts ("peers") in the subfield. Typically, when a research paper is submitted to an academic journal, the editors invite a group of scholars in similar subject areas to anonymously review the papers. The peer reviewers scrutinize the paper according to the scientific criteria and professional standards of their field. Based on the outcomes of the peer-reviews, research papers may or may not be published. Not all scholarly sources are peer-reviewed, as we will explain below.

Peer-reviewed Journal Articles

Peer-reviewed journal articles are scholarly papers that have been vetted by experts through peer-review, and published in academic journals. Having undergone a rigorous review process, they represent the highest scientific values. However, not all peer-reviewed journals implement the same level critical review process. Some journals agree to publish only a very small number of papers after putting them through several levels of critical review process; others accept a large portion of papers submitted to them after a less rigorous process. Obviously, the articles published in the highly selective journals are likely to be of higher quality since their scientific values are well-validated. In addition to providing the most substantive and valid information on a topic, peer-reviewed articles provide up-to-date knowledge. Peer-reviewed articles take relatively shorter time to write and publish, and the literature and data analyzed are likely to be more recent than those in books. Compared to books, journal articles also focus on a more specific and narrowly defined set of research questions. These are good reasons why peer-reviewed journal articles should be the main source of information for your research project.

Books

Books can be scholarly or non-scholarly. For example, a systematic comparative study of economic development strategies in developing countries in Asia, and a study of a catastrophic disaster and its impacts on communities using systematic collection and analysis of data would be scholarly books. On the other hand, a memoir of a survivor of domestic violence and an edited collection of newspaper feature articles on women's education around the world would be non-scholarly books. When you use books as sources of information on which you want to base your research, you should rely on scholarly books.

Scholarly books are usually based on systematic and scientific studies and are reliable sources of information for your research. But, books are usually long and comprehensive, and cover material in more depth than your research may require. While the rich details discussed in books will help you gain insights into various aspects of the issue, you may face an overload of information, which may confuse and sidetrack you. In addition, books tend to be not as up-to-date as journal articles are, because the writing and publishing of a book typically takes several years.

Theses and Dissertations

Theses and dissertations are based on in-depth studies that student scholars, such as Master's and Ph.D. students, conduct to fulfill their degree requirements. These are usually reviewed by a committee of faculty supervisors and experts to ensure that they meet scholarly standards. Theses and dissertations often cover new and unique topics about which little research has been published. They also have comprehensive literature reviews for a thorough overview of the topic, which you may find useful. But you should keep in mind that dissertations can also be overwhelming to undergraduate students because they are book-length projects and discussions often involve highly specialized details.

Typically the degree-granting institution has a bound copy of the doctoral dissertation. While most institutions do not circulate copies of dissertations, some may, if multiple copies of a dissertation were deposited to the library. You may ask your school library if you can use the inter-library loan service to borrow a bound copy of a dissertation from the degree-granting institution. In the United States, you may be able to access online text of dissertations if your school library subscribes to ProQuest Dissertations and Thesis Full Text library. In the United Kingdom, you can search for dissertation titles using the British Library's EThOS (Electronic Theses Online Service) database. Dissertation titles can also be searched in journal article databases or WorldCat.

Working Papers, Statistical Reports, and Government Reports
These are the types of studies usually done by experts, both academics and experts in applied fields, but published in venues other than scholarly journals. They are often published by research institutes (such as the Pew Center in the United States, the Joint Research Centre in the European Union, and university affiliated research centers), government agencies (such as the Census Bureau, the Environmental Protection Agency, the United Nations and its agencies), or independent research groups and advocacy organizations (such as the Greenpeace, Amnesty International, and Water Environment Research Foundation). These organizations publish working papers, reports, statistical yearbooks, and other periodicals either in print or as online publications.

Just like journal articles, these publications are usually based on scientific studies done by experts. The slight difference is that they may not have undergone the anonymous peer-review processes described above. While many of these papers are likely to have been reviewed and commented on by other experts before publication, the process may not be at the same level of critical questioning as anonymous peer-reviews. Also, some of them may reflect the particular perspectives of the agency or the institute. These types of report often focus on statistical and empirical reports and may lack much in-depth theoretical discussion. In general, working papers, project reports, and government documents are valid sources for statistical patterns, policy directions, and other empirical patterns about your topic. You will need to figure out how to integrate their empirical knowledge to the theoretical discussions in your literature reviews.

How Do You Go about Doing Library Research?

Searching for books and articles using your library account will require different processes. For books, you will search your university library's internal collections using its internal search system. Though libraries are increasing their e-book collections and other digital format resources, the vast majority of books are still in print form physically housed in your library. You will need to locate and check out these books in person. For this, you are likely to use your university library's internal catalog to obtain the call numbers and locations for these books within the library.

To search for journal articles, you will use journal article databases available through your university library website. The vast majority of academic journals today allow online access to the full-text of articles for paying subscribers. If your university library has a subscription to the online format of the journal, you will have instant free access to the online text of the articles found in your search. But bear in mind that your university library may purchase some journals in print format only, in which case, you need to go to the library and find the bound copies of the journals. If you find articles in journals to which your library does not subscribe, you can request your library to borrow them from another library through a service called, "inter-library loans." Ask your librarian about the library's inter-library loan policy and how you may request material from other libraries. Once the article is in your library, you will receive notification. Your library may give you a hard copy of the article or deliver it via school email in an electronic form.

These days, your library's internal search tool is often connected to a broader network of regional libraries or to a worldwide network such as WorldCat (www .worldcat.org) so that you can search for books and articles in different libraries in the worldwide network. In the United Kingdom, Copac National, Academic, and Specialist Library Catalogue (http://copac.ac.uk/) allows you to search for materials in over 90 major national, university, and specialist institution libraries in the United Kingdom and Ireland.

If your university library is a part of the international network, WorldCat, you will see the link for WorldCat with the list of catalogs and indexes on your library's website. Click on the link to reach the WorldCat website. If you are logged onto your library account, you are likely to be already inside the WorldCat's login page.

To conduct a search using WorldCat, click the "searching" tab in the middle of the screen. Enter your keywords, the title, or the author in the search box. For example, when we were working on this book in 2014, we tried a simple keyword search on genetically modified food as a test. We entered the term "genetically modified food" (with the quotation marks to treat the three words as one phrase) in the WorldCat search box and obtained a list of 1,535 sources. The list is also categorized into several tabs, "books," "internet," "visual," and so on. The "books" tab, for example, displays only books, but it also tells you whether your own school library has the book or not (but this feature may not be available in all libraries). To locate books available in your university library, use your library catalog to look up the call number. Or, click on the "Libraries Worldwide" link to list libraries that have the book you want. If another library has this item, ask your librarian to get it through inter-library loan. Figure 3.1 is a screen shot of a WorldCat search results.

Figure 3.1 WorldCat Search Results for "Genetically Modified Food." *Source*: © 2014 Online Computer Library Center, Inc. (OCLC). Used with permission of OCLC.

Your library may also give you an access to a large national library so that you can search from the vast collection of your nation's largest libraries. For example, in the United Kingdom, you can use the British Library's Explore the British Library (http://explore.bl.uk) search engine to look up scholarly journal articles and books. You can also use the Zetoc service provided by Mimas at the University of Manchester (http://zetoc.mimas.ac.uk) to access the British Library's electronic table of contents. Students in UK universities can log in to Zetoc using their university library account. Enter your university's name on the Zetoc Search-Access menu; it will take you to your own university's log in page. After entering your university login information, you will have access to over 29,000 journals through the British Library's electronic catalog (Figure 3.2).

In the United States, you can go to the Library of Congress (LOC) website (www.loc.gov) and search for sources without having an account (Figure 3.3). But if you want to borrow an item from LOC, you will need to use your library's inter-library loan services. Inter-library loan services are usually free of charge to students and take days to a few weeks to transport the item to your library. Library of Congress not only has a large number of books but also an extensive collection of digital format contents such as photos, media, newspapers, and other documents.

You probably are already familiar with article indices commonly used in your subject area. There are many journal article databases specializing in particular fields or disciplines. Box 3.1 below shows examples of journal index services in selected social science fields. Your university library website may have a web page with links to these databases and many more. There are overlaps among these databases. You will find many sources on health research listed in both PsycInfo and MEDLINE, for example. Academic Search Complete will include many publications found in

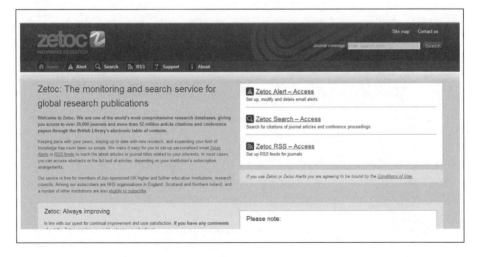

Figure 3.2   Zetoc by Mimas at the University of Manchester. *Source*: Zetoc Service by Mimas at the University of Manchester.

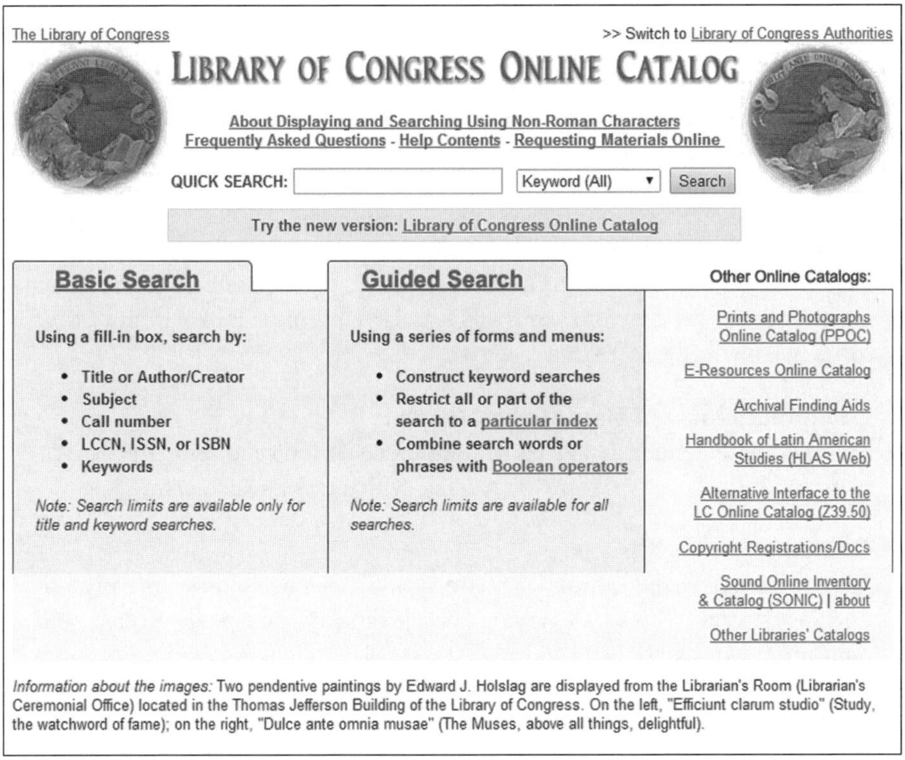

Figure 3.3 U.S. Library of Congress Search Screen.

other indices. If you know which databases work best for your topic areas, you may use just two or three of these services. Your university library may not subscribe to some of the more expensive databases; ask your school librarian whether there is an open and free alternative for the database you need to use. For instance, PubMed, offered free of charge by U.S. National Library of Medicine, can be a good alternative if your library does not subscribe to MEDLINE.

Box 3.1 Popular Article Databases for Social Science Research.

Below are journal article databases most commonly used in various social science fields.

Academic Search Complete
This is a large interdisciplinary database containing over 8,500 full-text publications. It is not limited to academic journals, and therefore your search results will include articles in magazines, books, and trade publications in

addition to academic journals. It covers disciplines including anthropology, area studies, biology, chemistry, ethnic and multicultural studies, food science and technology, general science, geography, law, mathematics, music, pharmaceutical sciences, physics, psychology, religion and theology, women's studies, and other fields.

Business Source Premier
This database focuses on business, economics, and related fields. You can access full-text articles for over 8,300 scholarly business journals and other sources.

Communication and Mass Media Complete
This is a full-text index to articles from over 200 periodical titles in the field of communications and mass media studies, with citations and abstracts.

Criminal Justice Abstracts
Subject areas covered by this database include crime trends, crime prevention and deterrence, juvenile delinquency, juvenile justice, police, courts, and punishment and sentencing.

Ebrary's Academic Complete
While e-books are relatively limited, Ebrary index gives full-text access to over 110,000 electronic books from a wide variety of academic publishers in a variety of fields.

ERIC
Most popular in education research, the ERIC database, sponsored by the Institute of Education Sciences of the U.S. Department of Education, provides access to more than 1.3 million bibliographic records of journal articles and other education-related materials. The database includes citation records, abstracts, and full-text links for journal articles (if available), books, research syntheses, conference papers, technical reports, policy papers, and other education-related materials.

MEDLINE
MEDLINE is widely used in health research. It provides access to the research literature of medicine and the health sciences: medicine, nursing, pharmacy, dentistry, veterinary medicine, and health care, plus links to full-text content where available.

PAIS International
The PAIS International database focuses on the literature of public and social policy, and it contains references to more than 1.7 million journal articles,

books, government documents, statistical directories, conference reports, publications of international agencies, and internet material. Newspapers and newsletters are not included. In addition to English, a subset of indexed materials is published in French, German, Italian, Portuguese, Spanish, and other languages.

ProQuest Central

ProQuest Central indexes over 160 subject areas including social sciences, business and economics, health and medicine, and more. It includes scholarly journals, dissertations, trade publications, and newspapers and magazines.

PsycINFO

PsycINFO is the main indexing database in the behavioral sciences and mental health. The database contains over 3.3 million records for articles from books, dissertations, and over 2,500 journals. The major focus of this database is psychology, but it also includes information about medicine, psychiatry, nursing, sociology, education, pharmacology, technology, linguistics, anthropology, business, law, and others.

Sociological Abstracts

The Sociological Abstracts database includes journal articles, books, dissertations, and conference papers, plus citations to important book reviews related to sociology and related fields of social sciences. The database records references cited in the source article from key journals in sociology since 2002. This function broadens research possibilities by providing related research and contextual material.

Worldwide Political Science Abstracts

The Worldwide Political Science Abstracts database provides citations, abstracts, and indexing of the international research literature in political science, international relations, law, and public administration and policy.

How Do You Conduct a Search Using Journal Article Databases?

Which database works best for your research depends on your subject. Your project supervisor can guide you in selecting what may be best for your project. We recommend that you conduct your search in more than one database. Even though there are large areas of overlap, journals may be indexed in some databases but not in others. Also, not all databases include books, book chapters, and/or conference papers. Databases may also include non-scholarly sources such as newspapers and magazines, which you may want to exclude.

Once you click on the link for a database you choose, you will see the search screen within the database. Use these steps to proceed with the search.

Keyword Search

Databases use search tools which look different, but they basically function in the same way. You will be provided with box areas (sometimes just one box) in which you will enter your search terms: keywords, author names, or parts of the title. If there is an option for advanced search, or guided search, we recommend that you use that option instead of the basic search. An advanced search allows you to use multiple terms at the same time and to designate the type of search (e.g., title, author, keyword in the text and so on). Use the pull-down menu to specify whether you want to search by article title, author names, or keywords, as shown in Figure 3.4. If you are just beginning your information search with keywords, you will be better off using the "all text" or "anywhere" menu; this identifies the search term in the title, abstracts, and even in the text of the article. If you have the full citation information of specific articles you know you want to access, use either the title search or author search options to find the exact articles you have in mind. In addition, with advanced search options you can limit your search to a certain time period, a particular language, or peer-reviewed articles. These options are helpful in excluding outdated or non-scholarly sources from your search.

When you enter your keywords into the search boxes, you can do it in a few different ways. Your results will vary depending on what you do. For example, suppose you are interested in searching for information on adolescent social media use. Key terms are likely to be "social media" and "adolescents." Using Academic

Figure 3.4   Designating a Search Field to Specify Your Search. *Source*: Reproduced with permission of EBSCOHost.

Search Complete database, try a few keywords and see how your search results differ. For example:

Enter the entire phrase, "social media and adolescents," in the first box and ask the search engine to find "all of my search terms." The database in this case treats "social" and "media" as separate terms and will find sources that have either the pair of words, "social" and "adolescents," or the pair, "media" and "adolescents." Using this search method, we came up with 63,170 items (Figure 3.5). Notice in this screenshot that the first two items happened to be on mass media and adolescents and not about social media. Because the search captured sources with the terms "media" and "adolescents," we ended up with references irrelevant to our topic, "social media." This search strategy casts the net very widely and may even include sources unrelated to the intended topic.

Use the two concepts as two separate keywords, which is a better strategy. Enter the key terms, "social media" and "adolescents" in the advanced search engine and choose the menu AND to connect them. This asks the search engine to capture references that have *both* of these two words in any part of the information (e.g., title, abstracts, text). Figure 3.6 shows that our trial using this technique resulted in 4,437 items. Here, we are using "Boolean logic" or a "Boolean Phrase," which link multiple search terms by defining logical relationships between them.

By using Boolean terms AND, OR, and NOT to link your search terms, you can designate the range of your search differently. When you use the Boolean term AND, the search engine will find sources that contain *both* the keywords. When used with different concepts/terms, as in our example above, the use of AND narrows your search to more specific areas. The Boolean term OR has the opposite effect, telling the search engine to capture *any one* of the terms entered in the

Figure 3.5 Keyword Search Using "All of My Terms" Option. *Source*: Reproduced with permission of EBSCOHost

Figure 3.6   Keyword Search Using Boolean Phrase. *Source:* Reproduced with permission of EBSCOHost.

search. For example, searching for "social media" OR "adolescents" will result in a list of all sources on social media as well as all articles on adolescents. As you can understand, it is counter-productive to link two different concepts with an OR. Your purpose of using two different keywords simultaneously is usually to narrow your search to specified areas; using an OR will make the search engine expand the search instead of narrowing it. We recommend you use *OR* when you are trying *similar* terms and *AND* for connecting two *different* terms. When NOT is used, the search will exclude the term that comes after the NOT. For example, a search using "young adults" NOT "adolescents" will capture sources on young adults excluding sources on adolescents. This technique also helps to narrow your search. But keep in mind that when you use NOT, the order of the terms you entered is important, as the term following NOT will be specifically excluded from the search. Figure 3.7 illustrates how Boolean logic expands or specifies your search.

Your search will produce different results depending on search options, even when you use the same set of search terms. Some options help you cast the net widely, while others help you to narrow your search to more specific areas. Boolean methods are useful, if you know that your search terms are clear and part of a common language among researchers in the field. On the other hand, if you are unsure of your search terms and are still in the process of clarifying and narrowing your keywords, try first entering the entire phrase. As illustrated above, you can see what other topics are related and sometimes confused with your specific ideas, and clarify your focus further. But even if you have a well-defined search, as was the case of our second search above with Boolean terms, you may still have a few thousand articles in your results. This is still an untenably large number of sources to skim through. There are a few more strategies to narrow your search even further.

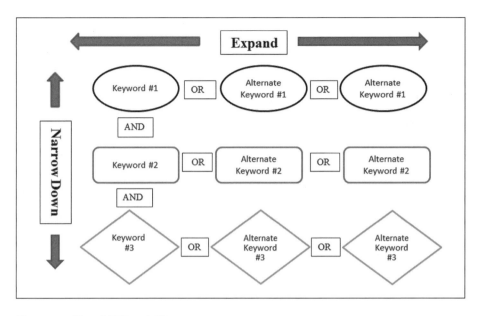

Figure 3.7 Use of AND and OR.

Zooming into a Refined Focus

For instance, you may narrow your search further by adding a third keyword. If you did a search with two keywords and your results had over a thousand articles, you probably need to zoom into a narrower scope. As shown above, you can narrow your search by linking key terms with an "AND." If a search using two keywords still has too many sources, adding a third word will narrow the search even further. A term representing your population, a country you focus on, or a particular aspect of your topic can be used as the third term. In the example of social media we used above, add "relationships" as the third term, if your focus is on how social media affects personal relationships among adolescents. Librarians generally advise against using more than three terms, as a fourth keyword will most likely result in an insufficient number of articles.

Some databases have a "search within" option in your initial search results screen. When your first search turns up too many items, you can choose to search within your list by entering an additional word into the "search within" box. For example, our search on "occupational therapy" using the Sociological Abstracts database resulted in 338 sources. When we entered "children" in the search within option we obtained 38 references focusing on occupational therapy on children or in pediatric contexts.

As discussed earlier in this chapter, you can "limit" options to restrict your search to particular document types (e.g., books, newspaper articles, peer-reviewed journal articles), languages (e.g., English, German, Spanish, etc.), or specified time periods (e.g., since 1990, 1990–2014, and so on). These limit options will exclude unnecessary sources and reduce the number of articles to a more manageable size. Figure 3.8 shows the limit options in ERIC database.

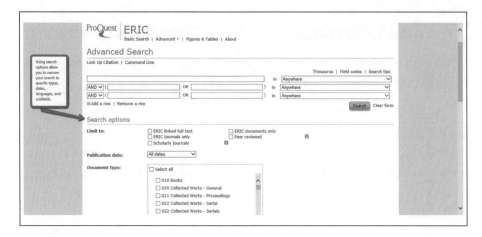

Figure 3.8   Limit Your Search. *Source:* Reproduced with permission of ProQuest, LLC.

Expanding Your Search

But what if your search results in less than ten articles and some of them appear irrelevant to your topic? What if you get zero results? One reason you may have too few results is that you entered a term not normally used by scholars in the field. For example, a student of ours searched for articles on "the influence of friends on drug use among middle school students" using three keywords "friends," "drug use," and "middle school." Her search found 22 articles. When she changed "friends" to "peers," she obtained a list of 262 articles. This shows that, even though "friends" and "peers" have similar meanings, researchers favor the latter term. You should substitute similar keywords until you find the terms most commonly used in the literature.

A similar strategy is to use two or three alternative terms in each search box and add OR. For example, if you enter "peers" OR "friends," the search will capture sources that have either of the two words. But remember that those words must be *synonyms* or similar words. Use this strategy with caution because if you link terms with different meanings with an OR, you may expand the search beyond your intention.

The thesaurus function (Figure 3.9) in journal databases is a helpful tool to identify alternative words. If you wish to find other terms for "friendship," for instance, click on the thesaurus feature of your journal search screen and enter "friendship." The thesaurus will then display related words, such as "interpersonal relations" and "peer relations." By checking off these terms, you can directly import the terms onto your search screen. The benefit of using a thesaurus function is that you will be able to find alternative terms that are not only synonyms but also frequently used in scholarly articles.

In addition, you can expand your bibliography by gleaning information, such as a subject word list or a list of other articles that cite this article, from within an article you find. For example, we looked for information on asylum seekers in Europe,

Figure 3.9 Thesaurus Feature in ProQuest Central. *Source:* Reproduced with permission of ProQuest, LLC.

and, using the keywords "asylum seekers" and "Europe," we found an article on Algerian immigrants in UK. We clicked on the title of this item to open the page with more detailed information about this article. As we illustrate in Figure 3.10, there are a few alternative terms in the subject word list you may want to follow up, depending on the exact focus of your topic. If the topic you have in mind is related to policies, click on the term "immigration policy" from this list and launch a new search on this term. But to be careful when you launch a new search like this, the criteria for your previous search will be removed. If your interest focuses on the experiences of asylum seekers, instead of policies, then expand your search using the term "refugee" in this subject word list. Since the subject terms are web links, you can launch a new search round by simply clicking on a subject word.

In addition, links for further reference information appear on the right hand corner of Figure 3.10. When you find an article closely related to the research questions you had in mind, finding its sources is as easy as clicking on those citation links.

In short, the search process is reflexive and circular, and you should be prepared to explore various sub-fields until you are able to zoom onto the most relevant literature on your topic.

Cast Your Net Several Times
Earlier in this chapter we recommended that you try multiple searches using a few different similar terms. A successful information search will provide a near complete list of all studies directly relevant to your topic. In essence, you want to capture studies investigating similar research questions as yours, focusing on the same set of variables, or using the same theory. Casting your net several times will maximize your chance of identifying all important studies. Use a few different keywords, but avoid the common mistake of changing all of the initial

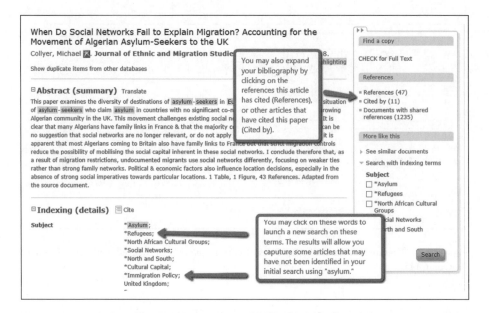

Figure 3.10   Using Information inside Your Citation to Expand the Search. *Source:* Reproduced with permission of ProQuest, LLC.

keywords when a search does not result in an adequate list of sources. Instead, we suggest you change keywords in a *systematic manner*. If your initial search was done using two main concepts, you should keep one term constant and substitute the other term.

For example, in a search for the literature on the influence of peers on adolescent delinquent behaviors, use several synonyms for "peers" (e.g., friends, cohorts, social network), while pairing them up with the same term "delinquent behaviors." Compare the lists you obtain while substituting this term and mark the studies that fit the above criteria in each search. Once you have tried all synonyms for "peers," choose the term with which you had most success. If "peers" was the term widely used in the scholarly literature, then keep it, and conduct a set of searches that pair it with synonyms for "delinquent behaviors," such as "deviance" and "crime." If you keep a log of the term changes, you can avoid missing terms or repeating the same pair. This process takes time, but will ensure a successful identification of all important studies in the field.

How Do You Keep Organized Records of the Information Found?

The list of scholarly sources you find in your search process becomes your working bibliography. These are the sources you will read, some more thoroughly than others, to be up-to-date on your topic. A working bibliography is not a fixed list, but a flexible list you revise as you add new sources and drop less relevant ones. You should note a few things as you refine your search. Keep the full citation information, abstracts, and a short note of your own ("annotation") about each source. Your annotation can include a short-hand summary of the research questions, methods, and findings, how the source is useful for your research, and how the source is related to other sources. To keep track of your search results, plan a systematic way to manage or organize your search results.

Notebooks and Index Cards

If the traditional note-taking on paper is your style, keep a notebook to record your working bibliography. We recommend that you take notes on the full citation information for the source (i.e., author's name, title of the source, year of publication, publisher, and journal title with the volume, and issue number, and page numbers if it is a peer-reviewed journal article), and a short annotation about how the source relates to your topic. Sort the references into smaller groups (e.g., empirical studies vs. theoretical studies, by different methods used, opposing views, or by theoretical perspectives), and mark them using tabs or sticky notes. Do you prefer index cards over notebooks? Write the information and a brief annotation on the index card for each source and organize them into different piles.

Computer File Notes

Note-taking using a word processing program is probably a preferred method today than using paper. Journal article databases usually allow you to email or download the selected source list, including abstracts, directly to your computer. All you have to do is to transport the list into a file, organize it, and add your annotations. You can arrange the list by authors' last names, in chronological order, or by groups representing different sub-themes or positions on the issue.

Citation Management Programs

Citation management programs (e.g., RefWorks, EndNote, Citavi, Mendeley Desktop) are convenient ways to manage your bibliography. They allow you to import the list of references you find in the journal databases into your account, store them in different folders, and pull them out for citation when you write. You may be able to use citation management programs from your mobile devices, too. These programs work similarly. Ask a librarian if your university library is connected to any of them. Using RefWorks, for example, you can export your search results from most journal databases to your RefWorks account, store them in an output format you prefer (i.e., APA, MLA, Chicago, Harvard British Standard, etc.) and organize the references into folders and sub-folders as needed. If you wish to add annotations to your references, write them onto a word processor and attach the file to the information on each reference. RefWorks has the Write-N-Cite plug-in program, which works with some word processor applications. This feature allows you to add formatted text citations and a bibliography while you write your paper. This may be helpful because you can automatically enter citations in the specific citation format required for your paper. You may have RefWorks access through your university library. More information on RefWorks and a tutorial on how to use it are available on the RefWorks website (www.refworks.com).

EndNote is likewise a citation management program that works similarly to RefWorks. You can search for information from your EndNote program by connecting to many popular article databases. Once you find the list of references you want to export to your EndNote folder, you can do so by simply clicking the "export" button. Just like RefWorks, EndNote allows you to send the reference list in various output formats. If it is available online, you can import the full-text of your source into EndNote. Tutorials for EndNote can be found at http://endnote .com/ or ask your librarian.

To use citation management systems such as RefWorks and EndNote, you need to first create an account. Your librarian can help you setting up an account to a management system linked to your school library system. Once you have an account, use your library's online database to conduct a search, select the articles you wish to store, and click on the export menu available on the results screen. Click on your citation management system, and click "export." Your selected references will be transported to and stored in your citation management account in a new folder. Figure 3.11 shows how you may export the search results to a citation management system.

Citavi (https://www.citavi.com) and Mandeley Desktop (http://www.mendeley .com/) are both computer applications to organize and manage references

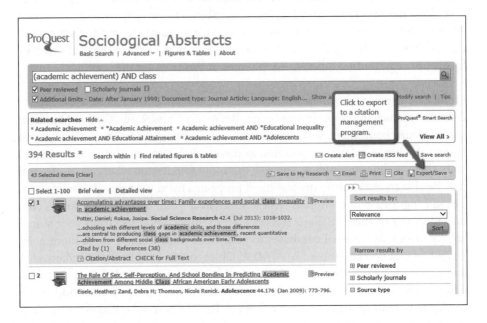

Figure 3.11 Using Export Menu to Send Results to a Citation Management System. *Source:* Reproduced with permission of ProQuest, LLC.

imported from research databases. Both have free versions downloadable from their websites. Once installed on your computer, you can export your search lists from a library database to a folder in these programs. The programs have features to add annotations, direct quotations for later use, and other contextual information on the reference.

How Do You Use the Information You Found?

The key to a good information search is selecting relevant and credible sources of information. What do we mean by "credible" sources? Credible sources provide valid and reliable knowledge based on scientific evidence. You may accidentally come across documents on the internet, which are well-written and compelling, but they may be written to represent only a particular side of a debate and not based on scientific studies. Selecting appropriate and valid information sources for your research depends on whether the sources are scholarly, and whether they are peer-reviewed. In addition, it is best if you use the most updated sources you can find. If a study provides you exactly what you wanted to know but was written in the 1980s, it is unlikely to be accurate accounts of today's society.

Considering these criteria, recent peer-reviewed academic journal papers are probably the best sources for the kind of scientific knowledge you want to use to inform your own research. Academic books, research reports and working papers by university affiliated research organizations can also be credible sources of information. These sources almost always include detailed descriptions of the evidence they use and their methods of data collection, making it possible to evaluate the scientific value of the claims they make. These are important details you need to pay attention to when you judge the validity and reliability of the information you find. Unreliable sources most often lack methodological detail and make it difficult to evaluate the credibility of the arguments they make. You should avoid relying on those sources.

Conducting information searches aids you in refining and clarifying research questions and topic ideas. As you are exposed to a variety of discussions, documents, and materials on your topic, you will gain more insights into specific aspects of your topic and be able to narrow your research focus further. As you search, you may discover that the initial questions you had in mind have already been answered by other studies; in their place, you may begin to form a new set of questions inspired by what you find in the literature. Or, you may develop a new direction in your thinking as various strands of discussion reveal new ways to think about your initial topic ideas. It is a reflective and interactive process that you will continue throughout your literature review.

Research is not isolated work. You probably have not thought about this often, but by doing this research project, you are actually participating in a giant dialogue involving scholars and students who have studied and are investigating the same topic. Thus, the beginning of social science research is usually searching for what is already known about your topic. If you do research properly, you will have made a new "discovery," i.e., uncovered new knowledge about an issue. When you write a paper and share your findings, you will help readers build on your work and develop more questions for further study. In Chapter 4, we discuss in greater detail how you may bridge existing knowledge on your topic and your research questions to explore in your project.

References

Mann, Thomas. 2005. *The Oxford Guide to Library Research*. 3rd ed. New York: Oxford University Press.

Schutt, Russell K. 2011. *Investigating the Social World: the Process and Practice of Research*. Thousand Oaks, CA: Pine Forge Press.

Further Reading

Badke, William. 2014. *Research Strategies: Finding Your Way through the Information Fog*. 5th ed. Bloomington, IN: iUniverse.

Hart, Christopher. 2011. *Doing a Literature Search: A Comprehensive Guide for the Social Sciences*. London, UK: Sage.

Internet Resources

Australian Library Gateway (ALG) is a "one-stop-shop" directory service for information and collection in 5,200 Australian libraries and cultural institutions. http://www.nla.gov.au/libraries/

Colorado State University (U.S.) library provides instructions on how to do library research online. http://lib.colostate.edu/howto/doing-r.html

Copac* search (UK and Irish libraries). http://copac.ac.uk/

Georgetown University library's internet source evaluation tutorial. http://www.library.georgetown.edu/tutorials/research-guides/evaluating-internet-content

Research Libraries UK (RIUK) provides links to 34 research libraries in the United Kingdom. http://www.rluk.ac.uk/

University of Illinois. Tips and tricks for evaluating websites. http://www.library.illinois.edu/ugl/howdoi/webeval.html

University of North Carolina (at Chapel Hill) libraries' research tutorial. http://www2.lib.unc.edu/instruct/tutorial/

Exercises for Chapter 3

Exercises below are designed to assist you with bibliographical research. Choose the exercises that best suit your goals. Doing all three exercises could also be useful, as they are designed as sequences. Exercise 3.1 will help you compile a list of potential search terms. You can then use these terms to conduct several rounds of keyword search to find relevant sources on the topic and build your working bibliography. Exercise 3.2 is intended to help you to organize and keep systematic records of multiple search attempts. Finally, Exercise 3.3 is useful to finalize your working bibliography for the literature reviews.

Exercise 3.1 Figuring out Search Terms

Before starting a search for information, you should think about which terms may best capture the relevant literature. Make a list of similar keywords so that you can try different search terms. For example:

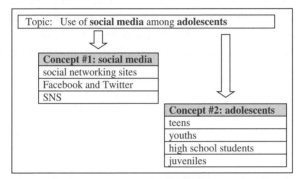

Now, let's try this with your own topic. Enter your topic phrase in the first box and highlight the concept terms in the topic phrase. For each of your concepts/ terms, list possible synonyms, or alternative terms in the smaller boxes below. Look up alternative words using the thesaurus option in your journal database, as described in this chapter; add them in the synonym list.

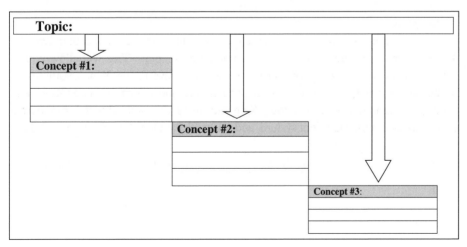

Exercise 3.2 Use of Boolean Terms

Boolean terms AND and OR will expand or narrow your search. In this exercise, let's map out how you may use your search terms using Boolean phrases. From

Exercise 3.1, list the highlighted key concepts/terms in your topic phrase. These will be your search terms.

Concept #1:
Concept #2:
Concept #3:

1 Using AND

Using AND to connect *different* concepts will narrow your search to documents containing all of the terms. In this chapter, we recommended using two terms— you can use a third term but only when you want to narrow your search even further. Use three key terms from your topic phrase to make a list of possible pairs you can use in your search.

Concept #1	AND	Concept #2
Concept #1	AND	Concept #3
Concept #2	AND	Concept #3

Enter each pair into your database (e.g., ProQuest Central, ERIC, Sociological Abstracts), and perform a keyword search. If your search results have roughly 1,000 citations or more, add the third term to narrow your search further. Save your search results onto a computer file or onto a citation management system and skim through the titles and a few abstracts to select relevant literature. We recommend you do this for all three pairings above.

2 Using OR

Use OR to connect *similar* terms (i.e., the synonyms listed for each concept in Exercise 3.1) in order to capture documents containing any of them. This will allow you to locate sources on the same concept but using alternative terms. When your search results are too few (less than 10 sources), add an alternative term with an OR for one concept and search again (see below). Save your research results onto a computer file or onto a citation management system, and select relevant literature from the saved list.

Concept #1	OR	Alternative Term for Concept #1

AND

Concept #2

Exercise 3.3 Creating a Working Bibliography

At the end of Exercise 3.2, you may have a list of a few hundred sources. At this time, we recommend that you skim through the titles and the abstracts of the sources you have saved, and select the sources you feel the most directly related to your topic (see step 1 below). Discard the ones that are not directly relevant to your questions. You will review the selected studies closely for your literature reviews.

1   After skimming through the titles and the abstracts of the references you have saved in Exercise 3.2, select the studies that are most relevant to your research. In general, references that fit the following criteria are relevant and you should include them in your working bibliography:
    • Does this study ask research questions that are the same or similar to your own research questions?
    • Does this study include the same set of concepts/variables as yours?
    • Does this study apply the same theory as the one you may use?
    • Does this study the same target population as yours?
    • Do other studies you are interested in cite this study?

2   Choose the references that fit the above criteria to compile a working bibliography. Your working bibliography may include 15–50 sources, depending on the topic, but there is no set rule about how many should be in your bibliography. We recommend that you show this list to your project supervisor and receive feedback on whether you have included appropriate literature for the scope of your research and whether your working bibliography should have a manageable number of sources.

3   In general, if after selecting the most directly relevant references, your working bibliography includes more than 50 sources, you may still have some less relevant studies in your list. Or, it could be an indication that you should focus on an even narrower aspect of the issue or a particular segment of your population. Discuss with your project supervisor, or your professor, to fine-tune your topic.

4   A library information search is an on-going process that lasts through the completion of your literature review. Once you identify relevant literature and compile a manageable *working bibliography*, you will be continuously adding to and subtracting from the list as you read and evaluate each reference more closely.

Your Project Outcome after Chapter 3

At this point:

• You have a working bibliography, or the initial list of 15–50 sources you plan to read carefully for the purpose of the literature review.
• Your working bibliography includes full citation information in the citation style you will use in this project.
• You have obtained full texts of the articles and books in your working bibliography. If your university libraries do not have some of them, you should have requested the inter-library loan service or other arrangements with your library so that you can access them.
• Begin reading the sources you have obtained from the library.

Chapter 4
Reviewing the Literature

The previous chapter discussed the process of searching for the literature and building a bibliography to read and review. In this chapter, we will discuss how to review the literature you have identified, focusing on the process of evaluation and assessment. The literature review plays an important part in your research. You can use it to improve your research topic and questions. If you have rough ideas about what you want to study but have not yet clearly conceptualized your ideas, a literature review will help you conceptualize them and refine your research topic.

After locating literature on your selected topic, you will read, analyze, synthesize, and summarize the literature. Writing a literature review is a major part of your research proposal, which will develop into a section of your final research report. In this chapter you will learn about some important ways of doing literature review, including how to handle sources and how to have a complete and accurate reference list. While searching for literature, reviewing it, and writing the review, you may encounter some questions. This chapter addresses the following frequently asked questions:

- What is a literature review?
- Why do I need a literature review for my research?
- What does the literature review entail?
- How do I sort my literature?
- How do I read my literature and take notes?
- How do I evaluate and synthesize my reviewed literature?
- How do I write a literature review for my research proposal?

After discussing these questions, the chapter will provide exercises to help you write a literature review for your research proposal.

Student Research and Report Writing: From Topic Selection to the Complete Paper, First Edition. Gabe T. Wang and Keumjae Park. © and Published 2016 by John Wiley & Sons, Ltd.

What Is a Literature Review?

When you read journal articles on your topic, you will find a section, usually in the beginning, describing theoretical frameworks and previous research findings about the research topic. This is the literature review section. The literature review section is the space where researchers show how their studies are connected to previous knowledge on the topic. The literature refers to all previous research done on a specific topic, including theoretical analyses and empirical research findings on the topic. Reviewing means you will read, summarize, assess, and synthesize the literature to build a foundation for your research. Reviewing the literature involves looking over published papers, reading, and evaluating them. It is more than merely summarizing the findings of previous research; it also involves critical reflection, grouping similar studies, and relating them to other groups of research. When writing literature review, you provide your readers with an organized overview of the existing studies on the topic and your critical evaluation of the state of the field of study. Ultimately, the purpose of reviewing the literature is to identify questions or areas in need of more research.

One of the most challenging tasks in your literature review process is to decide what to include and what to exclude in your literature review. In order to write a good literature review, you need to pay attention to two things. First, you need a clear idea about your topic, your research questions, and the concepts included in your inquiry. Second, you will carefully skim through the abstracts and outlines of each reference, and select the studies you should include in your review. Ask whether a source is relevant and useful for your research questions. But this is much easier said than done. We suggest you include the following types of studies:

- Studies whose topic or research questions are similar to yours or include the same variables as yours;
- Studies using your theoretical approach;
- Studies testing the same set of independent and dependent variables;
- Studies of the same issue or question but done on a different population from your target population; and
- Studies that other sources on your topic cite frequently.

Why Do You Need a Literature Review?

Of the many reasons to do a literature review, one is exploration and learning. Past and present research will clarify your topic. Reading books and research papers will give you a basis on which to brainstorm about questions you want to study. The accumulated knowledge you gain by intensive reading will provide you with comprehensive background information on the topic and point to ways to do your research.

Another reason for doing a literature review is to find out the principal theories, major empirical research findings, and research methods that have been used in studying your topic. Specifically, you will learn what theories social scientists have used in studying the topic, how they have developed and tested those theories, what concepts they have used in empirical research, what independent and dependent variables they have used, what research methods they have utilized, and what similar research on the topic has found. At the same time, you may also find how research on your topic has changed over time.

A literature review can also show potential pitfalls you may face. Previous research may have already shown that relationships between particular variables are not empirically confirmed or the correlations are weak. It may also tell you that some methods have proven inappropriate for researching your topic. Or, in contrast, areas related to your topic have yet to be covered adequately. Previous research will often point you in new directions.

Then, you can use a literature review to guide, rationalize, or justify your research. By learning how other researchers have done their research, you may rationalize both the methods you are using and the theory you are utilizing in your research. In other words, the literature review process should make you aware of the possible methods you can use, and assess whether the theory you are using is appropriate.

What Does the Literature Review Entail?

Review of the literature is a systematic process that entails a few steps. This process involves a thorough investigation of scholarly knowledge relevant to your topic, and an integration of such research knowledge into a coherent whole to foreground your research questions, and refine the questions you hope to answer in your research project. In general, the following steps are critical parts of the literature review (Figure 4.1).

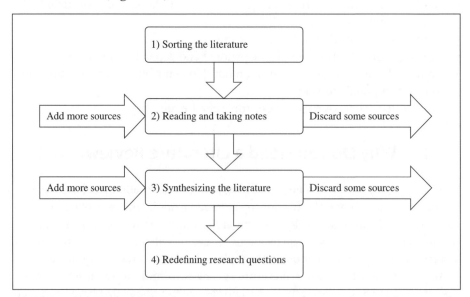

Figure 4.1   The Process of Literature Review.

Keep in mind that the literature review is also an iterative and reflexive process; as your research questions become more specific and clarified during the process of literature reviews, you will add more relevant sources and discard sources which turn out to be irrelevant.

How to Sort Your Literature

We know that sorting is a necessary step for organizing. If you were going to organize your desk drawer, you will divide the contents into groups of similar items and put each group in some sort of organized compartments. Likewise, your literature needs to be sorted into groups and categories of similar studies. A preliminary reading of abstracts, subheadings, and key findings will help you to sort the literature into groups so that you can summarize and evaluate it in an organized manner. Here are some commonly used methods for sorting your literature.

Opposing Arguments and Findings
You can sort the journal articles, book chapters, or notes by their points of view, such as pros and cons, or positive and negative findings. For example, some researchers find that the death penalty reduces violent crime while others find it has no effect on violence. Some researchers argue that population growth affects economic development while others insist that population growth is not related to economic development. In these circumstances, you may put the group of research which finds positive association between two variables and the group which finds negative statistical association into two different categories. When there are conflicting arguments in the literature, classify the sources by different arguments that are put forth. For instance, whether religion is a source of gender oppression or a source of strengths for women is a debated point in gender studies literature. If you are conducting literature reviews on this topic, you may sort the literature into two groups based on their arguments.

In separating groups of views or conflicting findings, think about what factors affect some systematic differences between the groups of studies. They could be theoretical assumptions, methodological differences, or some contextual factors. Sometimes, different study populations will yield different findings. For example, if you find that most research on juvenile behavior in the United States indicates that self-control is negatively related to juvenile delinquent behavior but most research in China indicates that self-control is unrelated to juvenile delinquency, you might want to explore whether culture influences the difference.

Different Variables Tested
You may sort your literature according to specific relationships examined in the study. For example, if you want to find out the relationship between youth crime and (1) family cohesiveness, (2) peer association, and (3) educational commitment, then you can separate the literature into sets of studies focusing on each of these

pairs. You will then be able to summarize what the prevailing findings are in each of the three groups and structure your literature review accordingly. You can also attempt to build an integrative model combining all three variables above and come up with hypotheses based on the combined theory to be tested in your own research.

Different Theories Applied

If the field of literature is divided into three different theoretical perspectives, such as conflict perspective, structural-functionalist perspective, and interactionist perspective, you may separate the papers into three groups according to the theoretical perspectives. In your review, you can evaluate how the perspectives may have led to different research foci and interpretation of findings. For example, some studies of juvenile delinquency guided by conflict perspective conclude that juvenile delinquent behaviors have been caused by the unequal socioeconomic status of their families. On the other hand, some studies of juvenile delinquency guided by interactionist perspectives conclude that juvenile delinquent behaviors have been caused by peer influence.

Similarly, the patterns of lower pay in female-dominated occupations have been common in many countries. There is a disagreement between different theoretical schools on why this is happening. Sociological theories of gender argue that this is due to gender segregation in occupation and devaluation of feminized work; economic theories such as human capital theory, on the other hand, explain that low wages are due to different skills levels, as women are concentrated in low skill specialization (Perales 2013). In your reviews, you may sort the studies into two groups depending on which of these two theoretical models they support. Sorting the literature and questioning where some discrepancies among existing studies come from are both essential steps for literature reviews. As Galvan summarizes below, theoretical or methodological "imperfections" in existing literature can be an appropriate focus for your own research project.

> If there are competing theories in your area, plan to discuss the extent to which the literature you have reviewed supports each of them, keeping in mind that an inconsistency between the results of a study and a prediction based on theory may result from either imperfections in the theoretical model or imperfections in the research methodology used in the study.   (Galvan 1999: 54)

Research Methods

You can classify your literature review according to the types of research methods that have been used. If the materials you are reading include qualitative and quantitative studies and the methods being used make a difference in findings, separate them and determine whether there are systematic differences between the studies. When researchers use different research methods, you may also notice the strengths and weaknesses of each method being used. Similarly, if your literature includes longitudinal and cross-sectional studies, put them into two groups and summarize their findings. Are there systematic differences between the two kinds of studies or omissions resulting from prioritizing one method over another?

Time Period

If you are interested in trends in research or social change, the literature can be classified according to the time of the research being conducted. You may put the books and articles into different groups according to the time period during which the research was conducted and published. For example, you may put the research done on the relationship between technology and organizational structure into groups organized by decades. You may find trends or changes in findings on the relationship between technology and organizational structure over the decades, an area worth studying.

Population

You may also classify the literature according to the population you study. If the research on the same topic is conducted on different study populations such as urban and rural populations, juvenile and adult populations, people of different ethnic groups, or people in Britain and France, separate the studies according to study population. You may detect systematic differences across different populations. The same research done in different areas or different organizations may produce systematic differences, which may give you ideas for your own research.

Sorting the literature will help you better understand and summarize existing studies. It will also help you recognize trends, similarities, and differences among studies, which is the first step for organizing and synthesizing them. When you organize the literature by positive or negative findings, by theories, or by variables tested, you will understand the field of study in a systematic and organized manner. Seeing "the big picture" in this way will make the review process easier and more enjoyable (see Exercise 4.2 for help in sorting your literature).

How Do You Read Your Literature and Take Notes?

After you collected and sorted your literature, start reading the articles and books more closely. If you have already had clearly defined research questions, pay attention to how other researchers have answered the questions. If you have already identified your independent variables (i.e., the causal factors) and dependent variables (i.e., outcomes), make note of the findings on the relationships which you want to study. If you are not quite sure about your research questions or your independent and dependent variables, make a list of questions and variables examined in other studies as you read; reading the literature should help you define your research questions and identify your variables.

Thorough note-taking is absolutely essential. Your memory is never as good as your notes. Today, computer programs allow you to take notes and organize your thoughts much more effectively. To take notes systematically and consistently, we highly recommend you to develop a template, or a list of standard items you will record for each of the studies you read (see Exercise 4.1 for a sample template). The basic things to record include the topic, the research questions or the hypotheses investigated, methodological details (e.g., the sample, data collection methods, and measures), key findings, and your evaluation of the study. It is always a good idea to summarize the researcher's important ideas or findings that are relevant to your research and write them down right away. Taking notes sounds simple, but you need to develop the habit when reading an article or book.

If you think you will quote a paragraph or a few sentences of what you have just read in your paper, copy that paragraph or the sentences carefully and make sure you copy them accurately. Remember to write down the page number or numbers of the paragraph for your future quotation in addition to the full citation information for the source. If you do not want to use the author's exact words, you can paraphrase the major ideas. Even if you paraphrase, the ideas are borrowed; record citation information to indicate that the ideas belong to the source document.

Remember to record the full citation information for the source you are reading. If you are reading and taking notes from a journal article, the information you write down should include the author(s)'s name(s), the year of publication, the title of the article, the title of the journal, the volume and the issue number of the journal, and the page numbers in the journal in which the article appeared. If you are reading books, the source information you write down should also include the place where the book was published and the name of the publisher. Such information normally appears on the copyright page of a book, which is on the inside of the title page. If you get the information from a website, you should write down the author's name, date of publication, title of the source document, date when the information was retrieved, and the web page's URL (Universal Resources Locator).

While taking notes, it is convenient to use your computer to type your notes and organize them according to subjects, authors, or your research questions. Then later, when you need your notes or citations, you can simply copy and paste them into your paper. You may spend a little bit more time taking notes when reviewing literature but save yourself a lot of time while writing your literature review. More importantly, you are less likely to make mistakes in indicating the sources in your text or in preparing your reference list.

How Do You Evaluate and Synthesize Your Reviewed Literature?

After reading the literature, you now need to evaluate, analyze, synthesize it and write a summary assessment of the field of study. Reviewing each study in the literature and synthesizing the whole field are two different processes. In your review of each study, you will carefully evaluate whether the study applied an appropriate theoretical framework, whether the study is further elaborating theory, whether the validity and reliability of the data are established, whether the methods of investigation is robust, and whether there is an agreement between the claims and the evidences.

When you attempt to synthesize the literature, you should pay more attention to the *relationships between the studies, and between groups of study.* Look for patterns, similarities, and differences between groups of study. Pay attention to any methodological inadequacies and unexplored themes in the field of study as a whole. These are often called "gaps and voids" in the literature. For example, reviewing the literature on the relationship between economic recession and suicide, you may find that high unemployment rates during economic downturns affected both male and female suicide rates in Taiwan (Chen, et al. 2010) while suicide rates only increased for males and not for females in the UK (Coope, et al. 2014). Such cross-national differences may be worthy of your attention, as it may indicate that social and economic contexts are affecting the relationship between these two variables. Similarly, when you review literature about juvenile substance use, you may notice some regional differences; surveys conducted in the U.S. state of Utah find that African American juveniles are more likely to use drugs than Caucasian American juveniles, while surveys conducted in the Buffalo, New York find that Caucasian American juveniles are more likely to use drugs than African American juveniles.

The "gaps and voids in the literature" indicate that there may be factors and variables unaccounted for, or there are "imperfections" in the theoretical applications and methodological executions in existing studies. If you do a good job with your assessment of studies you classified earlier, you will be able to point to under-researched areas, contradictions to be resolved, and new questions to be explored. These gaps or voids are what you would want to identify during your literature reviews. Sometimes, putting the groups of literature into a visual "map" can help the process of synthesizing.

Figure 4.2 is a sample mapping of the literature on children's well-being and family structure, which we created. First, we classified the studies into three groups based on the different variables which had been identified as factors affecting children's well-being in diverse structures of step-families. Then, we used arrows and shorthand notes to describe the associations and possible causal directions between groups of literature. We found that the literature does not tell much about some of the relationships in this map, and recorded those in the box at the bottom. If the field of study looks like this map, these questions are the questions we are likely to pursue as our research questions for a study.

As you evaluate the field, you may also look for problems, and inadequacies in methodologies of the study, and explore new directions for your research. In evaluating your literature, identify problems related to the sample size and quality, the adequacy of data collection strategies, and the validity of measures. If studies on medical cannabis use among cancer patients were mostly conducted using surveys, you may point out the need for more in-depth study using qualitative methods. If existing studies tend to use small samples, you may consider designing a study using a large-scale data set. If you find the measurements for certain concepts are

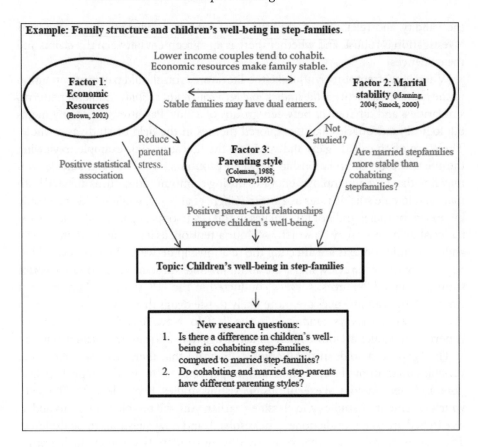

Figure 4.2   Synthesizing with a Visual Map.

not adequate, for example, using self-report as the measure of alcoholism, or using only income as a global indicator of quality of life, you can critique these methodological limitations. Most published studies have explicit discussions on the limitation of their research. Such limitations may come from using limited samples, flawed methods, or inadequate analysis. Any of these limitations may open a door for your research project and allow you to make contributions to the field.

Even when the literature you reviewed seems fine, you may still retest the theory with new data, or replicate past research on a new study population. You can design a study to confirm previous research findings, support an existing theory, or revise or reject an existing theory (see Exercise 4.4 for help in analyzing the literature).

Refining Your Research Questions and Variables
In the end, your literature review will help you refine your research topic and research questions. Generally speaking, you need to have an adequately defined topic before you start your literature review. Your review, however, may prompt you to revise your topic. It can help you make your topic more specific or more appropriate. You may also change the initial research questions and variables into

ones you determine understudied in existing studies. This is perfectly normal during the process of literature review. Conducting a literature review is a part of the process in finalizing the research questions for your study. Therefore, you may need to redefine your topic and revise your research questions several times throughout the review process (Galvan 1999).

As you fine-tune your research topic, research questions, and your variables, you may need to review more literature, if you find that your literature review in certain areas is insufficient. On the other hand, do not hold on to the studies which have become irrelevant along the way because you revised your topic or research questions.

How Do You Write Your Literature Review?

Since you will be expected to include initial literature reviews as part of your written research proposal, let's discuss how to write the literature reviews. Before you write your literature review, you should decide on its purpose and length. If your project supervisor or class instructor has a length requirement, then you should write accordingly. If you are doing literature reviews for a term paper for an undergraduate class you are taking, you need to show your awareness of the literature on the topic. If you are working on a thesis, a research proposal for postgraduate studies, or other comprehensive research projects, you will have to provide more comprehensive and up-to-date coverage; in this case, your literature reviews should include major studies or classic work on the topic, and all key research published in the past ten years. In this case, your literature review may be longer than a literature review for a term paper or a journal article format assignment.

Writing Formally and Using Appropriate Techniques
Though writing habits are different for everyone, we strongly recommend that you develop a detailed outline before you write your literature review. An outline will give you a sense of structure and help you maintain a coherent logic as you write. Of course, it is okay to revise your outline and edit your drafts as your thinking unfolds. Many published studies use subheadings to organize their literature reviews.

Literature reviews should be written in a formal language. There are technical tips to achieve this. For instance, limit the use of the first person in your writing, although it is all right to speak in the first person occasionally to indicate your analytic assessment or an argumentation (such as "My critique is that ..." and "I argue ..."). Leave out casual references to your opinions such as "I think," "I believe," "in my opinion." What you write is obviously your opinion and your ideas. Similarly, the use of the second person ("you") should be avoided as well. As is the case with any writing, avoid using the same words repeatedly.

Writing Evaluation and Synthesis, Not Mere Summaries
The key to a successful literature review is that it should be a *critical* and *organized assessment* of existing studies. It should not merely list summary after summary but

"evaluate, clarify and/or integrate the content of primary reports" (Cooper 1988: 103). Phillips and Pugh warn that "a mere encyclopedic listing in which all the titles are presented with only a description of each work and no reasoned organization and evaluation would not be adequate" (1987: 53). This means when you review the literature, you need to not only provide critical evaluations on the previous research theoretically and methodically, but *integrate* the previous research and organize it logically and systematically. Remember that literature reviews are "representation of *interaction* with the literature" (Bruce 2000: 75. Italics are our emphasis).

It is useful to make the distinction between a narrative review and a synthesized review here (Cooper 2010). A narrative review is a series of summaries of each article reviewed, typically in chronological order. This is sometimes called an "annotated bibliography." In narrative reviews, you may critically examine each study in the literature, but there is no sense of organization in your reviews, nor any internal logic in your presentation of the studies; a summary is simply presented in a paragraph or two for each study.

A synthesis of the literature on the other hand is an integration of knowledge learned from separate research into coherent statements of assessment about the field as a whole. A synthesis of literature will be able to show a "unified picture" of the field; it clarifies how different groups of study are distinguished from one another, and explains how they are related to one another. Are there unresolved debates in the literature? Begin with a statement that there are contradicting findings in the field, and then present what those are. Have you identified three groups of studies using different theoretical models? State in your own voice that there are three competing models; then your synthesized reviews should summarize what those three models are, how they have been tested, and evaluate the strengths and weaknesses of each group. We often recommend our students to use subheadings within the literature reviews to keep different groups of literature organized.

In some disciplines, a meta-analysis of the literature is done as a foundation for a synthesized literature review. Meta-analysis is a quantified summary of the types and groups of research in the defined topic area (Cooper 2010); this provides categorization of different studies in the field, and basic statistical counts of different studies in the literature, which are very useful for constructing a synthesis. In short, your literature reviews should be a holistic assessment of the state of the knowledge in the topic area.

The most frequent problem we have found in our teaching is that students tend to do a narrative review; in other words, they review a few articles, write a summary for each article, and then simply list them in separate paragraphs. This style of review represents a collection of literature rather than an evaluation or synthesis. If you have written your literature review in this way, work more on it to produce a synthesized literature review.

Another common error is including a review of literature that is not directly related to the research questions. This is sometimes due to the change of research questions, which occurs during the review process. For instance, including a review of the literature on rehabilitation of adolescent drug users would be inappropriate for a proposal of a study on gender and peer influence on drug use. Even though both are about drug use, literature on how to treat users has little to do with a study attempting to find the causes that lead to drug use among youths. As your review progresses, you should pay attention to the direction into which your research questions are crystalizing. If your research questions move away from your initial ones, eliminate parts that are becoming irrelevant to your current study direction.

Including Justification for Your Own Study

As an extension to this, your literature review will also tell your readers that research on certain areas is needed, should be done in a different population, or using a different research methods. This provides the rationale for your own research and the way you design and conduct your research project. For example, if the previous research is not conclusive, then your research is necessary. If the previous research missed certain sections of the society, your research that includes such missed societal sections will make the research more complete. If previous research is only cross sectional, then your longitudinal research will make a new contribution to the understanding of the issue. If your research will go beyond what has been done so far; then, your research may break new ground.

Your literature review will end with a paragraph about the specific research questions or hypotheses your own study will investigate. Your research questions or research hypotheses should have a logical connection to your reviews, as they are derived from your reviews and theoretical discussions. If you have several research hypotheses, we recommend listing them one by one as a numbered list.

Students often ask how research questions and research hypotheses are different. The difference is sometimes a matter of form; the former are stated as interrogative sentences (i.e., Does A cause B?) and the latter are declarative sentences (i.e., A causes B). But, generally speaking, research questions tend to be broader than hypotheses. For example, in light of the literature review, you may ask what factors influence the likelihood of high school students' dropping out of school. On the other hand, hypotheses are affirmative statements that contain more specific and theoretically informed predictions or assumptions. For example, you may hypothesize that the need to work to help the family's finance is likely to lead teenagers from lower income families to give up schooling. Notice that, in the above examples, the research question is open to a broader range of answers while the hypothesis predicts a relationship between two specified variables. You need not repeat the questions in both forms; state them either as a set of research questions or a set of hypotheses.

Documenting Sources and Creating Your Reference List

When you write your literature review, you should always indicate from which sources you borrow ideas, direct quotes, or statistics. Neglecting to do so opens you up to the charge of plagiarism. Plagiarism is commonly defined as trying to pass off someone else's work as your own. This not only applies to the entire paper, but also to parts of a paper. For instance, if you copied a paragraph from a source without quotation marks and citation, the reader of your paper is being led to believe that those sentences are your own writing. Thus, this constitutes plagiarism. Even when some passages are paraphrased, the ideas still belong to the author of the source you read, and therefore you must acknowledge it by properly citing the source. Plagiarism can be avoided by learning and practicing proper citation.

Citation is important for a couple of different reasons. First, citation is a way to acknowledge intellectual property rights of the author of the ideas and writing from whom you are borrowing. Just like physical properties, there are ownerships in materials created by intellectual labor. When you borrow these intellectual products, you must specify to whom they belong; intellectual products include written documents, images, and other forms of creative products. This is an ethical obligation. Second, citations can enhance your own argument. By citing published research, you are supporting your argument with proven evidence and increasing the credibility of your claims. Citations also help the reader of your paper by providing "breadcrumbs" to follow if he/she wants to read more in-depth about the ideas you paraphrased or quoted, or to evaluate the validity of your arguments. Thus, citation is not only a critical practice for academic honesty, but also an important part of communication between you and the reader of your paper. Do not forget this advice: Cite someone's work whether you use direct quotations or indirectly paraphrase.

There is a multitude of citation styles and different disciplines may use different formats. Your supervisor or instructor may require a particular style which you will need to follow. Or your university may have specific requirements for citations and reference lists for theses or dissertations. The guideline for citation style and formatting for your school should be available in the university's thesis handbook. Alternatively, another easy way is to check out a thesis or dissertation from your university library and follow the format that has been used.

In the social sciences, the citation styles provided by the *Publication Manual of the American Psychological Association* (APA) is perhaps most frequently used. American Sociological Association format (ASA) is used in sociology and related fields. Chicago Manual of Style is also commonly used. Whichever format you use, use it correctly and consistently throughout your work. Citation style guides include instructions for citations in the text as well as for preparing a reference list at the end of the paper. Whenever you cite something from a book or a journal paper, you should remember to add the source to your reference list. In other words, the sources cited in your text must match the reference list. The rule is to list *all* references you cite in your paper and *only* the references you cite in your paper.

There are computer applications that aid citation and referencing. Examples are EndNote, ProCite, and OneNote. It may be worthwhile to search for other products with similar features that are available free of charge online (Mendeley Desktop is one example and Citavi also has a free version with limited function). These applications will allow you to store reference information (i.e., author(s), publication date, title, journal title, volume and issue number, page numbers, publisher (in the case of books) and so on) to create your own reference list and find relevant reference information whenever you need. Whenever using a citation and referencing application, check to see that it works appropriately when you finish writing your literature review.

Box 4.1 A Sample Reference List in Various Citation Styles.

American Psychological Association Style (APA Style)

Bambra, C., Fox, D., & Scott-Samuel, A. (2005). Towards a politics of health. *Health Promotion International, 20,* 187–93. doi:10.1093/heapro/dah608.

Marmot, M. (2005). Public health social determinants of health inequalities. *Lancet, 365,* 1099–1104. doi:10.1016/S0140-6736(05)71146-6.

Weaver, J. B., Mays, D., Weaver, S. S., Hopkins, G. L., Eroglu, D., & Bernhardt, J. M. (2010). Health information-seeking behaviors, health indicators, and health risks. *American Journal of Public Health, 100,* 1520–1525. doi:10.2105/AJPH.2009.180521.

Chicago Manual of Style (Author-Date System)

Bambra, Clare, Debbie Fox, and Alex Scott-Samuel. 2005. "Towards a Politics of Health." *Health Promotion International* 20:187–93. doi:10.1093/heapro/dah608.

Marmot, Michael. 2005. "Public Health Social Determinants of Health Inequalities." *Lancet* 365: 1099–1104. doi:10.1016/S0140-6736(05)71146-6.

Weaver, James B., Darren Mays, Stephanie Sargent Weaver, Gary L. Hopkins, Dogan Eroglu, and Jay M. Bernhardt. 2010. "Health Information-Seeking Behaviors, Health Indicators, and Health Risks." *American Journal of Public Health.* 100: 1520–25. doi:10.2105/AJPH.2009.180521.

American Sociological Association (ASA Style)

Bambra, Clare, Debbie Fox, and Alex Scott-Samuel. 2005. "Towards a Politics of Health." *Health Promotion International* 20:187–93.

Marmot, Michael. 2005. "Public Health Social Determinants of Health Inequalities." *Lancet* 365:1099–1104.

Weaver, James B., Darren Mays, Stephanie Sargent Weaver, Gary L. Hopkins, Dogan Eroglu, and Jay M. Bernhardt. 2010. "Health Information-Seeking Behaviors, Health Indicators, and Health Risks." *American Journal of Public Health* 100:1520–25.

References

Bruce, Christine Susan. 2000. "Research Students' Early Experiences of the Dissertation Literature Review". *Annual Editions: Research Methods* 01-02. Guilford, CT: McGraw-Hill/Dushkin.

Chen, Ying-Yeh, Paul S. Yip, Carmen Lee, Hsiang-Fang Fan, King-Wa Fu. 2010. "Economic Fluctuations and Suicide: A Comparison of Taiwan and Hong Kong." *Social Science and Medicine* 71(12): 2083–2090.

Coope, Caroline, David Gunnell, William Hollingworth, Keith Hawton, Nav Kapur, Vanessa Fearn, Claudia Wells, and Chris Metcalfe. 2014. "Suicide and the 2008 Economic Recession: Who Is Most at Risk? Trends in Suicide Rates in England and Wales 2001–2011." *Social Science & Medicine* 117: 76–85.

Cooper, Harris. M. 1988. "The Structure of Knowledge Synthesis". *Knowledge in Society* 1: 104–126.

Cooper, Harris. M. 2010. *Research Synthesis and Meta-analysis: A Step by Step Approach*. 4th ed. Thousand Oaks, CA: Sage.

Galván, José L. 1999. *Writing Literature Reviews: A Guide for Students of the Social and Behavioral Sciences*. Los Angeles, CA: Pyrczak Publishing.

Giarrusso, Roseann, Judith Richlin-Klonsky, William G. Roy and Ellen Strenski. 2008. *A Guide to Writing Sociology Papers*. 6th ed. New York: Worth Publishers.

Machi, Lawrence A., and Brenda T. McEvoy. 2012. *The Literature Review: Six Steps to Success*. 2nd ed. Thousand Oaks, CA: Corwin.

Perales, Francisco. 2013. "Occupational Sex-segregation, Specialized Human Capital and Wages: Evidence from Britain," *Work, Employment, and Society* 27(4): 600–620.

Phillips, E. M., and D. S. Pugh. 1987. *How to Get a Ph.D.* Milton Keynes: Open University Press.

Further Reading

Galvan, Jose L. 2012. *Writing Literature Reviews: A Guide for Students of the Social and Behavioral Sciences*. 5th ed. Glendale, CA: Pyrczak Publishing.

Orcher, Lawrence T. 2005. *Conducting Research: Social and Behavioral Science Methods*. Glendale, CA: Pyrczak Publishing.

Pan, M. Ling. 2008. *Preparing Literature Reviews: Qualitative and Quantitative Approaches*. 3rd ed. Glendale, CA: Pyrczak Publishing.

Patten, Mildred L. 2010. *Proposing Empirical Research: A Guide to the Fundamentals*. 4th ed. Glendale, CA: Pyrczak Publishing.

Internet Resources

North Carolina State University library has a video tutorial for postgraduate students. http://www.lib.ncsu.edu/tutorials/litreview/

University of North Carolina Writing Center online guides on literature reviews. http://writingcenter.unc.edu/handouts/literature-reviews/

University of Nottingham's website provides links to many study resources for managing reading and writing literature reviews. http://www.nottingham.ac.uk/studentservices/supportforyourstudies/academicsupport/studyresources/dissertationsandprojects/managingreadingandwritingaliteraturereview.aspx

University of Reading (UK) Study Advice webpage offers several helpful tips for reading and organizing information. http://www.reading.ac.uk/internal/studyadvice/StudyResources/Essays/sta-undertakinglitreview.aspx

Exercises for Chapter 4

Use some of the exercises to sort and organize the literature you are reviewing. Exercise 4.1 provides a template for thorough note-taking while reading the literature. Exercise 4.2 helps you to group and organize the literature; consider how you will sort and classify the literature based on some criteria in this exercise. Exercise 4.3 suggests a way to lay out groups of literature in a conceptual map and to clarify the relationships between groups. Exercise 4.4 will help you analyze the literature as a whole. Your answers to the guiding questions will be the foundation for your assessment of the state of the knowledge on this topic. At the end of the exercises, you will be able to identify some understudied areas in the literature, which may become your own research questions for your project.

Exercise 4.1 Reading the Literature and Taking Notes

Note-taking is essential for a good literature review. The template below identifies key information to record about the articles and books you read.

SUMMARY INFORMATION

Citation information (author(s), year of publication, full title of the article, journal title, volume and issue numbers, and page numbers)	
What is the topic? What are the research questions or hypotheses studied?	
List the theories reviewed in this article. Write down the main concepts and claims of each theory. Ask yourself which of the theories may be a good framework for your study.	
Identify independent and dependent variables examined in this article.	
What is the study design? Describe its methodology (the sample, data collection methods, measures used, dataset used)	
What were the answers to the research questions? For each of the research questions, summarize the findings.	
What are the theoretical conclusions of this study?	
Your evaluation or critical comments on this study.	
Questions which can be addressed by future studies	
Key references to look up	

IMPORTANT QUOTES FROM THE ARTICLE

Quotes from the article (Indicate direct quotes with quotation marks)	Citation information (Author, Publication Year, and Page(s))	Your own interpretation of, and comments on the quotes

Exercise 4.2 Sorting Your Literature

We offer four different sorting criteria to group and organize your literature. You do not need to use all four criteria; choose one which makes the best sense given the literature. Classify your material into groups using the selected classification system and add your notes and reflections following the guiding questions.

1   Sorting by Theory

Among the literature you reviewed, are there competing theories or perspectives to explain this topic/issue? If there are, briefly summarize: a) what they are, b) what claims each theory makes, and c) what studies apply which theories. Prepare a table like the one below to visually summarize the different positions and theoretical frameworks you will discuss in the literature review section.

Theory/Perspective #1	Theory/Perspective #2	Theory/Perspective #3
Name of the Theory/ Perspective:	Name of the Theory/ Perspective:	Name of the Theory/ Perspective:
Main Claims:	Main Claims:	Main Claims:
List of studies using this framework:	List of studies using this framework:	List of studies using this framework:
Main points of debates and contrast between the theories:		
The theoretical framework to be used in your study and the reasons why you choose this framework:		

2   Sorting by Variables

Another way to sort and organize the literature review is by variables investigated in existing studies. Researchers often examine several factors or independent variables for one dependent variable which may be your topic. Prepare the table below to organize the literature by the variables studied. Construct a similar table with multiple dependent variables if your topic is the independent variable and you are interested in its various outcomes.

Variable #1 (for example, family cohesiveness and delinquent behavior)	Variable #2 (for example, peer association and delinquent behavior)	Variable #3 (for example, educational commitment and delinquent behavior)
Main findings about this association:	Main findings about this association:	Main findings about this association:
Major studies cited:	Major studies cited:	Major studies cited:
Your critiques on this group of studies:	Your critiques on this group of studies:	Your critiques on this group of studies:
Are there new hypotheses to be tested about this topic? Which ones you can examine in your own study?		
Are there methodological flaws in these studies (e.g., sample, measures)?		
Can you create a study rectifying these flaws?		

3   Sorting by Methods

What methodologies are predominantly used in existing studies? Sort your literature by the types of research methods – quantitative studies and qualitative studies. Is there a need for a study using the under-used methods (depending on what the predominant methodology is in the literature)? Briefly summarize the ways a new methodology can remedy the shortcomings of existing studies.

Quantitative Studies	**Qualitative Studies**
List major studies and record sample and data collection methods used:	List major studies and list sample and data collection methods used:
Key findings:	Key findings:
Your critique on this group:	Your critique on this group:

Is there a need for a study using a different/under-used method?

What new research questions can be addressed using a new method?

4   Sorting by Population Studied

Is there a particular group/population that has not been studied by other research-ers? Is there a need to examine this topic/issue within an understudied group? Is there a need for a comparative study between different groups of people?

Group/Population #1	Group/Population #2
Major studies on this population:	Major studies on this population:
Key findings:	Key findings:
Your critique:	Your critique:
Are there understudied groups? How does this void affect the field of study? What group should be studied?	
Is there a need for comparative study? What groups would be appropriate for a comparison?	
What new research questions can be examined using a different population?	

Exercise 4.3 Visual Mapping of the Literature

Visualizing the relationships between different groups of literature helps you to organize your reviews. Using the blank space below, lay out the "map" of the literature you have read, as we showed in Figure 4.2 of this chapter. Use the grouping mechanism you used in Exercise 4.2 to sort out the groups. Based on the findings in the literature, indicate statistical associations and causal directions using arrows and notes. Describe in shorthand notes the relationships between groups and record any unexamined relationships in the literature.

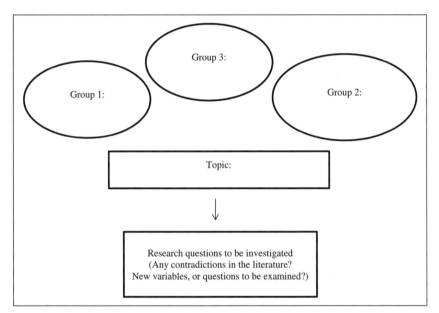

Exercise 4.4 Evaluating the Literature

You now have a good basic foundation to start the next step in the literature review: your evaluation. Evaluating the literature involves 1) understanding the overview of the relevant field of study, 2) clarifying the relationship between different subgroups of literature within it, and 3) identifying the "gaps and voids" and what new information you can add to the existing literature. Once you decide on your research questions or hypotheses and determine what contributions you will make with this study, make those points explicit in your literature review.

Guiding Questions to Evaluate and Synthesize the Literature

1   Are there debates or competing theories about this topic? Which theory or side of the debate is more convincing to you?

2   Is there a need for an integrated theory that combines all or some of the existing theories? Is there an integrated theory you can test in your research?

3   Taking the literature as a whole, what are the gaps and voids about this topic/issue? Are there unexplored research questions or new hypotheses to be tested? Is there a new variable you can introduce to improve our understanding of your topic? Can you focus on these understudied issues in your study?

4   What methodologies are predominantly used in existing studies? Is there a need for a qualitative study or a quantitative study (different from the predominant methodology) to address some particular aspects of this topic/issue?

5   Is there a particular group/population that has not been studied by other researchers? Is there a need to examine this topic/issue within an understudied group?

6   Is there a need for a comparative study?

Your Project Outcome after Chapter 4

At this point:

- You have read and made notes about the sources in your bibliography.
- You have constructed a set of clarified and revised research questions which you are ready to investigate in an empirical research.
- You have revised bibliography which includes some newly added references according to the revised research questions. References which have become irrelevant are eliminated from the list.
- You have an organized literature review.
- Your research questions are finalized.

Chapter 5

Research Questions and Methods

Having carefully selected a research topic, reviewed relevant literature, and decided on the objective of your research, now is time to design your research. First, refine and finalize your research questions and select your research methods. Here are questions students frequently ask when developing their research questions and selecting their methods:

- What are my research questions?
- What is the goal of my research?
- Should I use quantitative or qualitative methods in my research?
- How do I use theories in my research?
- Are ethical matters important in my research?
- To what ethical issues should I pay attention?

This chapter addresses these frequently asked questions. To help you work out your research design, we will first focus on things you should consider in order to choose the right research design for your study. Then, Chapter 6 will discuss more details on different data collection methods. Exercises placed at the end of the chapter are designed to help you develop your research questions and move forward with your research design.

What Are Your Research Questions?

Now that you have specific research questions you are ready to study, it is time to think about how to answer them. Conducting research is like building a house. A blueprint is essential and will facilitate its construction. Similarly, a well-designed research project is a good beginning and will enable you to get the research done.

Student Research and Report Writing: From Topic Selection to the Complete Paper, First Edition. Gabe T. Wang and Keumjae Park. © and Published 2016 by John Wiley & Sons, Ltd.

When you design a house, you need to decide on what kind of house you want to build. Similarly, when you design your research project, start with your research questions. In finalizing your research questions, we want you to consider a few more important things to determine whether they are ready.

Research Questions Are Related to Your Literature Reviews
Research questions are directly connected to the conclusions of your literature reviews. In Chapter 4, we described the process of literature reviews. They present a summary and critique of existing studies on the topic and identify any unresolved debates or understudied areas ("gaps and voids") in current scholarly dialogues. Ideally, your plan is to address these areas with your own research so that your own study can add something new to the existing knowledge. In other words, literature reviews provide rationale or justification for your research questions. The connection between your literature reviews and your research questions should be apparent and clear to yourself and your readers.

Research Questions Are Theoretical Questions, Which Require Data Analysis to Answer
Sometimes students conflate research questions with the actual questions they will ask respondents. For example, "what is respondents' self-identified class?" is not a research question. This is a question to be directed to the respondents during your research. Similarly, "Why did the respondent vote for the Labor party in this year's election?" and "What jobs do you wish to pursue after graduation?" are questions which you will use in the surveys or interviews. Simply put, survey or interview questions are the questions intended to obtain specific information about individual respondents' opinions, attitudes, and behaviors.

Your research questions, on the other hand, are questions about more general patterns commonly found in the population, or about broader concepts and the *relationship*s between concepts and issues. If you have questions such as "does social class affect individuals' voting patterns?" and "do the students in elite universities (such as the Ivy League schools in the U.S. or the Russell Group universities in the UK) have different job aspirations compared to their peers in non-elite schools?," then you can see that no individual respondents can provide you with direct answers to these questions. You will need to analyze the data on the two concepts, class and voting choice, or university affiliation and job aspirations, to see whether they are connected. These are examples of what count as research questions. An easy way to tell if your question is a suitable research question is to ask whether you need to analyze the data to answer it. If the answer to your question can be obtained directly from individual respondents, it does not qualify as a research question.

Research Questions Should Be Clear and Specific
This is a repeated point, but we will emphasize again. A common problem students confront is that their topics are not fully and appropriately conceptualized. They ask research questions that do not accurately reflect the topics that they select for research. For example, a student selected "Student Athletes' Problems"

as his research topic. When asked to put his research topic into research questions, he wrote "What are student athletes' problems?"

Asked exactly what "problems" he had in mind and how he was going to do his research, the student responded that he was thinking about cannabis and alcohol use among students playing sports in university teams and their effects on academic performance. He was thinking about conducting surveys among athletes in nearby universities to collect data. The professor asked the student to conceptualize his ideas and narrow them down to a clear topic that would more precisely reflect his ideas and then develop specific research questions based on his topic for his research.

After careful thinking, the student changed his topic to "Student Athletes Substance Use and Academic Performance." Accordingly, the student developed a research question, "How does student athlete substance use affect academic performance?" Asked to make his question even more specific so that he could design his survey questionnaire accordingly, the student changed his question to "How do cannabis, alcohol, and cocaine use affect student athletes' class attendance and their grade point average?" This question is much more conducive to his questionnaire design than the question the student first raised.

The above example illustrates the process of identifying concepts and specifying a topic idea into concrete research questions. In finalizing your research questions or specific hypotheses for testing, you need to identify the precise definitions for the concepts so that they represent your research ideas. In the above example, our student had to clarify what he meant by "problems" student athletes faced. When you write hypotheses for a quantitative study, you may have to specify your concepts even further into observable variables. The student above came up with "class attendance" and "grade point average" as variables representing the concept "academic performance." This is a process called "operationalization" in research terms which we will explain more in Chapter 6. For now, remember that variables refer to concepts that can take different values across cases. For example, gender, whether someone is a university student or not, work hours per week, favorite sports, average grade earned last year, and so on, are all variables because each individual / case in your study will have different answers / values for these questions.

Research Questions Ask Complex Questions
When you develop your topic into research questions, avoid asking "yes/no" questions, such as "Do students use drugs?" or "Does family income affect school performance?" Instead, ask research questions starting with why, what, and how. Questions starting with why, what, and how provide answers more sophisticated than a simple yes or no. The following research questions can be good examples:

- How do family relationships affect student school performance?
- How do overseas work assignments affect white collar workers' future career paths?
- In what ways can women in corporate boards affect company policies and practices on gender equality?

- Why are university students politically active in some countries and not in others?
- What factors affect marital satisfaction?
- What factors influence experiences of depression among elderly population?
- Why do some democratic revolutions fail?
- How does social class affect health outcomes for patients with cardiovascular diseases?
- Why is education migration more pronounced in Asia than in other regions?
- What factors affect teachers' attitudes on ethno-religious minority pupils?
- How do the new social media affect patterns of adolescent friendship formation?

What Are the Goals of Your Research?

It helps to have clear objectives for your research. Research objectives are usually implied in research questions. Do your research questions ask about the distribution of attitudes or behaviors? Or do they inquire about the relationships between variables? There are several kinds of research, but the following four are most common. What method of field research you want to choose depends on the goals of your research and the scope of the research question you ask.

The first type of study is an **exploratory** study. If the questions you asked are about a newly emerging issue in the field or something that is inadequately studied, your goals are finding some basic information for further study. For example, if you want to find out how emails shape the way office gossip develops and affect people in the workplace, you may design an exploratory study using a small sized sample. In this case, your main purpose is to provide some basic insights about this question, identify some empirical patterns of behaviors, and investigate some potential connections to other issues in the workplace such as clique formation, fair treatment and equity, work satisfaction, and productivity. Identifying good research questions for future study is an important benefit of exploratory studies.

For instance, social media are a relatively new phenomenon. As an exploratory study, you may conduct in-depth interviews with young people about how they use Instagram, Facebook, Twitter, LinkedIn and other social media and how their usage affects their interactions with others. Or you may observe, with the participants' consent, a handful of personal profiles, images, and exchanges of comments on a particular social media site to explore the significance of social media on people's lives. Or you may want to conduct surveys, especially with open-ended questions, asking a small sample of students about their use and the perspectives on social media to understand this form of social interaction. All of these designs can achieve the goal of an exploratory study.

Keep in mind, however, that exploratory research often has few guideposts. That means you have to figure out how to give meaning to your findings. You may break new ground in your exploration, but you may also get stranded somewhere without finding any substantive answers to your initial inquiry. Therefore, think carefully before you decide on exploratory research. By definition, it has limited generalizability and your findings need to be examined further.

A second type of study is a **descriptive** study. If your goal is to provide information on the distribution of characteristics, behavioral patterns, attitudes, or opinions, your study will be considered a descriptive study. This is a "fact-finding" type study. You probably have seen some large scale descriptive studies done by governments and mass media organizations. For example, population surveys, statistical reports on economy and labor trends, and health risk surveys among youths are routinely conducted and published by governments and their agencies in many countries. In a descriptive study, you may ask specific factual questions, such as what percentage of the study population support or oppose a particular side of a controversy and what is the distribution of public opinion on a specific social issue or government policy, or you simply collect data on health, or demographic and social characteristics of a group. Descriptive research usually does not tell you the causes or effects of something but describes what it is. Questionnaire surveys may be most appropriate for descriptive research.

A third type of research is an **explanatory** study, which is more common in social science research. Explanatory research addresses the "why" question; if the goal of your study is to find out what is causing a particular issue or phenomenon; then it will be an explanatory study. For example, if you want to examine why girls do better in language and literature courses than boys, you will conduct an explanatory study and investigate the possible causes for the gender gap in language learning. Or, if you want to explain why some people are happier than others, then you will test what factors are related to subjective feeling of happiness. You may even be able to assess what factors have stronger impact than others. In social sciences, testing on such relationships is often done using statistical analysis techniques. For explanatory studies, quantitative questionnaire surveys using a large representative sample or experimental research designs are commonly used.

The fourth is an **evaluative** study, research frequently conducted for policy and program evaluations. If you are interested in finding out whether a social policy or an intervention program works, or how it works, conduct an evaluative study. In evaluative studies, you compare the data before and after the implementation of a policy or an intervention program so as to assess what effects the intervention had on the outcome. You will evaluate if the program has effectively reached its goals. For example, when a school is interested in exploring whether using tablet devices and interactive apps will improve children's reading skills, an evaluative study design can be implemented to measure baseline reading skills before the use of tablet devices and the skills after using the devices for a certain period of time. You may also evaluate if the program has been implemented appropriately and what steps are necessary to implement the program better. If a new social program has been suggested in your region, you may conduct needs assessment research and decide if the new program is actually needed. You may also perform an assessment to find out if an existing program should be continued.

What Method Should You Use in Your Research?

After determining the goals and objectives of your research, it is time to consider what research design is most appropriate to answer your research questions. There are several commonly used methods, including experimental research, questionnaire surveys, ethnographic research, in-depth interviews, content analysis, secondary analysis of existing data, historical research, and comparative study. These research methods are usually categorized as quantitative and qualitative research methods.

What Is the Difference between Quantitative and Qualitative Research?
The broad categorization between quantitative and qualitative research is something you should think about first, before you consider specific methods to collect your data. **Quantitative research** has been developed from the philosophy of logical positivism, and it is based on a systematic use of quantified empirical information to study human behavior. Quantitative research methods include questionnaire surveys, content analysis, experimental tests, and other methods that you can use to quantify information for numerical analyses. Quantitative researchers employ statistics to analyze and summarize the data collected.

Qualitative research is a research strategy to collect data about a person, a group, or a community from the participants' own perspectives. Locke et al. describes it as "a means for describing and attempting to understand the observed regularities in what people do, or in what they report as their experience" (Locke et al., 2000: 96). Qualitative research is premised upon the idea that interpretation is a key to the understanding the social world, and that social reality is a constructed reality and experienced differently by individuals, ideas largely attributed to such theorists as Max Weber and George Herbert Mead. Qualitative research methods include in-depth interviews, observations, ethnography, and focus group discussions. In qualitative research, data include transcribed interviews, texts, images, and field notes. Qualitative researchers systematically interpret, analyze and summarize non-numerical data to report the patterns and relations between different themes in the data, and describe the population, or the setting in question in great detail.

For example, consider how a student's research interest in studying romance will be addressed differently, depending on the research strategy used. As you can see in Box 5.1, the data collected using different research methods will yield quite different data to analyze. Quantitative data such as the answers collected in survey questionnaire like the one in Box 5.1 will allow the student researcher to collect quantifiable numeric data; there is a number code for each answer choice in the survey. The student will be able to report what percentage of the respondents have experienced love, what was the strongest feeling people felt, and if romance is likely to change people. The student researcher can also compare the answers by gender, age group, and levels of education.

The interview data in this example have other details not captured by the survey data; as you can see, the transcript includes descriptions of emotions in the respondent's own words, ambivalence and self-reflection, and complicated explanations for his romantic interests. Notice here that there is also information volunteered by the respondent (e.g., "Jackie" was non-white) without being asked. These details are difficult to be captured if you use quantitative data collection methods such as a survey questionnaire illustrated here. On the other hand, the narrative data are too detailed to allow clear-cut comparisons between men and women, or between different age groups, as you would be able to do with quantitative data.

Box 5.1   Quantitative and Qualitative Data.

Data collection on "being in love": how would quantitative and qualitative data be different?

Quantitative data collection using surveys

1   Tell us about who you are:

Gender: 1) Male _X_ 2) Female____
Age (Please write down) *35*
Highest School Completed (Please write down) *2-year college*

2   Have you ever felt you were "in love"?

1   Yes _X_ 2) No ____

3   How many times you felt you were in love in your life?

1   Never ____ 2) 1–3 times _X_ 3) more than 3 times ____

4   What was your emotional state when you were in love?

1   Nothing different from usual ____
2   Happiness _X_
3   Excitement ____
4   Sadness or heartbreak ____
5   Anxiety ____
6   Other ____

5   Thinking of your first love, what was the most important thing to you?

1   Appearance _X_
2   Personality ____
3   Similarity or common experiences ____
4   Difference or newness ____
5   Trust and friendship ____
6   Other ____

6   Do you agree that the love relationships influenced you to take a different direction in life?

1   Strongly agree ____
2   Agree *X*
3   Disagree ____
4   Strongly disagree ____
5   Other ____

Qualitative data from an in-depth interview

Interviewer: Have you ever been in love? Yes? Tell me about your first love? What was it like? What was s/he like? How did you act?

Respondent: Oh, it was in my high school. Jackie was her name and she was a beauty. I began to ride on the school bus for the first time in tenth grade. The first year in high school, my mother drove me to school every day on her way to work. Riding on the school bus was a whole new experience. Jackie was the prettiest girl in our bus route, well, I thought in the whole school, basically. Jackie was the first girl who talked to me on the bus. She was new to town. She was from a big city. My town was kind of small. She had these stories of crazy people in the big city. My town was like, everyone was the same. Look alike houses, same pick-up trucks, and so on. I grew up in Vermont. I rarely had close friend who was not white until then ... She was different and very warm. I was fascinated by her, you can say. I was happy but more excited ... We were friends first then began to do things more like date when we grew older, but I think there was already some attraction when we first met ... Her family moved when we were senior in high school and that was the end of our relationship. It was heart-breaking. I know I changed because of this experience. I became very curious about the world outside my hometown. I was interested in meeting people from different places ...

Which approach is appropriate for your research? It all depends on what kinds of questions you ask. If your research questions ask about the distribution of opinions, behaviors, or characteristics, or include phrases like "how many" or "what percentage," quantitative research methods may suit your purpose. Quantitative designs are also appropriate when you plan to test hypotheses, or relationships between clearly defined variables. Quantitative methods can involve a large number of respondents. Because of their efficiency, quantitative methods such as surveys can take advantage of probability sampling techniques (see Chapter 6 for details on probability sampling techniques), findings likely to be generalizable to a larger study population. Quantitative research follows standardized data collection and analysis procedures. Research needs to be well planned, and uniform standards must be maintained in the research process.

If your research questions focus on processes, complexity of meaning, and contexts, use qualitative research strategies. Qualitative methods are also suitable when you have somewhat broad and loosely defined research questions. Qualitative research will allow you to gain an in-depth understanding of attitudes and behaviors of participants from their own perspective. Since the resulting data do not lend themselves to easy quantification as illustrated above, qualitative researchers usually report on themes and trends using words instead of statistics. Because of its nature, qualitative research methods are more appropriate for exploratory research (Patten 2010).

However, do not feel you must choose one and completely abandon the other for a given project. You should think of them as rather complementing each other. Use both strategies in one research project, if your research questions call for both types of information. This strategy is called "mixed-methods," and you can combine the benefits of quantitative and qualitative data by using mixed-methods.

Some students have the perception that quantitative data analysis is complicated and qualitative research is relatively simple. This perception is inaccurate. Either method has its challenges and benefits. The techniques for quantitative data collection and analysis are well developed and their use is well established, but some statistical models may require a higher level mathematical understanding. In contrast to quantitative research, the techniques for collecting and analyzing qualitative data are much more diverse and flexible. Qualitative research requires the researchers to think creatively and yet systematically. Published qualitative research papers may suggest some models for student researchers like you. Sometimes, qualitative data analysis can be time-consuming. Transcription of voice data, multi-stage coding, and theorizing with the seemingly scattered information require long and hard work. You should inform yourself about the different benefits of quantitative and qualitative methods, and choose your research strategy that fits best for your research questions, the objectives of your study, and your skills.

Which Method Should You Use to Collect Your Data?

There are several quantitative and qualitative data collection methods that may suit your research projects, and each has its advantages and disadvantages. For example, **experimental research** is well suited to research projects involving relatively limited and well-defined concepts and propositions. Experimentation that is often used in psychology research is appropriate for hypothesis-testing and explanatory studies as well as small group interactions (Babbie 2013). An advantage of experimental research is that the researcher can manipulate the independent variable to see the change in or impact on the dependent variable. For example, if you want to find whether placing flowers in areas where the elderly frequent in a nursing home affects their mood, you can test your proposition using an experiment. In a typical experiment design, you will assign the residents randomly into two groups, measure the baseline scores relating to their mood, expose one group to flowers and let the other group conduct their routine life without flowers. After a certain period of time, you can measure again the mood scores and see if there was a difference between the two groups. Another way of conducting this experiment would be to measure the residents' mood before and after you place flowers and see whether there was an improvement after the exposure to flowers.

Questionnaire surveys are widely used in social sciences today and are appropriate for descriptive, explanatory, and exploratory studies of a large number of people about their values, attitudes, opinions, and behaviors. For example, if you want to find out how many university students are reading journal articles on computer screens instead of in prints, how many people support a social welfare program reform, or what percentage of the population think globalization is good for their national economy, you can use a questionnaire to survey and collect information on a large number of people within a relatively short period of time. You may also use a questionnaire survey to collect data on some variables and then use statistical analyses to find out if and how they are related to each other. Nowadays, you can easily conduct surveys via emails, or using online survey sites and collect data through the internet. Questionnaire surveys, however, may not be suitable for an in-depth understanding of the issues being studied.

Content analysis is appropriate for virtually any form of communication, including published books, magazines, newspapers, songs, paintings, speeches, letters, laws, and constitutions (Babbie 2013). Data collected from these media are likely to be texts and images, which are qualitative data. Content analysis is a type of study in which such qualitative data are analyzed by way of coding; a process of summarizing text and image data using short-hand labels ("codes"). Coding schemes are constructed either based on theories or based on some regular patterns and themes you find in the media data collected. For example, if you want to find out which television stations airs more violent programs, you can conduct a content analysis of a sample of programs from several television channels; first, develop coding schemes for violence by defining what you consider indicators of violent acts (e.g., use of weapons, harming a person, verbal abuse, glorified destruction, and so on), and observe the shows in the sample while counting the occurrences of violent elements according to your coding scheme. Your data then can be statistically summarized using percentages and frequencies.

You may analyze data already collected by someone else to answer your research questions. This is called "**secondary data analysis**" which is another option you may consider. Nowadays, government organizations, research institutes, professors, and sometimes students collect all kinds of data. Some data sources are well-known, such as census data and other omnibus surveys on attitudes and behaviors. In the United States, there are the General Social Survey (GSS), Monitoring the Future Trend (MFT) data on juvenile behaviors, and the Uniform Crime Report (UCR) on crime. Center for Disease Control (CDC) also has multiple series data on health related issues. In Europe, in addition to the European Social Survey, there are multiple datasets collected by the European Statistical System, such as the European Community Household Panel, the European Health Interview Survey, and EU Statistics on Income and Living Conditions. General Social Survey in Australia provides data on the country. These are high quality data sources for quantitative analyses, since they are collected from larger representative samples using well-tested measures. If you have access to such data, they will prove useful in your research. But you need to check the requirement of your assignment before choosing to do secondary analysis. Some assignments may require you to collect original data so that you would have the training for constructing instruments and collecting data in the field.

Your professors might have also collected data and be willing to let you use them. If an existing dataset has the information you need, it is always a good idea to do your research with the dataset. The disadvantage of using existing data, however, is that their variables may not be the exact measures for the concepts you are studying. Therefore, there is a possibility that they may not be able to fully answer your research questions. In some circumstances, you may have to make your research fit into the existing data.

In contrast to questionnaire survey research, **qualitative field research** is effective in obtaining an in-depth understanding of a particular experience, an on-going event or social process in its natural setting. If you are interested in finding out what it is like to live on the street as homeless, you may design your field research combing some observations and in-depth interviews with homeless people. If you wish to study how political rallies, such as the recent "Occupy ..." movements in several countries unfold and continue, you may observe the unfolding demonstration in person.

In-depth interviews are one of the most common qualitative data collection strategies. If your research questions require in-depth information on some experiences, attitudes, or life histories, or you need to gather as many basic details as possible about a topic or a question, this is a suitable research strategy. In-depth interviews allow you to gather detailed stories from the interviewees' own perspectives. Moreover, you can spontaneously probe any unexpected "twists and turns" in the answers and stories given by the interviewee.

Interviews can be unstructured, semi-structured, or structured. The differentiation is based on how flexible your prepared questions are. An example of an unstructured interview will be a general life history interview, asking "can you tell me the story of your life?" On the other side of the spectrum, a structured interview will have a list of prepared questions which you will ask to all interviewees. Interviews used to be done in face-to-face settings. But, these days, interviews can be done via online media such as emails, synchronized chatting, and video-calls. These technologies enable you to recruit participants beyond the geographical confines of your research.

Participant observation and ethnography are types of research in which the researcher becomes a temporary member of the community/site and conducts observations of everyday practices as they occur naturally in a community/site. In-depth interviews with the community members are usually combined with observations. What separates participant observation from other types of qualitative data collection is that social processes, interactions, and cultural practices are observed within the actual context in which they occur. Naturally, the method allows the researcher to see better the interconnectedness of events, behaviors, and social relations (Bogdewie 1999). Participation in the same routine activities as the group members helps you to build social relationships with the members and learn the cultural values and norms of the group with ease. While an observer may not be fully immersed in members' perspectives, being a participant member allows you to understand and anticipate members' actions in ways outsiders cannot.

Focus group studies use small group discussions as a way to collect qualitative data. A focus group is a relatively small group of people (usually less than 12) gathered by the researcher for a discussion on the topic of interest. Focus groups are usually made of people sharing some commonalities, for example people with similar life experiences, consumers of a particular product, children in a particular age group, and so on. The researcher leads the discussions with a set of prepared questions while moderating the exchanges of opinions and ideas. Often, another researcher observes and takes copious notes on the focus group discussions. This is a widely used method in marketing research for product evaluation, or assessment of consumer reactions to advertising.

If you want to find out how things change over the years, engage in **historical research**. For example, if you want to find out how a social welfare program developed in a society, look up documents and descriptions from historical sources and trace the program's development over the years. Find out how the program developed and changed over the years, and what factors have influenced its evolution. Your comprehensive understanding of the program may give you insights for the improvement of the program.

In today's globalizing world, cross-cultural or cross-national **comparative research** may help you understand the similarities and differences between different nations, societies, and cultures. For example, climate change is a global issue and yet there are different opinions on the urgency of climate change and the extent of reduction in the use of fossil fuels. A comparative study on support for fossil fuel reduction between countries, between social classes, or between different age cohorts can shed light on the state of the debate on this critical issue. This is just one example. There are many routine cross-cultural and cross-national studies on economic indicators, social inequality, health, political participation, and social change. During the 1980s, there was much cross-cultural research that made systematic comparisons between the United States and Japan. Recently, more cross-cultural comparative research has been done between China and the United States, between China and India, and between other countries. Such research may serve as good examples for your cross-cultural study. If you have a different cultural or ethnic background, you may be privileged to conduct cross-cultural or cross-national comparative studies. If you have lived in several different countries, your past and current experiences or observations may give you insights into comparative research.

Box 5.2   Summary on Data Collection Strategies.

Which data collection strategy is suitable for your project? Here are summaries of different data collection strategies. Sample research questions and citation for recently published research are provided for each type of research. The publications are listed in the reference list at the end of the chapter.

1   **Surveys:** If your research questions inquire relationships between relatively well-defined variables, or you have some theoretically predicted relationships you wish to test, consider a quantitative study using surveys as data collection methods. Surveys will also allow you to assess prevalence of opinions, attitudes, and behaviors among the population. Example: What are the impacts of parents' migration and types of guardianship arrangement on children's test scores? (See Zhou, Murphy, and Tao 2014.)

2   **Experiments:** Similar to survey research, experiment designs are suitable for testing theoretically predicted association between clearly defined variables. The main difference between survey research and experiment research is that the latter allows you to manipulate the independent variable to examine whether a cause-effect relationship between the two variables exists. If testing causal relationships is your main goal, experiment designs will be suitable for your project. Example: Are family sizes likely to decline when family planning services and credit on contraceptive use are provided by community-based programs? (See Desai and Tarozzi 2011.)

3   **Secondary data analysis:** The goals of secondary data analysis are the same as surveys. Choose this strategy if you find a dataset collected from a large sample, which includes the exact variables implied in your research questions and hypotheses. Examples: Has the two-child family ideal been persistent and universal in European countries during the last three decades? (See Sobotka and Beaujuan 2014.) Are people without siblings more likely to choose to live nearby their elderly parents than those with siblings? (See Holmlund, Rainer, and Siedler 2013.)

4   **Historical study:** If your research questions concern a particular historical period in the past, or how things have changed over time, historical study will be the research design of your choice. For such research, you will collect data from archival documents and secondary data sources. Example: What environmental factors affected family formation and family size in the Great Plains of the United States during the period of its initial Euro-American settlement? (See Gutmann, Pullum-Piñón, Witkowski, Deane, and Merchant 2012.)

5   **Comparative study:** If your main goal is to compare two or more groups, regions, or countries, your research will be a comparative study. Comparative study is not a data collection strategy. Comparative study

means that your focus in your analysis is comparisons between groups or countries. Comparative study can use original surveys to collect data, or use secondary data from existing data sources. Example: How do family clinicians in four different countries perceive the impacts of information and communication technology on family life? (See Bacigalupe, Camara, and Buffardi 2014.)

6 **In-depth interview study:** A popular qualitative research design geared toward collecting detailed data. If your research questions require in-depth information on personal experiences, attitudes, opinions, or expert knowledge related to a topic, interviews may be suitable data gathering strategy. It requires longer research time per case than survey research, and therefore is done using a relatively small sized sample. Example: How do first generation immigrant children cope with school transitions in the host country? (See Moskal 2014.)

7 **Participant observations and ethnography:** This data collection strategy is suitable if you are interested in studying a group, a community, or a group in rich depth, or studying the complex contexts in which an event or an issue occurs. Observations and ethnography require relatively long time during the field research, and are suitable for more serious research projects such as theses and dissertations. Example: In what ways do Japanese school teachers help parents accept and cope with their children's cognitive and behavioral disabilities? (See Kayama and Haight 2014.) How do older women in sub-Saharan African communities organize themselves in response to the effects of HIV/AIDS, poverty, violence and illness? (See Chazan 2014.)

8 **Focus group:** Data collection using focus groups will allow you to quickly assess opinions, reactions, and thought processes related to your topic. Focus groups enable you to collect information on individual perspectives as well as common ideas shared among the group. Example: What are urban residents' attitudes, perceptions, and justifications regarding reproductive behaviors observed in their locality? (See Sahleyesus, Beaujot, and Zakus 2009.)

Use the above information to think about which method will suit your project. In Chapter 6, we will discuss more detailed steps of each of these various research designs.

How Do You Use Theory in Your Research?

Your research may take either a deductive or an inductive approach. That means using a theory to guide your research, or developing a theory based on the data collected in your research. Without utilizing a theory or theories to guide your research, your research can become a blind-folded chase. Similarly, without an effort to develop a theory in your empirical research, your research may not fully come to fruition. Think of theories relevant to your topic when you plan your research, and how your research design may relate to them.

> Note that being able to say in a proposal that the research either will test some aspect of an important theory or has its origins in such a theory is usually an excellent way to help justify proposed research. This is true because the results are less likely to be viewed as isolated data. Instead, they are likely to contribute to understanding behavior in a large context. Thus, you will want to consider whether your research questions, purposes, or hypotheses can be related to one or more theories.
>
> (Patten 2010: 23)

You may conduct a **deductive research** and test a theory in your research. That means you will develop research questions or hypotheses based on a theory, operationalize the relevant concepts, and collect empirical data to answer your research questions or test your hypotheses. For example, Travis Hirschi has developed a version of social control theory. Accordingly, juvenile social bonds, including attachment to society, commitment to the conventional lines of action, involvement in conventional activities, and belief in traditional values are negatively associated with deviant behavior (Siegel and Welsh 2014). If you want to test whether Hirschi's social control theory is valid, construct some measures for the concepts of attachment, commitment, involvement, belief and deviant behaviors. Then collect data on these concepts, analyze the data, and perform statistical analyses to see if social bonds are indeed negatively associated with juvenile deviant behavior. In such research, you apply a theory to specific cases or population to see if the theory is applicable and valid.

You may also conduct **inductive research** and develop a theory based on your data. For example, if you are curious why women university students tend to have higher grade point averages than men students, conduct open-ended interviews on students' time management, study habits, course selections, extra-curricular activities, and general social life to figure out what factors may contribute to the gender gap in academic performances. If your data analyses indicate that, on average, women spend more time studying than men because they spend less time socializing with friends, then, you may attempt to make a theoretical conclusion that women and men may hold different perspectives on their years in universities and they end up developing different skill sets from university education. You may even interpret that this is because higher grades are more critical for women than men for their chances in the job market, if you have supportive data from your interviews. Of course, this would be an exploratory theory which would have to be tested further in later studies.

Some students think that theory is too complicated for them. In fact, a theory is simply a statement of the relationships between two or more variables. Therefore, you can develop your theory in your empirical research. When you engage in either deductive or inductive research, theory should be part of your research. You may either use it to guide your research or use it to summarize your research. You may also use an existing theory to support your findings and make your argument more convincing. Generally speaking, there will be different theories related to your research topic. What you need to do is to deliberately consider them when you design your research and use them in your research when they are appropriate.

Are Ethical Matters Important in Your Research?

Last, but not least, you should carefully consider how to design an ethical research. Social science usually involves people as the subjects of its research. In your research, you are likely to collect information about people and from people. You may have to ask sensitive questions which could upset the participants or collect information about private matters. What if a participant has an emotional breakdown because your interview makes him recall some painful memories from the past? What if your research design requires that you not disclose your real research purpose? What if you collect information that can be used in legal matters against research participants? As you can imagine, there are many issues that can create ethical dilemmas for you as a researcher.

Research participants, when they agree to participate in your research, agree to share information about themselves (sometimes very private information) with you or agree to participate in activities you control and can manipulate. By agreeing to participate in your research, participants may become vulnerable. You should be most careful not to cause the participants any harm or disadvantages because of their willingness to help your study. If you have taken a course in research methods, you probably are familiar with the background history of research ethics. In the past, researchers had sometimes misused their power in the name of science to cause disturbing consequences to participants. Some of the well-known cases are highly controversial, including the U.S. Health Service's Tuskegee Syphilis Study, Harvard University Professor Stanley Milgram's experiment on obedience to authority, and Zimbardo's Stanford prison experiment.

In the Tuskegee study, participants, mostly poor African-American men from rural areas, were not told the true purpose of the study; in addition, they were not given beneficial medical treatments (penicillin) for the purpose of study. In the Milgram experiment, participants were led to believe that they were causing extreme pain to other participants behind a wall. Zimbardo's study caused enough distress for some participants to leave the study in a few days. Also, the emerging interactions among participants became so volatile that they had to end the study early. These research projects have obviously indicated that ethical matters are extremely important. Though the Zimbardo study's follow-up sessions reported that no lasting negative effects were found among participants one year after the experiment, its provocative research design makes us ask a question: can participants' exposure to potential risks be justified when a study has the promise of producing insightful knowledge that will advance the field of the study and benefit society? This is not a simple question to answer. Answering the question will require careful consideration of different issues involved in each case. When you begin to design your field research, there are a few ethical issues that you should pay attention to and handle carefully.

What Ethical Issues Should You Pay Attention To?

Ethics are about the principles of doing right and wrong. In research they guide you in determining how you should relate to participants and the information you collect when you are in a position of power as a researcher. In the United States, research ethics are guided by the principles declared in the *Belmont Report* which is a federal document; the principles include respect for persons, beneficence, and justice (National Commission for the Protection of Human Subjects of Biomedical and Behavioral Research 1978). Medical and science researchers are bound by the Declaration of Helsinki by World Medical Association (adopted in 1964, and amended in 1975, 1983, 1986, 1996, 2000, 2002, 2004, 2008, and in 2013) to comply with international ethical standards. In different countries, professional associations in academic disciplines, university review boards, and ethics committees in research organizations are likely to have published codes of ethics. While there are slight variations in the guidelines of different organizations, there are common standards to which you need to pay attention.

Voluntary Participation
Participation in research as subjects should be voluntary and based on decisions by the participants. You cannot, for example, ask a friend who is a leader in an organization to use his authority to force subordinates to participate in your study, either directly or indirectly. If you are in a position of authority, you cannot influence your associates to participate in your study. A professor or a tutor cannot use his or her authority to pressure students to participate in the study.

Informed Consent
Before agreeing to be involved in a study, participants should be informed of the nature of the project and the activities in which they are asked to be involved. Participants should be capable of fully understanding the information about the research and consenting to it based on their own free will. Informed consent is typically ensured by obtaining a signature from the participants on informed consent forms. People who are unable to make decisions on their own behalf, such as children or the mentally ill, cannot consent, and you will need to obtain consent from their guardians.

Anonymity and Confidentiality
The identities of participants should be protected since research may include private and sensitive information. Anonymity means participants' identities are completely unknown to the researcher (you) as well as to the public. If you conduct

surveys without any participant identification, participants will remain anonymous. In a study requiring in-person interviews, the identity of the participants is likely to be known to the researcher, but you as the researcher can keep information confidential by not revealing it to anyone else. Maintaining confidentiality is an important ethical obligation. Your research plans should include measures to protect confidentiality such as the use of pseudonyms, separation of biographical information from the contents of interviews, locking interview records, and plans for destroying records at the conclusion of the study. In addition, a statement should be included in your informed consent form about how you will ensure confidentiality.

Assessment of Risks to Participants

What are the likely "risks" of participating in your study? Does your research involve sensitive questions which may stir negative emotional reactions from participants (e.g., shameful experiences, volatile political opinions, personal biases, etc.)? Does your research invoke some traumatic past experiences (e.g., victimization of violence, surviving torture, etc.)? Is there a potential for physical harm to your participant because of the information he/she provides to you (e.g., being subject to retaliation, etc.)? When designing your research plans, you should carefully assess potential risks for your participants, whether they are psychological, physical, or legal risks. Obviously, you cannot predict every possible risk before the actual research begins. But do your best and consider different scenarios.

Benefits Outweighing Risks

When you judge there are risks for participants, you should consider the magnitude and the likely duration of the risks and how likely the risk factor will appear during the study. The risks may be minimal, but at other times, there could be significant risks to participants. Also, there are risks that are reasonably preventable, but others may be too unpredictable to proceed with them. You should carefully weigh these risks against the potential benefit of your research to the participants and its contribution to the field of knowledge. If there are predictable risks for the participant, you need find out how to include protective measures into your study. You should discuss any risks involved in your study fully in your application for ethical clearance and explain how the benefits from the study may outweigh the risks.

Debriefing

Sometimes, you may have to temporarily deceive participants to make an experiment work, which was the case with the Milgram research. While lying to participants does not sound ethical, you may be able to conduct research involving deception, if it does not cause grave harm to the participants and if you can "undo" the deception through debriefing sessions. During debriefing explain how the experiment worked and address any participant's concerns and questions. If the deception caused emotional strain between participants, they should be given opportunities to reconcile and resolve any negative emotions. We would advise you be extremely careful about such research projects and get approval from your professor or supervisor and your university.

Protection of Vulnerable Populations

Some groups are particularly more vulnerable to coercion or to the pressure imposed by research situations. These groups are identified as "vulnerable populations" in the ethics guidelines of your institutions. Examples of vulnerable population include, but are not limited to, children, prisoners, mentally impaired persons, and socioeconomic minorities. If your research subjects are vulnerable populations, specific measures and procedures to protect their rights and privacy should be built into your research design. Consult your project supervisor, mentor, or office of research ethics for further guidance. Before your research design is finalized, you should assess the above issues to come up with an ethical research plan.

Once you complete your research design including sampling strategies, data collection methods, and instruments for data collection, your research protocol must be reviewed by people trained in these matters to ensure the research plans protect the participants of the research. This is a process called ethics review. We will revisit the research ethics review and clearance at the end of the next chapter, at which point, your research project will have clearly defined field research protocol.

References

Babbie, Earl. 2013. *The Practice of Social Research.*13th ed. Belmont, CA: Wadsworth/Thomson Learning.

Bacigalupe, Gonzalo, Maria Camara, Laura E. Buffardi. 2014. "Technology in Families and the Clinical Encounter: Results of a Cross-national Survey." *Journal of Family Therapy* 36(4): 339–358.

Chazan, May. 2014. "Everyday Mobilisations among Grandmothers in South Africa: Survival, Support and Social Change in the Era of HIV/AIDS." *Ageing & Society* 34(10): 1641–1665.

Desai, Jaikishan, and Alessandro Tarozzi, 2011. "Microcredit, Family Planning Programs, and Contraceptive Behavior: Evidence from a Field Experiment in Ethiopia." *Demography* 48(2): 749–782.

Gutmann, Myron P., Sara M Pullum-Piñón, Kristine Witkowski, Glenn Deane, and Emily Merchant, Emily. 2012. "Land Use and Family Formation in the Settlement of the US Great Plains." *Social Science History* 36(3): 279–310.

Holmlund, Helenam, Helmut Rainer, and Thomas Siedler, 2013. "Meet the Parents? Family Size and the Geographic Proximity Between Adult Children and Older Mothers in Sweden." *Demography* 50(3): 903–931.

Kayama, Misa, and Wendy Haight. 2014. "Disability and Stigma: How Japanese Educators Help Parents Accept Their Children's Differences." *Social Work* 59(1): 24–33.

Locke, Lawrence F., Waneen Wyrick Spirduso, and Stephen J. Silverman. 2000. *Proposals That Work: A Guide for Planning Dissertations and Grant Proposals.* 4th ed. Thousand Oaks, CA: Sage.

Moskal, Marta. 2014. "Polish Migrant Youth in Scottish Schools: Conflicted Identity and Family Capital." *Journal of Youth Studies* 17(2): 279–291.

Patten, Mildred L. 2010. *Proposing Empirical Research: A Guide to the Fundamentals.* 4th ed. Glendale, CA: Pyrczak Publishing.

Sahleyesus, Daniel Telake, Roderic P. Beaujot, and David Zakus. 2009. "Attitudes toward Family Size Preferences in Urban Ethiopia." *Journal of Comparative Family Studies* 40(1): 97–117.

Siegel, Larry J., and Brandon C. Welsh. 2014. *Juvenile Delinquency: Theory, Practice, and Law* Belmont, CA: Wadsworth.

Sobotka, Tomáš, and Éva Beaujouan. 2014. "Two Is Best? The Persistence of a Two-Child Family Ideal in Europe." *Population & Development Review* 40(3): 391–419.

Zhou, Minhui, Rachel Murphy, and Ran Tao. 2014. "Effects of Parents' Migration on the Education of Children Left Behind in Rural China." *Population & Development Review* 40(2): 273–292.

Further Reading

Neuman, W. Lawrence. 2011. *Social Research Methods: Qualitative and Quantitative Approaches*. 7th ed. Boston, MA: Allyn and Beacon.

Patten, Mildred L. 2011. *Questionnaire Research: A Practical Guide*. 3rd ed. Glendale, CA: Pyrczak Publishing.

Wolfer, Loreen, 2007. *Real Research: Conducting and Evaluating Research in the Social Sciences*. Boston, MA: Pearson Education.

Internet Resources

British Health Research Authority research ethics review process. http://www.hra.nhs.uk/resources/before-you-apply/

Inter-university Consortium for Political and Social Research (ICPSR) at University of Michigan provide hundreds of data series from all around the world.

https://www.icpsr.umich.edu/icpsrweb/ICPSR/index.jsp

Zimbardo's Stanford Prison Experiment website is a good resource to look up ethical issues in experiment research. http://www.prisonexp.org/

Exercises for Chapter 5

Exercises in this chapter help you to make informed choices on the goals and styles of your research. Exercise 5.1 may help you clarify what type of inquiry you are making in this study, and what research objective you have. Exercise 5.2 is intended to help you make a decision on whether to pursue quantitative or qualitative research. Exercise 5.3 provides guiding questions to design an ethical research. Finally Exercise 5.4 is a template to summarize the directions of your research design thus far.

Exercise 5.1 Clarifying the Objective of Your Inquiry

By now, you will have clearly defined research questions and/or hypotheses for your study. First, let's make a list of them.

Research Questions

1

2

3

4

5

Look at the first box of each row in the diagram provided below. Which box includes the kinds of question you have in mind? Follow the arrow to find out what your research goal is.

Which of the following set of questions best describes your inquiry?

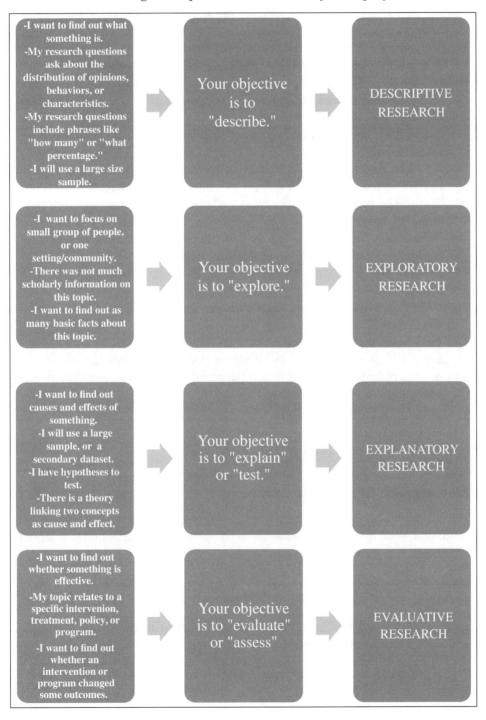

-I want to find out what something is.
-My research questions ask about the distribution of opinions, behaviors, or characteristics.
-My research questions include phrases like "how many" or "what percentage."
-I will use a large size sample.

Your objective is to "describe."

DESCRIPTIVE RESEARCH

-I want to focus on small group of people, or one setting/community.
-There was not much scholarly information on this topic.
-I want to find out as many basic facts about this topic.

Your objective is to "explore."

EXPLORATORY RESEARCH

-I want to find out causes and effects of something.
-I will use a large sample, or a secondary dataset.
-I have hypotheses to test.
-There is a theory linking two concepts as cause and effect.

Your objective is to "explain" or "test."

EXPLANATORY RESEARCH

-I want to find out whether something is effective.
-My topic relates to a specific intervenion, treatment, policy, or program.
-I want to find out whether an intervention or program changed some outcomes.

Your objective is to "evaluate" or "assess"

EVALUATIVE RESEARCH

Exercise 5.2 Quantitative or Qualitative Research?

Consider the following questions to determine whether quantitative or qualitative research is suitable for your project.

Diagnostic questions to determine quantitative and qualitative orientation of your research

1   Are your research questions very specific? Do they require clear-cut answers?
2   Are you interested in general patterns among a relatively large number of people?
3   Is your research likely to be descriptive research or explanatory research?
4   Do you have hypothesis statements or predictions on the relationships between two concepts or variables?
5   Do you have research questions asking whether two concepts or variables are connected in some ways?
6   Are there ways to measure the concepts in your research questions or hypotheses with a few closed-end questions, or multiple-choice questions?
7   Will you be able to collect data from a relatively large sample (over 100 cases at the minimum)?
8   Do your research questions require in-depth information on something?
9   Is your research likely to be an exploratory research?
10 Are you interested in learning in-depth about a particular group, or a community?
11 Do your research questions begin with the word, "how," "why," or "in what ways"?
12 Are you interested in the contexts in which things occur?
13 Are you likely to have a very small sample (for example, under 30 cases)?
14 Are you collecting data without any particular theoretical expectations or any predictions about the findings?

Quantitative research: If your answers to the questions 1–7 are mostly "yes," then your study has quantitative orientation.

Qualitative research: If your answers to the questions 8–14 are mostly "yes," then your study has qualitative orientation.

Mixed-methods research: If you have answered "yes" to several questions in both sets, your research questions are likely to require using both quantitative and qualitative data.

Exercise 5.3 Research Ethics

Once you complete your research protocol in the next stage, you will apply for ethics clearance using the forms required by your institution. At this stage, use the following self-guided questions to consider ethical issues and design an ethical research plan that protects human subjects.

1   What is your study population?
2   Are they able to understand your study and consent on their own?
3   Are they vulnerable population? If this is the case, what plans do you have in order to safeguard their well-being?
4   Are there any potential psychological, physical, or legal risks for the participants of your study?
5   What are potential risks? List them all.
6   Are the risks minimal or significant?
7   What is the expected duration of the risks?
8   What benefits does your study yield for the participants?
9   What benefits does your study have for the field of knowledge?
10 Are the benefits of your study much greater than the risks for the participants?
11 Do you have contact information for any counseling or other service organization to which you can refer your participants if needed?
12 Do you have plans to protect participants' identities?
13 Do you have plans to keep the data secure?
14 What can you do to minimize or avoid the risks?

Exercise 5.4 Checklist before Moving on to the Next Chapter

Let's record the progress you have made so far with your project.

1   A working title for your research project:

2   Your project supervisor and contact information:

3   Theory(ies) on which your research is grounded:

4   Your finalized research questions and/or hypotheses:

5   Key concepts and definitions:

6   Research objective or style of research:

7   Quantitative or qualitative orientation:

8   Potential ethical concerns:

9   Plans to minimize or avoid the risks:

Your Project Outcome after Chapter 5

At this point:

- You have finalized your research questions.
- You have determined the goals of your research (e.g., a descriptive study, an explanatory study, an exploratory study, an evaluative study).
- You know if your research goals call for quantitative research, qualitative research, or mixed-methods research.
- You have carefully considered ethical issues involved in your research and are confident that you will design a study conforming to the professional ethical standards.

Chapter 6

Steps of Quantitative and Qualitative Research Designs

Since the guiding principles and procedures for quantitative and qualitative research are quite different, the two kinds of research design call for somewhat different knowledge and skills. In this chapter, we are going to illustrate more detailed steps of quantitative and qualitative research designs and some issues to consider at each step. We will first discuss steps of quantitative research designs. Qualitative research designs will be discussed in the second half of the chapter. If you have already determined that your study calls for a qualitative research design and are only interested in qualitative research, skip directly to the section on qualitative research design.

Quantitative research designs include various methods including surveys, experiments, and content analysis. Since the most commonly used quantitative research method is questionnaire survey, we will focus on the steps involved in survey research and assume the discussion will help those interested in other quantitative research methods as well. Students frequently ask us these questions when designing their survey research projects:

- What are my independent variable and dependent variables?
- How do I select a sample to study from my target population?
- What is an acceptable sample size for survey research?
- How do I turn my concepts into variables in survey questionnaire?
- What are levels of measurement and why do they matter?

The first half of this chapter responds to these questions and relevant issues. In designing a survey research, the following steps are usually necessary:

Student Research and Report Writing: From Topic Selection to the Complete Paper, First Edition. Gabe T. Wang and Keumjae Park. © and Published 2016 by John Wiley & Sons, Ltd.

What Are Your Independent and Dependent Variables?

The term "independent variable" is commonly used in social sciences to refer to the cause, or the variable that affects the other in a hypothesized relationship. The term "dependent variable" refers to the effects or outcomes in a hypothesized relationship. For example, let's consider the research question, "How do relationships with parents affect teenagers' school performance?" Suppose you expect that teenagers who do not have the typical quarrelsome relationships with their parents will do better in school than those who have a lot of conflicts with their parents. The independent and dependent variables are already implied by your research questions. The independent variable in this example would be relationships with parents and the dependent variable would be school performance. Similarly, if your research question is "Are teenagers' grades negatively affected by gravitation toward social media?" then your independent variable is "gravitation toward social media" and your dependent variable is "grades." Since you are likely to have more than one research questions in your study, you may have multiple independent and dependent variables.

Sometimes, you may have several independent variables and one dependent variable, and vice versa. For example, questions such as "Do regular medical check-ups, exercise, and sufficient vegetable intakes reduce the likelihood of cancer?" and "Do cigarette bans in public buildings and higher cigarette taxes encourage smokers to quit smoking?" have multiple independent variables and a single dependent variable. On the other hand, a research question on the academic and emotional effects of bedtime reading during early childhood assumes one independent variable ("bedtime reading") and multiple dependent variables (the various "academic and emotional effects"). It is a good practice to write down your research questions and label your independent and dependent variables.

When you identify and label your independent and dependent variables, you should be quite clear in your mind that an independent variable is the cause of the dependent variable and a dependent variable is the effect of the independent variable. A dependent variable must be able to vary or be affected when it is influenced by the independent variable. In another example, if you use education as an independent variable and salary as a dependent variable, then, you are anticipating that the salary of your respondents will change when their level of education changes. If a variable cannot vary or cannot be affected, then it cannot be used as a dependent variable. For example, someone's race and gender cannot be changed by the influence of other variables; thus, they cannot be used as dependent variables.

In the examples above, abstract concepts such as "relationship with parents," "gravitation toward social media," and "emotional effects," need to be more specified and **operationalized** into measurable indicators so that you can quantify them. Operationalization is a step where you identify very specific indicators or measures for your concepts. For example, "relationships with parents" are not something you can directly observe, but you can use some very specific indicators for a good or a bad relationship. Quantifiable indicators, such as "number of arguments a teenager had with his/her parents within a month," "number of times a teenager received a punishment from parents within a month," and "number of times a teenager violated rules set by parents" are all good ways to measure whether a teen has a good relationship with his/her parents. Or, you can simply ask the teen respondents to rate the quality of their relationship with parents on a scale of one to ten. The concept, "gravitation toward social media" is hard to measure itself. You will need to use tangible measures such as "time spent on social media each night." Likewise, the concept "emotional effects" can be specified into multiple questions gauging how happy the child is, how social the child is, or how energetic and curious the child is, and so on.

How Do You Select a Sample to Study from Your Target Population?

What group of people or cases is your research about? Do your research questions concern the general population, a particular group of people, countries, schools, or other social organizations? The answer to these questions will be your study population, or target population; the term refers to the group of people or cases about whom you will conduct your study and to whom you will apply the findings of your study (Babbie 2013). Your population is also the pool of cases from which you will select a sample, or a subgroup of the cases you will actually study. As you can imagine, if you select a sample that resembles your population closely, you will be able to use your findings to tell something about your study population. But if your sample does not resemble your study population, your ability to use your study findings to predict the patterns in the study population is limited. Suppose you have selected a group of students from your university whose average grade is an A. You know it is unlikely that this sample will reflect what the average grade is in your university. The extent to which your sample "looks like" your study population is called "**representativeness**"; study findings from a representative sample can be **generalized** to the study population. For instance, if a group of spectators selected by random drawing of numbers happens to have the same demographic characteristics as the spectators in the entire stadium, this sample will be representative of the crowd in the stadium. This means that, if there is more rooting for Team A in this sample, you can generalize that there will be more support for Team A among the entire stadium crowd.

How do we select a representative sample? Social science methods teach us that we can approximate a representative sample by reducing systemic selection biases in sample drawing process. In general, a selection method which only relies on random chance is considered as having no systemic selection biases (Babbie 2013). There are a variety of different ways to draw a sample from the study population: simple random sampling, systematic random sampling, stratified random sampling, cluster sampling, quota sampling, snowball sampling, purposive sampling, and availability sampling. Some of these sampling techniques select participants using random drawing while others do not. The specific steps and details of different sampling strategies are beyond the scope of this book. If you need to refresh your memory on how to draw a particular type of sample, consult some of the references listed in this chapter.

In the broadest sense, sampling methods fall within two groups: probability and non-probably sampling. In the above list, all the variety of random sampling and cluster sampling fall in the probability sampling category. Quota sampling, snowball sampling, purposive sampling and availability sampling are non-probability sampling. Probability sampling methods select participants based only on random chance. Sampling theory considers this as the best way to obtain a **representative sample**. To use probability sampling methods, you need access to the **sampling frame**, which refers to the roster of all units in your study population (e.g., an approximate list of citizens of a country, a list of residents of a community, a list of all schools, organizations, student roster, and so on), so that everyone is in the pool of available subjects and only random chance can determine whether someone is selected to be included in the sample.

Non-probability samples are used when researchers do not have access to the sampling frame, or do not have a clearly identifiable study population (such as undocumented immigrants, homeless population). Research done by students like you often has to resort to non-probability sampling methods simply due to insufficient time and resources. Non-probability sampling methods are likely to introduce sampling biases because factors other than random chance will affect the selection process. It is okay to study a non-probability sample, especially for a small scale exploratory study, or if you are conducting qualitative research. Just keep in mind that your findings will have limited generalizability, and the limitation should be included in the discussion of your findings.

When you select your study population, make sure that you can gain access to them. If your study population is minors (such as children or juveniles) or people with limited power (such as prisoners), you may face particular difficulties obtaining informed consents from guardians or getting permission from the heads of the institutions to enter the sites to collect data for your research. Therefore, think carefully about access before you decide to study a particular population.

After you decide on your study population, decide on what your unit of analysis is. It may be individuals, universities, organizations, or countries, depending on what is most appropriate for your research.

What Is an Acceptable Sample Size for Surveys?

Another issue to consider is sample size. Regardless of whether you use probability sampling or non-probability sampling, the size of the sample is an independent issue which requires your attention. If you want to conduct surveys and use computer software to do data analysis, you need a sufficient number of respondents in your sample. As a general guideline, a minimum of 400 cases will be amenable for statistical data analysis. This suggestion is to reduce sampling error due to sample size. If you have a sample size of 400 cases, the standard sampling error will always be 5% or smaller no matter what the variation is in the study population (Babbie 2013). In reality, however, it may be unrealistic for a student researcher to be able to draw a sufficient size sample; you are more likely to work with much smaller size sample due to the time and resource constraints. In deciding your sample size, consult with your project supervisor, or professor, as they may have specific guidelines or requirements for sample size. Generally speaking, three principles are useful in determining sample size.

First, the larger the sample size, the smaller your standard sampling error will be. At the same time, your sample is more likely to resemble the characteristics of your population and you will be able to generalize your findings to the target population.

Second, if you are conducting a quantitative study, most statistical analysis techniques used in social sciences assume a normal, or the bell-curve distribution of data. If the sample is too small, say less than 100 cases, there is a good chance that you will not meet this assumption of a normal distribution. Our advice is to obtain at least a sample size of 100 respondents, if you plan to use statistical analysis techniques. With that number you will be able to use commonly used descriptive and inferential statistical techniques such as cross-tabulation analyses, chi-square tests, t-tests for comparison of means, and so on. Keep in mind that you may receive invalid answers, which you will exclude from your analysis; to obtain a sample size of a 100 valid cases; you may need to go slightly beyond your targeted sample size when you collect the data.

Third, a small sample size may produce insignificant statistical results simply as a function of the sample size. Sometimes, small samples require you to use special statistical measures other than the commonly used measures mentioned above. According to probability theory, when sample size decreases, the standard error increases. For example, if you do a chi-square test with a very small sample, you may find that many of the cells in your cross-tabulation have fewer than five cases and your chi-square value is not statistically significant. If you have more than 25% of the cells with fewer than five counts, your chi-square analysis is not acceptable (George and Mallery 2000). If this is the case, you cannot use chi-squire analysis to test whether two variables are statistically independent of each other. On the other hand, if you only intend to use simpler descriptive statistics such as percentages and graphs to answer your research questions, a sample size smaller than 100 can still work.

A "robust" sample, or a sufficiently large and representative sample, is needed if your goal is to perform an explanatory study. This is one reason why many researchers turn to secondary data, data collected by governments or large organizations with resources, for explanatory studies. As a student researcher, you are likely to conduct a study on a modest size sample using non-probability sampling strategy. This is quite all right, as long as you are mindful of the limitations of your methods, make cautious interpretation of your findings, and discuss the limitations in your report. If you and your supervisor decide to work with very small sized sample, say less than 50 respondents, you may consider it as a pilot test for a full-scale study at a later time.

A pilot study can yield valuable information; you can get a sense of how survey questions are interpreted by the respondents, gauge whether the length is appropriate, estimate what response rates you can anticipate, and detect any potential problems in administering the surveys. These are important learning experiences and skills-building processes which make your project meaningful. You will also obtain some descriptive statistics about the patterns of behaviors and attitudes you are investigating with a pilot study. If you must resort to very small sample sizes due to the constraints in time and resources, consult your project supervisor about designing a well-planned pilot study which will give you a good foundation for future projects; this can be more meaningful assignment than a poorly conducted research on a larger sample.

Also, the above guidelines are for quantitative studies requiring statistical data analyses. Qualitative research is most often done on a sample much smaller than 100. Sampling issues in qualitative research will be further discussed later in the chapter when we review steps of qualitative research.

How Do You Turn Your Concepts into Variables in Surveys?

If you conduct a survey, develop your survey questionnaire to include questions on the independent and dependent variables and demographic information needed for your research. Most surveys include demographic questions to collect basic information about your study population. Typically, you ask about gender, age, level of education, and socioeconomic status, and race and ethnicity. However, which information is needed depends on your research questions. For example, if you study university students' adjustments to campus life away from home, it may be relevant to ask how many years they have attended university. Before you start to construct your survey questions, you should have a clearly identified list of your independent, dependent, and demographic variables. If you have an abstract concept in your research question, you need to operationalize it as we described earlier in this chapter. In surveys, most concepts are measured by one or a set of questions. For example, if your research question is "How do gender, race and age affect student school performance," then you will need to specify and measure school performance. In this case, you cannot directly ask your respondents what their school performances are. Instead, you need to identify indicators such as student Grade Point Average, class attendance, or time spent on study to measure school performances.

Since you need to include measures for all your concepts, you should have at least one question for each of your concepts in your survey instrument. Some simple variables such as gender, age, whether or not one is in university, whether or not one supports a political candidate can be sufficiently measured by a single question item. But for abstract concepts, or concepts that have a broader range of meaning you may need more than one indicator. For example, if your variable is depression, a composite question consisting of several items asking about different symptoms of depression may be a far better measure than a single question asking whether one experiences depression. The key idea is that the indicators in your survey instrument should capture the full meaning of your concepts.

In the U.S., students in university classes participate in teaching evaluation surveys at the end of the semester. The purpose of the surveys is obviously to measure "good teaching." Imagine that schools use just one question, "does your professor demonstrate good teaching?" This single item indicator would be not only too simplistic, but also vague as each student may have different ideas about what good teaching is. Typical teaching evaluation surveys thus include several questions on various aspects of teaching, such as knowledgeability, organized presentation, use of examples, interaction with students and so on.

In developing survey questions, please pay attention to the **validity** of your questions to make sure that you will get what you intended to get, or measure what you mean to measure. For example, student GPA is a good indicator of academic performance. How many times students visit the library may not be a direct measure of academic performance. It may affect academic performance, but library use itself is not a valid measure of academic performance. Your measures should also have **reliability** which refers to the quality of a measure that produces the same value or observation repeatedly. For example, reading a thermometer is a much more reliable measure for fever than feeling the temperature with your hand on someone's forehead, since the judgment from touching one's forehead can be capricious. Likewise, asking "how many times did you drink last week?" is more reliable measure than asking "do you drink often?"

What Are Levels of Measurement and Why Do They Matter?

When you design your survey questions, think about what kind of data analysis you are going to conduct after you collect your data. Statistical data analysis procedures are often closely related to the mathematical property of your variables, called "**the levels of measurement**." Given that statistical analyses are based on mathematical computations of various statistics, the mathematical qualities of the numerical data you collect will influence data analysis.

Let us use a simple example. For the demographic variable, gender, researchers often give the numeric code "1" for male respondents and code "2" for female respondents. Computing what percentage of your sample is men or women would be an appropriate thing to do, but computing the mean score for this variable is not, as there is no such thing called "average gender." You would not want to use statistical technique "mean score" when you perform an analysis of variables such as religion, nationality, or favorite Thai dish. This is because all of these examples are variables with no mathematical meaning, or no variations in amount. On the other extreme, if you ask respondents to write down their age, or their salaries in precise currency terms, then you know that the different values you will obtain can be compared in quantity; computation of mean scores (e.g., average age, average income) makes perfect sense with these variables.

These examples illustrate the different mathematical qualities of the numeric data you will obtain from different types of variables. As we mentioned above, statistical tests assume that the variables entered into the computation have certain type of mathematical property. The types of mathematical properties are expressed in levels of measurement. In statistical analysis, **four levels of measurement** are differentiated, **depending on the level of mathematical precision of the measure:** they are **nominal, ordinal, interval and ratio** levels. A nominal level of measurement has the lowest level of mathematical quality, because its values are number codes that do not represent actual quantities, but simply different qualities. A ratio level of measurement on the other hand is the highest level of mathematical precision because its values actually correspond to mathematical quantities, just like natural numbers. Let us explain each of these with some examples.

Nominal level measurements pertain to those variables whose attributes are simply different in type, not in quantity, from one another. In other words, the numeric codes assigned to the respondents' different answers for a nominal level measure have no implied order or quantity. The difference between categories of a nominal scale is a qualitative difference (Graziano and Raulin 1999). For example, gender, race, occupation, and marital status are usually measured at a nominal level, as different attributes respondents can take in these variables are different kinds, and not different amount. Here is an example of nominal level of measurement:

Question: Which of the following racial groups do you identify yourself with?

1   ___African American
2   ___Asian American
3   ___Caucasian American
4   ___Native American
5   ___Hispanic American
6   ___Other

In this case, the number 1 is arbitrarily used to represent the African Americans and the number 3 is used to indicate the Caucasian Americans. The numbers assigned to each category, however, do not mean any higher or lower social value relative to one another. In addition, the attributes of a nominal level variable are mutually exclusive (i.e., no overlap between attributes) and exhaustive (i.e., they cover the full range of possible attributes for all respondents).

Ordinal level measurements assess a variable in its order of magnitude. They have the property of magnitude (Graziano and Raulin 1999), or a rank-order. In other words, variables that are measured at the ordinal level have categorical attributes like those of nominal level measures, but they also have the advantage that the categories can be ordered or ranked from low to high or from one extreme to the other. Thus, the numbers assigned to different attributes, or categories signify different point in a system of order. For example, social class, people's attitudes, or students' academic standing are usually measured at the ordinal level. For example:

Question: Which social class do you belong to?

1   ___Lower class
2   ___Lower middle class
3   ___Middle class
4   ___Upper middle class
5   ___Upper class
6   ___Other

In this example, the respondents' social class is rank-ordered from what are socially deemed lower socioeconomic statuses to higher ones. The numeric codes do not mean exact quantities, but they indicate a rank-order between categories and identities. The difference between lower class and lower middle class is not the same as the difference between upper middle class and upper class. Nor, the lower middle class (Numeric value "2") is exactly half as rich as the upper middle class (Numeric value "4"). In order to make it exhaustive, "other" has been provided for those respondents who are not sure about their socioeconomic status or who do not want to reveal their socioeconomic status.

The interval level of measurement measures a variable's attributes that are not only rank-ordered but also are separated by a uniform distance between them. Interval level variables are measured in terms of a standard unit of measurement, and therefore the categories of an interval measurement have equal intervals between the categories. For example, temperature can be measured on an interval level.

Question: What is the temperature in your city today? _____ $C°$

In this example, the measurement indicates an equal difference between any two units of the measurement. That is, the difference between $18C°$ and $19C°$ is the same as the difference between $10C°$ and $11C°$. But notice that there is no absolute zero, or absence of a value in this scale. A temperature of $0C°$ is still a temperature indicating a relative location in this scale, and it does not mean that there is no temperature.

Ratio level of measurement is the same as interval level of measurement, except that ratio level of measurement is also based on a true zero point or an absence of the quantity. In other words, variables that are measured on a ratio scale have the characteristics of an interval scale plus a real zero. For example:

Question: How much money do you have in your pocket now? _____ Euros

In this example, if a respondent answered zero, he/she has absolutely no money at all in his/her pocket. Likewise, if someone answered zero, for a question about years of schooling, you can interpret this as a lack of any formal schooling.

In social science research, you will find very few, if any, true interval level variables; most measures are ratio level measures. Also, the distinction between interval level and ratio level measures does not make a difference in statistical computations for social sciences. Therefore, you may treat interval and ratio level of measurement as if they are the same level. This is a common practice and the reason why many people lump the two together as "interval-ratio" level measures. If you use software packages for statistical analysis such as IBM's SPSS program, you will notice that there is no option for designating a variable as an interval level measurement. Instead, interval and ratio levels of measurement are both indicated with the term "scale."

Since the levels of measure will enable or limit the statistical procedures you can apply at a later stage, it is important to understand different levels of measurement at this stage and operationalize your variables into adequate levels of measurement. For instance, you can use bar charts or pie charts, frequencies and percentages, and cross tabulations to analyze your data when your independent and dependent variables are nominal level of measurement. If you want to calculate means, correlations, or multiple regressions, however, your independent and dependent variables need to be interval or ratio level measures. Similarly, to use means or variances to compare two groups (t-test) or several groups (one-way analysis of variance), your dependent variables should be measured at the interval or ratio level. All of these procedures are explained in Chapter 9.

If you are not sure about what kind of data analysis you will eventually use at the time you design your survey questionnaire, we advise you measure your independent and dependent variables at the interval or ratio level whenever possible. Of course, some variables, such as gender, ethnicity, and religious affiliation, are naturally nominal level and cannot be measured as ratio level variables. But there are many variables that can be measured on an ordinal scale or a ratio scale; for example, salaries from work can be measured as an ordinal level variable ("Which of the following range does your monthly salary belong to?") or as a ratio level variable ("Please write down the exact amount of your monthly salary in U.S. dollars."). In this case, we recommend that you use a ratio level variable. We suggest this because statistical software packages allow you to transform ratio level variables into a lower level measurement after the data are entered, but you cannot do the reverse.

For example, if you collected your income data in real dollar amount (i.e., a ratio level measure) but later decide to use simple cross-tabulation technique for analysis, you can recode the income variable into a new four- or five-category income range variable (i.e. an ordinal level measure). No information is lost in this recoding process, and you can still keep the data on your original variable (the exact dollar amount for each respondent) as a separate variable. If your original variable was an ordinal level income range variable, however, there is no way you can estimate what exact dollar amount each respondent earned. The lesson here is that mathematically higher level measures tend to contain more minute information. Therefore, you should measure at the highest level possible because you may need information with more precision at the data analysis stage.

Similarly, it is a good idea to use ordinal level measures when you have an option to choose either nominal level or ordinal level. For example, students often construct questions with simple "yes" or "no" answer choices. You may ask yes/no questions but after collecting data, realize that the procedures you can use to analyze data are quite limited. Yes/no questions contain far less information than asking, for instance, about the frequency of particular behaviors or the degree of support on specific issues. To illustrate this point, let's compare how the following two questions treat the same variable. When asking about college student drug use on campus, student researchers have a tendency to ask:

Did you use marijuana on campus last month?

1____Yes 2____No

But rephrasing this into an ordinal level question offers more precise information on each respondent and allows a greater range of statistical analysis procedures later on:

How often did you use marijuana on campus last month?

1 ____ Never
2 ____ Seldom
3 ____ Sometimes
4 ____ Often
5 ____ Always
6 ____ I do not know

You can use even more computer data analysis procedures, if you measure student drug use on a ratio level:

How many times did you use marijuana on campus last month? _____

The lesson is that, in designing your questionnaire, consider what kind of data analysis you will conduct and determine the appropriate level of measurement for each of your variables. Quantitative research designs are suitable to pursue relatively straightforward questions and clearly defined hypotheses. If your research questions call for the in-depth understanding of a complex problem, a deeper examination of a particular experience, or comprehensive knowledge of a group of people, you will be better off collecting detailed qualitative data for your empirical research. We now discuss some methodological issues relevant to qualitative research.

There are more issues related to survey designs which we have not covered in this chapter. Some are beyond the scope of this book. We hope that you will find more in-depth details from your research methods textbooks. One issue we have not discussed in this chapter is how to write clear and effective questions. There are many tips for properly wording survey questions. *Essentials of Research Methods: A Guide to Social Science Research* (Ruane 2005) has two excellent chapters on this issue.

What Do You Need to Know about Qualitative Research Designs?

The main benefit of qualitative data collection methods is two-fold: 1) they allow you to obtain data reflecting the participants' own perspectives, and 2) they are conducive for a wide range of observations without a pre-conceived notion about the issue or the situation. These methods are designed to have participants' voluntary information in their own words, or let you make observations in the natural setting of a situation. There are various ways of conducting qualitative research, and each way may be appropriate for a specific type of research project. As we discussed in Chapter 5, some of the popular qualitative data collection strategies include in-depth interviews, participant observations, ethnography, and focus groups. Since in-depth interviews are most frequently used by students, we will focus on the steps and concerns involved in in-depth interviews. When designing their qualitative research project, students frequently ask us these questions:

- How do I construct my interview questions?
- How do I select people for interviews?
- What should I do during the interviews?
- What other qualitative data collection methods can I consider?

The remaining part of this chapter responds to these questions and relevant issues. In designing in-depth interviews, the following steps are usually necessary:

How Do You Construct Your Interview Questions?

In-depth interviews are based on open-ended questions that reject pre-conceived predictions and allow participants to express themselves in their own words. They offer you a better sense of what respondents feel and think. For example, suppose you are interested in understanding the challenges new immigrants face in adjusting to their host country, your research question may ask: What are the main problems new immigrants and refugees face in integrating into their receiving country?

This question is broad and open-ended. You have no independent or dependent variables, nor is there a need to identify them.

But you are not approaching this question blindly, either. Having reviewed existing literature, you probably now know something about issues that concern new immigrants. For example, you know that the literature on immigrants and refugees discusses legal barriers for work permits and citizenship, cultural differences, language barriers, prejudice and discrimination based on race, ethnicity and religion, and economic difficulties. With this knowledge you can identify focal areas in designing your interview research and constructing interview questions.

In-depth interviews are not usually highly structured and allow you to spontaneously explore emerging new issues and themes as the interview unfolds. To collect relevant information consistently across many interviewees, however, you need to have some standard set of broad questions you want to ask everyone. This set of questions is called an "interview schedule." Depending on how many specific questions you have in your interview schedule, and how closely you plan to adhere to the prepared list, you may have highly structured interviews, semi-structured interviews, or unstructured interviews. Which one you choose to do depends on the goals of your study. Here are a few tips for constructing an interview schedule.

First, keep the questions open-ended and allow your respondents to answer them in their own way. Questions leading to a yes/no answer are not productive in interviews. For example, if you ask, "Did you have a lot of difficulty finding jobs after you came to this country?" your interviewee is likely to simply answer, "Yes, I did" and stop. Instead, if you ask, "Tell me about how you tried to find work when you arrived here, and how you found your first job," you are inviting your respondent to tell you about his experiences and difficulties with his job search.

Some immigrants may not have had much trouble finding a job because a relative had a job offer already lined up while others lacking connections may have had a long period of unemployment and economic hardship. Respondents may voluntarily tell you stories about demanding and unrewarding work or share their experiences of discrimination while telling their job search stories. You will be in a better position to collect these varying accounts on work when you use open-ended phrases like the second example. Moreover, you will be able to assess what issues matter most about work and job opportunities by paying attention to the issues your interviewees mention first. These rich details will not surface, if you ask "yes/no" questions.

Second, for each interview question, you should think about "probing questions," or follow-up questions for more details or information on a closely related issue. Probing is a critical skill in interviews since your respondents are unlikely to pour out details about their experiences right from the beginning. In our example about the job experience, your interviewee may give you a relatively short answer, for instance, "I have a friend who worked in a restaurant. He told me that his manager may give me a job. So, I went with him one day and started to work there." At this point, probe further in a few different directions. If your research focus is job market conditions and opportunities for immigrants, ask follow-up questions about how long he searched before getting his first job, what he did to search for work, what types of job were available, and so on. If your research question concerns the role of social networks for new immigrants, which many scholars consider important, then probe more about this "friend" who helped your interviewee. Ask: "Who was that friend? Was he someone from your country? Did you meet him here?" These questions will help your respondent elaborate on his relationship with his friend and possibly other resources and information that may be vital to his settlement into a new community.

Third, keep your interview schedule flexible enough so that you can pursue new leads or switch the order of your questions as the conversation unfolds. Depending on your research questions and style, interviews can be more or less structured. You may feel skilled and comfortable conducting interviews only with an outline of themes in mind (unstructured interviews). Or you may be concerned about forgetting some important questions and would prefer to stay close to the prepared interview schedules (structured interviews).

Most of you are likely to be somewhere in-between and follow a style called "semi-structured" interviews. In semi-structured interviews, you will prepare an interview schedule including some probing questions but you will also let yourself explore a different theme or direction as new clues emerge in the conversation. Be ready to embrace newly found issues in the course of the interview. In our example of an interview an immigrant, suppose your interviewee told you that one day he got into a fight with another immigrant worker from Africa because he did not like the African song this man was singing to himself all the time. This may prompt you to ask about possible conflicts between workers of different ethno-religious backgrounds in places where many immigrants work. Even if you had not planned to ask questions about this issue, this may well be a relevant focal point in your research. Do not hesitate to add new questions, if there are newly emerging interests as your interviews progress.

Fourth, interviews are conversations and the flow of the interviews may affect the amount of information you obtain. In general, it helps the interviewees' thought process if you move from one question to the next with a sense of continuity. For instance, ask about marriage and then about children; there is a close connection between these themes and your interviewee is likely to stay focused and remember more relevant details. But if you ask about marriage first, then educational background and old school friends, and finally about children, it may be difficult for your respondent to recall information, jumping back and forth on different periods of the life course. This consideration of smooth flow can guide you in constructing your interview schedules as well as carrying out the interviews.

Overall, having a prepared interview schedule / guide offers at least two advantages. One is that you will have a clear direction before you start your interviews and will be able to include all your main questions. The other is that you are likely to collect consistent information from all interviewees. As long as you use the interview guides with flexibility, you will enhance your chance of obtaining richer and more useful data.

How Do You Select People for Interviews?

Just as in quantitative research, qualitative studies require careful thoughts on sample selection. Selecting appropriate participants for your research will have an impact on your data, since you are likely to have a relatively small sample in an in-depth qualitative study. It may be unrealistic to gather a sample that is truly representative of your study population. One way to handle this limitation is to attempt to select a sample heterogeneous enough to capture the diversity of experience and perspective on the topic you are studying. Selecting interviewees parallels the process of sampling in quantitative research, except that you are highly likely to rely on a non-probability sampling methods. When you select participants for an interview-based study, carefully consider the heterogeneity of the sample, a minimum threshold of interviewees, and the pros and cons of different sampling methods.

For the heterogeneity of your sample; you probably want to select people of different demographic attributes so that you can collect accounts from diverse points of views. For example, if you want to know about experiences of homeless people in a large city, include people of diverse demographic backgrounds, with dependent families and without, from different service facilities, and from different geographic sections of the city. Beginning researchers often resort to interviewing those who are easily available. But if you select people solely in the same social network, you may obtain similar stories; people in the same social network tend to have common characteristics. It is convenient to recruit participants from one support group for recovering alcoholics, for instance, but this is not the best strategy for discovering a range of patterns, experiences, and stories about this population. To increase the heterogeneity of your sample, you may purposively reach out to participants with diverse social characteristics (e.g., by gender, age, nationality, ethnicity, level of education, race, and so on). Selecting participants from multiple geographic locations is one strategy to increase diversity and improve representativeness within your sample.

Second, even if a relatively small size sample is acceptable for qualitative studies, you need to have a minimum number of participants in your sample. If you interview only four or five individuals, you will be unable to find enough commonalities, or draw any generalizable conclusions. In this case, the outcomes become little more than five individual stories. If you are conducting a case study which is the type of qualitative study zooming into comprehensive and in-depth examination of a single or a few cases, then five individual stories would still be good for case-oriented analyses. But if your objective is to summarize some theoretical themes, then you may need a minimum number of interviews to represent a common story of your study population.

The sample size in qualitative research is usually not pre-determined, but a "**saturation point**" is often recommended as the threshold for concluding the data collection. The "saturation point" is defined as the moment when additional interviews no longer produce new information (Schutt 2011); in other words, when you feel that you are getting the same story over and over, you may have reached the saturation point. The saturation point can come earlier or later in your interviews depending on the scope of your research questions and the heterogeneity of your sample.

In our experiences, published qualitative studies tend to be based on more than 30 interviews and rarely go over a sample size of 100 unless secondary data sources were used. For semester-long undergraduate research, we think a minimum of 13–15 interviews is realistic, although you may not be able to reach the saturation point. If you have a year or longer to work on your research project, you will have a better chance of getting enough interviews to reach the saturation point. We strongly recommend that you consult with your project supervisors and faculty mentors who are familiar with the scope of your research questions and the constraints of resources under which you are conducting this research. Since most qualitative research is exploratory in nature, a non-representative sample itself does not disqualify the entire research. You just need to interpret its findings with caution and avoid an overgeneralization.

A few non-probability sampling methods you may want to consider, instead of availability sampling, include purposive sampling, quota sampling, and snowball sampling. **Purposive sampling** involves selecting individuals who fit certain criteria required by your research questions. Individuals may be selected because they belong to certain groups, demographic categories, or they are likely to have special information or knowledge that can help your study. For example, for a study of a city's sanitation services, you may purposively interview people involved in sanitation services including the city's director, managers of various divisions, and street cleaning crew. If it is important for you to include in your study various types of business organizations, you may also set a quota in your sample for various business categories and reach out to different business sectors according to your quota. This strategy is called "**quota sampling**." Quota sampling helps you to ensure a representation of various groups of cases in your sample and to achieve a make-up of the sample that is similar to your target population. **Snowball sampling** is a strategy to recruit additional participants by utilizing referrals from earlier interviews. Just as a snowball grows in size by rolling it, you will rely on earlier interviewees to introduce new participants to you. In snowball sampling, you will ask each interviewee to introduce you to other potential participants who meet the criteria to be included in the study; the chain of referrals will enable you to amass growing numbers of people into your study, like an enlarging snowball. Snowball sampling is especially useful if your study population is not easily identifiable, such as homeless people, victims of intimate partner violence, or undocumented immigrants.

Although non-probability sampling methods are commonly used in qualitative research, this does not mean that you cannot use a probability sampling strategy. If your study population is a small sized group and if you have a list of everyone in the population, you can pursue the random sampling strategy described earlier in this chapter. For instance, if you are conducting a case study of a business corporation and you can obtain the list of all employees in this organization, make a random selection using the list. But bear in mind that if the sample size is small, random sampling does not promise any greater representativeness than the non-probability sampling strategies listed above. You may even use a combination of different selection strategies to recruit participants for your qualitative study. The key is to select a group of participants from which you will be able to collect a maximum amount of information for your research questions. Thus, the scope and goals of your research will determine the best methods for selecting interviewees.

What Should You Do to Have Productive Interviews?

Since interview research entails face-to-face interactions between the interviewer (you) and the interviewees, paying special attention to the following aspects of the interviewing process will positively affect the quality of your interviews.

First, you want to have a nice introduction. A proper and friendly introduction will set the tone of the entire interview. One of the main purposes of the introduction would be to create a comfortable connection with the interviewee. There is another important purpose, which is to ensure ethical process. During the introduction, you need to let the interviewee get to know you and learn about your study, so that he/she feels comfortable in agreeing to participate. Here are some very important things to include in your introduction: information about yourself (e.g., your name, institutional affiliation, position/title etc.), information about your study (e.g., the objectives, sponsorships of the study if any, the purpose of the interview, the use of data, etc.), and information about the recruitment of the respondent (e.g., how his/her name was found, why he/she was selected, what makes him/her a suitable interviewee for the study, etc.), and what you will ask of the respondent (e.g., types of question to discuss, length of the interview). Following the research ethics protocol, you should also clarify whether the interview will be tape-recorded, how confidentiality is guaranteed, and how you will safeguard the information collected. If there is a potential emotional risk for the interviewee, you must disclose it before he/she agrees to sign the informed consent statement. Also, ask the interviewee if she has any other questions about the study.

Openness and respect are important guiding principles in this process. Remember that the participant is doing you a huge favor by agreeing to give you his/her time sharing personal experiences and thoughts. At the same time, this favor puts her in a vulnerable position vis-à-vis you. It is critically important that you should build a sense of trust in the first few minutes so that the interviewee can comfortably open up to you. Use thoughtful and non-judgmental language. Sometimes, it will be necessary to avoid using certain words that may affect your interviewees. For example, you may avoid telling your interviewees that this research is about low self-esteem or drug abuse, which may make some interviewees uncomfortable or feel defensive. In such cases, you may use more neutral terms. For example, you may use "substance use" instead of "substance abuse." On the other hand, do not tell them anything that is untrue. Your use of the data collected from your interviewees must avoid hurting your interviewees, and you must tell them the purpose of your research and how you are going to use the data before the interview begins.

Second, interviewees may be nervous because, after all, you are a stranger, and they do not know what you will ask them. Creating a comfortable and relaxed atmosphere for the conversation will enable your interviewee to remember better and to feel more inclined to give honest and more detailed stories, which will enhance the richness of the data collected. Something as simple and mundane as dressing appropriately can affect the interaction. If you dress too formally or too casually, it could become a cultural barrier to your conversation with your interviewees. You should try to talk in a similar style as your interviewee, using a level of vocabulary with which your interviewee will feel comfortable. If an interviewee feels either inferior or superior to you, the conversation may be affected and become unproductive.

Ask questions in a conversational style. If you read questions as if you are reading from a book, you may sound like you are testing your respondent rather than inviting him/her to talk. Practice your questions before you meet your interviewee so that you sound personable and welcoming in your questions. Also, since interviewees often ask for clarification, you should be able to explain the questions in different ways. During the entire interview, you should maintain a genuine interest in the interviewee's stories. A good listener is the best encouragement for the story-teller. Keep in mind that your level of engagement with the interviewee's story will affect how much information he/she will be willing to volunteer and share with you. Smiling, nodding, short words of agreement, encouragement to go on, and taking notes are all good gestures to show your support and interest. Be careful about any subtle expressions or gestures you may give off, and make every effort to avoid value judgments. You should eliminate any personal biases before and during the interview; for example, you should not assume that if your interviewee is from a poor neighborhood he/she will be unhappy or have low self-esteem. Likewise, if you say, for instance, "how do you feel about wearing hijab since it is a symbol of Muslim women's subordination?" then your interviewee may feel that you are biased against her religion.

Third, your interview schedule may include questions regarding sensitive issues or traumatic experiences. In this case, we suggest you start the interview with more general and not-too-personal questions and move onto the sensitive questions later once a rapport is established. For example, if your research is related to marriage, you may first ask your respondents general questions: when they got married, where and how they were married, and what their general perspectives on marriage are. Then move on to ask about problems and difficulties with their marriages.

Fourth, remember that the main purpose of your interviews is to gather information, and your primary task is to listen. Keep your talk to a minimum. Say enough to maintain a comfortable conversational atmosphere but you should not talk more than your interviewee. In addition, be careful not to make statements or ask questions that will "lead" your interviewees. What you want to get from your interviewees is accurate information, not something you like or with which you agree. People tend to agree, rather than to disagree, with the partners of interactions. If your interviewee picks up clues about your own thoughts on the topic discussed, it could influence his/her responses. For example, during an interview about a national health insurance system, let's suppose you asked, "Given the problems with the long-wait and overcrowding of hospitals, what are your thoughts about this country's national healthcare system?" Because the way you mentioned those negative issues as given, the respondent will lean toward saying negative things. If this happens, the answers you obtain are not necessarily the respondent's genuine thoughts.

Interviews essentially involve building a partnership with your respondent. Thus, the cultural expectations for respectful and professional social interactions should generally apply. In addition, since your goal is to obtain truthful and valid information, you should make continuous efforts to make the interactional dynamics conducive for a focused and productive conversation. But bear in mind that, ultimately, safeguarding your participant from any emotional or physical risks should be a prevailing priority in in-depth interviews.

What Other Qualitative Data Collection Methods Can You Consider?

So far, we have focused on the techniques and processes used in interviews, which are widely used data collection methods in qualitative research in many social science disciplines. There are several other common qualitative data collection methods that are useful for other research purposes. Participant observation and ethnography are widely practiced data collection methods in fields of study such as anthropology and cultural geography. These methods require careful planning and execution. The guidelines for field research are extensively covered in many discipline-specific methods books. We recommend you to look at some of the books listed in the Reference and Further Reading section of this chapter for detailed guidelines for these data collection methods. Here, we would like to offer a little advice which we have not covered in the above discussions on interviews in general.

Participant Observation and Ethnography
If you intend to conduct participant observation research, there are a few things you need to consider. First, you should determine what your role is in the research field, whether it is in a community or in an organization. The dual role of

researcher-member can range from being a complete outsider researcher to being a covert participant who completely hides his/her research role from the in-group members. Conducting research without disclosing your research purposes can entail difficult ethical dilemmas. Since you are a student, we recommend that you let your identity as a researcher be known and conduct your observation research either as an outsider researcher, or as researcher-member. This is a safer option with fewer ethical complications for student researchers.

Even when your researcher role is disclosed, ethical dilemmas are still possible, especially when you are invited to participate in group members' routine activities that are against your own cultural norms or involve risky behaviors (e.g., binge drinking, extreme hazing, spying on someone else's privacy). Sometimes, you may use your status as a researcher to excuse yourself from having to participate in activities that will present an ethical dilemma for you. But such episodes may also highlight your outsider status to the group members, which may affect what they are willing to share with you in the future. You should understand that the line between a participant and an observer is a precarious one and be aware of the ethical and practical problems that may emerge as a result of your dual role.

Second, you will need to set aside a regular time and even space to take notes of what you have observed, reflect on them, and record your reflections. After all, you will not achieve your data collection goals if you do not set aside time for data-recording and evaluation. You should have a notebook or an electronic device to take notes and record your observations and thoughts basically round the clock, for you never know what you may encounter or when. Most often, you will take many short notes on the spot, as jotting down a few things is all you can do at the moment. You need to make sure that you revisit these shorthand notes (typically during a break or at the end of the day) and write them up into more detailed "field notes." Field notes should be detailed and including your own reflections, interpretations of things observed, and even direct quotes from conversations you had with an informant.

Third, as a researcher you will typically develop close relationships with a few people ("key informants") who are willing to share access to insider knowledge and help you make connections within the community. Along with leaders of the community/site you are studying you will want to conduct in-depth interviews with your key informants. In general, you should not interfere with naturally occurring interactions within the community and follow the cultural norms and expectations in interactions with others. Try to avoid sensitive questions or questions that will provoke group members; and you should only ask these questions of key informants with whom you have developed a trusting relationship.

Focus Groups

In essence, focus group research is grounded on the principles of interview techniques, except that you are asking questions to a group of individuals, instead of to one interviewee. If you plan to conduct a focus group discussion, you need to prepare an interview guide similar to one used in interview research. Just as in interview, you should manage focus group discussions with flexibility.

Content Analysis of Image Data

All of the data gathering techniques discussed in this section are methods for collecting text-based data. Field notes and interview transcripts produce narrative data the meaning of which will be interpreted and summarized during the data analysis phase. With the increasing popularity of smartphone photos, YouTube videos, social media, and the abundant storage capacity of digital files, images are becoming a routine part of the social world today. As more people use images to chronicle personal life, maintain relationships, and record historic moments, you may find images to be good data sources to address research questions about people's attitudes, cognitive process, and experiences in contemporary society.

Images have been used as data in content analyses of magazine advertisements, films, news clips, TV shows, and other mass media. But explore other types of image data: Instagram photos, cartoons, video diaries, and drawings. You will undoubtedly find symbolic meanings embedded in images. Your task is to interpret the social patterns and human conditions of contemporary society (e.g., an analysis of gender stereotypes in magazine advertisements, an analysis of emotional state using Instagram photos). Or ask participants to use images to express their thoughts and attitudes (e.g., use drawings for an analysis of personality traits). While the potential is great, there are not too many models of image-based studies in the social sciences. If you are interested in using images as your data, you will need to think creatively about how to use them to address your research questions.

The above list is a far from exhaustive list of data collection methods. Which method is most appropriate for your research depends on the objective of your study, the nature and scope of your research questions, and the feasibility of the method.

References

Babbie, Earl. 2013. *The Practice of Social Research*. 13th ed. Boston, MA: Cengage Learning.

Bogdewie, Stephan P. 1999. "Participant Observation." Pp. 33–45 in *Doing Qualitative Research*. 2nd ed., edited by Benjamin F. Crabtree and William L. Miller. Thousand Oaks, CA: Sage.

George, Darren and Paul Mallery. 2000. *SPSS for Windows: Step by Step, a Simple Guide and Reference*. Boston, MA: Allyn and Bacon.

Graziano and Raulin, 1999. *A Process of Inquiry*. 4th ed. Boston, MA: Allyn and Bacon.

Orcher, Lawrence T. 2005. *Conducting Research: Social and Behavioral Science Methods*. Glendale, CA: Pyrczak Publishing.

Ruane, Janet M. 2005. *Essentials of Research Methods: A Guide to Social Science Research*. Oxford, UK: Blackwell.

Schutt, Russell K. 2011. *Investigating the Social World: the Process and Practice of Research*. 7th ed. Thousand Oaks, CA: Pine Forge Press.

Further Reading

Dillman, Don A. 2000. *Mail and Internet Surveys: The Tailored Design Method.* 2nd ed. New York: John Wiley & Sons, Inc.

Nardi, Peter M. 2006. *Doing Survey Research: A Guide to Quantitative Methods.* Boston, MA: Pearson Educational, Inc.

Neuman, W. Lawrence. 2011. *Social Research Methods: Qualitative and Quantitative Approaches.* 7th ed. Boston, MA: Allyn and Bacon.

Patten, Mildred L. 2011. *Questionnaire Research: A Practical Guide.* 3rd ed. Glendale, CA: Pyrczak Publishing.

Internet Resources

American Association for Public Opinion Research website offers tips for quality surveys. http://www.aapor.org/Best_Practices1.htm#.VHuHzDGG_-s

University of Michigan Institute for Social Research (IRS) Survey Research Center offers an online guide

book for cross-cultural survey research. http://ccsg.isr.umich.edu/index.cfm

University of Vermont Writing Center provides tips and reading lists for qualitative research. http://www.uvm.edu/wid/writingcenter/tutortips/anthrointerviews.html

Exercises for Chapter 6

Exercises in this chapter are designed to assist you in constructing survey instruments and interview schedules. Exercise 6.1 will help you to operationalize your concepts into measurable indicators to be included on your survey. Exercise 6.2 provides you element of introduction statements for your surveys or interviews. Exercise 6.3 will help you practice writing clear survey questions and provide guidelines for a good survey instrument. Once you complete your survey instrument, use Exercise 6.4 to evaluate the overall flow and organization. Exercise 6.5 provides a set of guidelines for interview questions for qualitative research designs.

Exercise 6.1 Specifying Concepts into Measures

The example in the table below illustrates how you can first clarify definitions of the concept you are using and then translate the concept into observable measures and survey questions. In the first column of this table, list all variables in your study. Give each variable a clear definition (i.e., conceptualization) in the second column, and then operationalize it into a specific measure or question which will appear in your survey instrument. Make a note on what level of measurement each item is.

Your Concept/ Variable	Definition/ Conceptualization	Survey Question/Measure (Some concepts may require multiple measures)
Example: Income	Annual household income	Annual household income before taxes (in US dollars): 1___Under $25,000 2___$25,001–$50,000 3___$50,001–$75,000 4___$75,001–$100,000 5___Over $100,000 Level of this measure: Ordinal level
(Add as many rows as needed)		

Self-check Questions

Once you complete the list, review the measures using these questions.

✓ Does this table include all of the concepts/variables for my research?
✓ Do all of my concepts/variables have at least one measure/operation?
✓ Are the levels of measurement for each variable appropriate for the purpose of my research?

Exercise 6.2 Questionnaire Design: Preparing an Introduction

When you design your survey or interview questionnaire, you need to include an introductory paragraph. Introductions to surveys can function as informed consent statement. The following elements should be included in your introduction:

1 Title of the survey
2 The purpose of your research
3 Statements that participation is voluntary
4 A polite request for participation and truthful answers
5 Guarantee of anonymity and/or confidentiality
6 Guarantee of ethical use of the data
7 Time needed to complete the questionnaire
8 Your contact information for any questions or concerns
9 A sincere appreciation for the respondent's participation

Now, let's write these into a paragraph statement directed to your respondents. Once you complete your draft introduction, have someone read it, and ask if the passage includes each of the above elements and sounds personable and inviting.

Exercise 6.3 Questionnaire Design: Writing Clear Questions

A clear and well-constructed survey questionnaire enhances the chance of valid data collection. When you write survey questionnaires, pay attention to the following:

1 Make sure each question is clearly stated
2 Avoid using negative or double-negative sentences
3 Avoid double-barreled questions, or two questions in one
4 Answer choices must be mutually exclusive and exhaustive
5 Use impartial language

To become familiar with these guidelines, look at sample questions below. Each question in the box has an error. Identify the error and rewrite the questions to correct the problem. After practicing with these sample questions, review your own survey instrument according to the criteria above and revise them.

1   Do you disagree that letter grades for college courses shouldn't be abolished?

    ___ strongly agree ___ agree ___ disagree ___ strongly disagree ___ don't know

    Problem:

    Rewrite:

2   Do you think that cigarette smoking is harmful to health and favor laws that ban smoking in all public places?

    ___ strongly agree ___ agree ___ disagree ___ strongly disagree ___ don't know

    Problem:

    Rewrite:

3   How often do you attend religious services?

    ___ more than once a week ___ once a week ___ a couple of times a year ___ on holidays

    Problem:

    Rewrite:

4   What subject field is your major?

    ___sociology ___psychology ___social science ___science ___other

    Problem:

    Rewrite:

Exercise 6.4 Questionnaire Design; Final Review of the Questionnaire

Once you finish writing survey questions/measures for all of your variables it is time to put them together and review them for flow. This is a checklist for reviewing your survey instrument.

1   Does my questionnaire have an introduction that includes informed consent statements?

2   Does my questionnaire include ALL of the variables for my research?

3   Are questions clearly written and free of grammatical errors?

4   Is there biased language that may influence the respondent's answer?

5   Is the spacing of the questions adequate? Does the questionnaire look visually professional (in case you are using print surveys)?

6   Does my questionnaire have proper transitional directions for the respondent? (If your survey questionnaire has several parts, you should have a transitional sentence to take your respondents from one part to another. For example, after asking about school life, tell your respondents "Next, I would like to ask you questions about your family life" before inquiring about family life. In this way, you help your respondents move from one section of questions to another and enable them to answer your questions more easily and accurately.)

7   How long will it take an average respondent to complete this questionnaire? Is the time you ask of respondents adequate and reasonable?

Exercise 6.5 Evaluating Preparedness for Interviews

Questions for semi-structured and structured interviews and focus group interview questions can be evaluated using the following guidelines.

1 Have I prepared a proper introduction to establish a comfortable and safe environment for the interviewees? (e.g., Explain who I am, the purpose of the interviews or focus groups, and what I ask of the participants.)

2 Have I prepared an informed consent form for the participants?

3 Am I familiar with the culture of the participants and prepared to communicate comfortably with them? Am I sure I have no biased or judgmental opinions about the participants or the communities I am about to study?

4 Does my interview schedule cover all of the themes and issues relevant to the research questions of my study?

5 Are my interview questions open-ended? Are they phrased in such a way to encourage detailed stories and answers?

6 Does any of the questions lead to simple yes or no answers? (If so, revise them.)

7 Do I have probing questions?

8 Are the questions written in non-biased language?

9   Does the interview schedule have a smooth flow? Are the transitions from one question to the next natural?

10 Am I prepared to ask the questions in several different ways in case the interviewee does not understand them?

11 Do I have a functioning voice-recording device and have an access to a transcribing machine?

12 Have I obtained ethical clearance on my project?

Your Project Outcome after Chapter 6

At this point:

- You have clearly specified the definitions of the concepts used in your research questions and hypotheses.
- You have determined which data collection methods you will use.
- You have identified the study population and determined the sampling strategy to select participants from this population.
- You have constructed your survey questionnaire, or pre- and post-test measures.
- You have established contacts with the site or the community in which you wish to conduct qualitative research.

Chapter 7

Writing a Research Proposal

A research proposal is a plan or blueprint of your research. When you do a research project for your thesis, a final year project, or a senior seminar class, you may be required to write a proposal as a part of the assignment. A research proposal is a document which contains details of your research plans including why you are doing your research, what questions it asks, and how you are going to collect data and analyze them to answer the questions. Once your project supervisor, committee, or professor reviews and approves your research proposal, it becomes a protocol which you will follow in order to complete your research. In writing a research proposal, students often ask the following questions:

- What should I include in my research proposal?
- Do I need a title for my research proposal?
- What should I write in my introduction?
- How should I write my literature review?
- What should I write about my research methods?
- What else do I include in my proposal?
- What format should I use to list my references?
- What writing styles are appropriate for a research proposal?
- How do I handle the comments and suggestions of my supervisor or professors?

This chapter addresses these frequently asked questions and relevant issues. At the end of the chapter, we provide exercises that will help you write a solid research proposal.

Student Research and Report Writing: From Topic Selection to the Complete Paper, First Edition. Gabe T. Wang and Keumjae Park. © and Published 2016 by John Wiley & Sons, Ltd.

What Should You Include in Your Research Proposal?

In essence, your research proposal includes any relevant details of your research plan. The research proposal serves two main purposes. First, it spells out every detail of your plan, and by showing it to your professors, supervisors, and ethics review committee, you will have a chance to obtain valuable feedback to improve the overall plan. Second, a written proposal helps you maintain focus despite any new developments and distractions you may encounter in the research process. You will be able to remember important details for each phase of the research and keep track of your progress against your initial plan. A good research proposal lays a solid foundation for a successful execution of your research and a meaningful research report or thesis.

There is no universally applicable format for a research proposal; different universities have different requirements. But there are some standard items common to proposals. If your university has a unique format or requirements, follow them. If your university and your project supervisor do not have specific requirements, we recommend you include the following parts. You can use these as subheadings in your proposal.

Key Elements of Research Proposals

1 Title of research project
2 Introduction
3 Literature Reviews
4 Research Methods
5 Research Timeline
6 Potential Problems and Remedies
7 References
8 Appendix

Do You Need a Title for Your Proposal?

Yes. The title of your proposal is likely to be the same or similar to the title of your research project. We do not recommend using "Research Proposal" as the title of your proposal. Use a title that tells you something about the whole project. It should be direct and accurately reflect the contents of your proposed research. For example, if your research is about the relationship between family's socioeconomic status and children's educational achievements, then the title for your research proposal could be "A Study of the Relationship between Family Socioeconomic Status and Educational Achievement." If your research explores distribution of bank branch locations in higher income and lower income areas, a suitable title could be "Bank Branch Locations and Income Inequality." Of course, you may also add "A

Research Proposal" as the subtitle so that the readers would know this is just a proposal and not the final report of the findings. For example, "Bank Branch Locations and Income Inequality: A Research Proposal."

As you can see in the examples, your title should be **descriptive and concise**. Descriptive titles convey the topic of your research so that readers immediately understand what your research is about. It is a common practice to include main concepts or variables in the title. Concise titles are short and effective. If your title is more than two lines long, think of how to shorten it without reducing what it is telling.

If you choose to, you can also include your research methods and population in the title. When your research employs a unique research method, it may be worth highlighting in your title. For example, if you use longitudinal data tracking a group of families to study how family relations affect children's development; you could have the proposal entitled, "A Longitudinal Study of How Family Relations Affect Children's Development." Similarly, if your proposed research is on a special and narrowly defined group of people, you may also indicate that in the title. If you are focusing on judges' attitudes towards the death penalty, you could choose "Judges' Attitudes towards the Death Penalty."

An effective title actually helps you in clarifying the research focus to yourself. Think of a title, even a tentative one, when you start to write your research proposal. After you have completed writing your proposal, you should take another look at your title to see if it really matches the contents of the research. You may need to revise your title at that point to accurately reflect the contents you end up writing.

After deciding on a title, write your introduction and literature reviews. They can be combined into one section or written as two separate sections. Whether you write them separately or as a combined section may depend on the convention of your discipline, any format requirements you need to meet, the type of research you do, and the advice of your project supervisor. Either way, you will cover similar information necessary for your research proposal. In this chapter, we will discuss your introduction and literature review separately.

What Should You Write in Your Introduction?

Make your introduction (or statement of the problem) succinct and to the point, but include these four items:

First, write an explicit topic statement. Introducing your readers to the problem or issue you are about to investigate is the most important mission of your introduction. Background knowledge may include a brief history of how the issue has developed, or the extent to which the issue has affected or been important to society. Basic statistics may help to establish that your topic is worthy of investigating. For example, if you are researching adolescent substance use because you believe it seriously affects school performance, give your readers the percentage of adolescents using substances, what substances they use, and how serious the problem is for the society. You might include the percentage of adolescents whose school performance has been affected by their substance use and how serious the impact has been. You can emphasize the significance of your topic by discussing the inadequacy of our understanding of the issue and the need for your study.

Second, if your topic statement includes theoretical concepts, you want to provide clear and specific definitions of these concepts in the introduction. It is a good idea to draw upon the definitions researchers use in their published work. For example, if you wish to use the terms "intrinsic work value" and "extrinsic work value," the meaning of these terms may not be self-explanatory to your readers, or there may be multiple definitions scholars have used for these terms. Wang (1996) defined *intrinsic work values* as the primarily psychological needs that employees desire and seek directly from their work activity. *Extrinsic work values* are the physiological and social needs that employees desire and seek from their work organization and working context. If this is the way you want to use these terms in your proposal, you should state them upfront so that you will establish a common ground for understanding your research. Similarly, if you are conducting deductive research and would like to start with a theory, you should briefly explain the theory even if you assume many of your readers already know it. After establishing a common understanding of the terms and theories, you may discuss why it is necessary and appropriate for you to test the theory with your research project.

Third, inform your readers of the objectives or purposes of your research, and tell them what you expect to find out from your research. Do you intend to provide some descriptive data on a social issue or a phenomenon? Are you testing the relationship between two variables, or testing a theory? Are you investigating a new issue which has not been studied by other scholars? Or, are you planning to evaluate the effectiveness of an intervention program? Use the introduction to communicate what you want to achieve in the research project. Do you have two objectives for your proposed research? List them both.

Fourth, explicitly state the significance of your research. Tell your readers why the proposed research is worth doing and explain its social or academic significance. For example, if your research project may increase our understanding of an important social problem or a timely policy issue, state it in the introduction. If your research project will have a great social applicability, let readers know that your research project may help a great number of people.

What Should You Write in Your Literature Reviews?

Most student research proposals require a literature review. As we explained in Chapter 4, your literature review should be comprehensive, up to date, and include all major studies on your topic. The quality of your literature review will depend on whether you have spent sufficient time completing a comprehensive literature search and a thorough review of the literature, and whether you were able to synthesize, rather than simply list and juxtapose, the literature. When you write your literature reviews, include the following elements.

Show Your Knowledge of the Field

Your literature review should demonstrate that you have a firm grasp of up-to-date knowledge in this field. More specifically, you should demonstrate that you know the seminal works on your topic, the most important studies to which other studies refer. Your review should show that you are familiar with the most important theories in the field and how they have been developed or applied to the topic. You need to show that your knowledge is up to date and you have read the most recently published papers and books. If you can locate a recent (i.e., less than two years old) review article, it would be very helpful to summarize the state of the knowledge on this topic, and pinpoint understudied areas which merit your attention. Discussions of the methods that have been used for the research on your topic, and problems or deficiencies in previous research also need to be included in the literature review. Below are a few more helpful tips on writing a strong literature review section.

Include Theories

As a student researcher, you are often asked to include theories in your literature reviews. In social science research, research questions are frequently derived from theories. There are usually several theories that have guided the scholarship in the topic area you are studying. Reviewing the competing theories or explaining a theory or theories that will guide your research questions is one of the main elements in your literature review.

Present with a Clear Focus

When you write your literature review, classify, evaluate, synthesize, and summarize the applicable literature. Determining what range of literature to include in your review is very important. For a larger project such as dissertation or a Master's thesis, you may need to include a broader range of literature and write a long and comprehensive literature review. In doctoral dissertations, literature review is usually the length of a book chapter. For a journal article style empirical paper, however, the literature reviews are much shorter and to the point. If you are working on a term paper, or an undergraduate research project, an appropriate range may be about 15–30 studies which are directly related to your topic. Identify studies which examine the same sets of variables as yours and ask similar research questions as yours. If you are testing hypotheses in your research, your literature review should focus on the relationships which you are going to test.

Synthesize the Literature

Avoid narrative reviews, and instead, synthesize the literature as we discussed in Chapter 4. You need to figure out what is the story the literature tells as a whole. Following the grouping you came up with while sorting the literature, write a systematic literature review. For example, in your research on the relationship between the death penalty and violent crime, you may have found that the relationship is inconclusive; some researchers find positive relationships while others find negative relationships between the two variables. In this case, you can start the literature review with a statement that the literature is divided, and then present the two groups of argument, while critically evaluating the sources of the conflicting findings. Was it because of different measures used in different studies? Was it because of the lack of individual level data? Or, was it because of the difficulty to separate out the influence of complex contextual variables? In order to evaluate and synthesize, you need to take each study as a puzzle piece, ask how it fits with the rest, and find out what the emerging picture is when all of the puzzle pieces are put together.

Think about Effective Organization for the Review

When you have an idea what the "big picture" looks like after putting the puzzle pieces together, think what would be the most effective way to present it. We often recommend our students to use subheadings, when they find sub-groups of research within the literature. For example, if the literature that you reviewed can be categorized into the study of urban population and the study of rural population, you may discuss the studies on urban populations first, and then review studies on rural populations. If the articles you reviewed are published over several decades and you want to indicate the historical development of the research on the topic, follow a chronological order by decades while summarizing the research trends in each decade. If your literature reviews include several relationships, such as the relationship between gender and marital satisfaction, between religion and marital satisfaction, and between communication styles and marital satisfaction, then, you may present the findings in these three groups.

You can use tables, diagrams, or figures to summarize, make comparisons, and organize the results of your literature review when they are appropriate. In fact, it is not unusual to find diagrams and tables in the literature review section of published research. A Venn diagram can vividly demonstrate a series of causal relationships among variables. A table with multiple columns presenting competing theoretical perspectives or methods may be effective for certain projects. Use subheadings when your review is long or when there are clearly separate issues that classify the literature. In doing so, you may "place them strategically to help advance your argument and allow the reader to follow your discussion more easily" (Galvan 1999: 97). After you finish your review, you should edit and revise it several times to improve your argument's flow, coherence, and clarity.

Write Optimal Length

How long should your proposal literature review be? Generally speaking, it should be brief enough not to become tedious but extensive enough to inform proposal reviewers about the study's topic. The actual length of your literature review should be determined by what it takes to provide sufficient theoretical grounds for your proposal. Sometimes, even if you ask your supervisor or professor how many references are required, or how may pages they expect, you are unlikely to receive a definite answer because it is almost impossible to give a set answer. The number of pages in your literature review or the number of references in your proposal should be determined by the scope of your study.

Limit the Use of Quotations

If you look at published articles carefully, you will notice very few direct quotes appear in the literature review section. We recommend you to avoid direct quotes in the literature review, if you can. Paraphrasing with citation is always a better style in literature reviews. Do not start paragraphs with a quotation. Your review of a study should be comprehensive, instead of highlighting particular quotes which can be taken out of context. The rule of thumb is to paraphrase or rephrase, whenever possible, the ideas you borrow from sources. If you use acronyms, spell them out for the first time you use them, and never assume that your readers will understand them as you do. Avoid using slang, colloquialisms, and idioms in your writing (Galvan 1999).

End with Your Own Research Questions

In short, your literature reviews serve as a theoretical justification for your research proposal, and thus should end with a set of your own research questions. After systematically summarizing the literature, you should have conclusions for your literature reviews which identify the understudied areas or unresolved debates in the literature. Following the conclusions of the reviews, add your own research questions which can make new contributions to the field by filling the gaps and voids you have identified. Galvan summarizes this process:

> The end of your literature review should provide closure for the reader, that is, the path of the argument should end with a conclusion of some kind. How you end a literature review, however, will depend on your reasons for writing it. If the review was written to stand alone, as in the case of a term paper or a review article for publication, the conclusion needs to make clear how the material in the body of the review has supported the assertion or proposition presented in the introduction. On the other hand, a review in a thesis, dissertation, or journal article presenting original research usually leads to the research questions that will be addressed.   (1999: 73–74)

What Should You Write about Your Research Methods?

A substantial part of your research proposal will be dedicated to the methods section, as you need to detail a step-by-step plan for conducting your research. Your research plan should be carefully worked out and systematic because your research methods will determine the reliability and validity of your data. Similarly, an appropriate and well-executed data analysis will produce findings that are reliable and valid. When you write the methods section of your proposal you should sufficiently and clearly answer all of the following methodological questions:

1   What is your study population?
2   What is your sample size?
3   How are you going to draw a sample from the population?
4   What are your variables?
5   What are the measures for your concepts?
6   What methods will you use to collect data from your selected sample?
7   Are there any ethical concerns, and if so, how are you going to address them?
8   How will you make sure that your subjects will not be harmed?
9   What completion rates do you expect for your survey?
10 What follow-up procedures will you employ, if response rates are low?
11 How are you going to control the quality of your data?
12 How will you analyze your data?

As you can see from this list, the methods section of the research proposal includes a description of the **population and the sample** (e.g., size, sampling techniques, representativeness, limitations), **site information**, if applicable, **variables and measures** to be used in the study (e.g., conceptualization, operationalization, inclusion of survey or interview instruments), research **ethics and informed consent procedures**, **data collection techniques,** administrative details and types of data (e.g., data collection methods, response rates), and plans for data analysis. Keep in mind that you should include enough details about your methodological plan so that anyone reading your proposal can replicate your study. It may be a good idea to ask a peer (e.g., a classmate, a postgraduate student) to read your methodological protocol and give you his/her feedback; s/he can tell you whether the research plan is clearly explained and looks feasible. The details in your research design also show your supervisor and review committee that you have carefully considered all aspects of research methodology and constructed a solid plan.

What Else Do You Include in Your Proposal?

Your Research Timeline
To complete your research on time, you need a specific working schedule for your research project. For example, you should list the date when you will have all your data collected and when you will have the analyses done. In this way, you can show your project supervisor that you will be able to meet the deadline and that you can carry out your research within a reasonable time frame. Allow extra time, as some parts of your research may not go as planned. Having your schedule specified in your proposal will help you focus on your goal and keep you motivated.

Potential Problems and Remedies

Any research has potential problems. Although you cannot predict them 100%, try to anticipate possible problems and include a "plan B" in your research proposal. In this way, you can show that you have a planned remedy to avoid or minimize the potential problems. Usually, there are three sources of potential problems. One is related to your research design itself. Although you strive to design the most careful and methodical research plan under given circumstances, no research design is perfect. Furthermore, even if you have planned your research well, things may not turn out the way you had anticipated. For example, if you mail out 400 survey questionnaires, you may get only a small percentage of them back. If this is the case, you either have insufficient data for the analysis, or low response rates may introduce biases to your data.

You may experience a problem with your sample. Suppose you plan a snowball sampling design for an interview-based study of people who run marathons to mark milestones in their lives. Snowball sampling is a method of increasing sample size by acquiring references from participants who completed interviews. As a byproduct of its design, it has the potential of producing a relatively homogenous sample since new participants are usually friends or relatives of previous participants. If you use a snowball sample, you should anticipate the potential lack of diversity within your sample and prepare strategies to resolve this problem; you may try to recruit interviewees from multiple geographical locations, or try to only select acquaintances, instead of friends and family of old participants who will share more commonalities.

If your research is related to highly sensitive topics, such as death, stressful family conflicts, traumatic past, or criminal behaviors, you may run into difficulty obtaining information from the participants. Many people may choose not to answer some of the key questions you wish to ask. Think beforehand about how this may affect your research outcomes. Extra measures to protect anonymity and confidentiality, or using other means than face-to-face conversations such as writing can be helpful to address this type of challenge.

The second type of source involves issues arising as matters of routine social life during the field research process. For example, your key informant may experience personal difficulties which prevent him/her from helping your research. Or, the social service program where you were conducting your research was cut off from its funding source and closed down in the middle of your field research. Other times, you may realize that your presence at a research site alters participants' behaviors, and you feel that the validity of the data is compromised. It is also possible that you have to suspend your research for personal reasons and the first batch of data you collect becomes too old and obsolete. These are not problems inherent to your research design, but they are things often happen in real life. Even if you can never fully prepare yourself for events like these, it would be helpful at the proposal stage to think carefully about possible back up ideas for any changes in informants, research sites, or your personal circumstances that can affect the course of your research.

The third type of problem is ethical issues which develop in the process of research, especially in qualitative research. This could include obtaining consent for vulnerable populations, and conflicts between the need for data and the protection of the participants. For example, if you are surveying or interviewing people with limited power, such as prisoners or minors, you must obtain permission from prison authorities or the guardians of the children; this could cause unexpected challenges and long delays. In Chapter 8, we present more discussions on various types of ethical issues you may run into while conducting field research.

By including your strategies for these occasions in your proposal, you are making yourself fully prepared for the field research. You can also show to your supervisor how likely you are to carry out effective research. By preparing remedies to your potential problems, you will be ready for more smooth and successful execution of your research.

Appendix

It is customary to attach any relevant supplementary documents to your research proposal. What may be included in appendices varies widely. It is best that you consult your faculty supervisor to understand which documents you should submit. For example, if you are going to use a questionnaire to collect data from your respondents, you should include a copy of your survey instrument in your proposal. Your project supervisor or professor is likely to read carefully your survey questionnaire or interview guides to evaluate your measures for the study. Institutional Review Boards and ethics committees also require survey instruments, interview questions, or other measures and coding schemes for ethics reviews. If you have research site information which you could not include in your methodology section, you may also attach that as an appendix to your proposal. If an itemized budget statement is required as part of your assignment, you may submit it as an appendix document.

What Format Should You Use to List the References?

At the end of your proposal, provide a complete list of references you cited in your proposal. The list will include the cited literature in your literature reviews as well as cited works elsewhere in your proposal. As in any scholarly writing, the reference list must be complete and match the citations in your text. Use an appropriate format for your reference list. Find out what citation styles are typically used in your field. (For APA reference style, refer to the *Publication Manual of the American Psychological Association*, Sixth Edition, published by the American Psychological Association in Washington, DC in 2014. For ASA format, consult the *American Sociological Association Style Guide*, Fifth Edition, published by the American Sociological Association in Washington DC in 2014). If you are not sure which style to use, consult your project supervisor.

What Writing Styles Are Appropriate for Research Proposals?

Though writing styles vary, research proposals are generally succinct and to the point. Clarity is a key to a good proposal as your goal is to show to others what you are going to do. If you follow the format we suggested above, you are likely to have a well-organized proposal that includes all information necessary to your research. When you write your research proposal, you should write it clearly, logically, and formally. Clearly means you state your ideas unambiguously so that your readers will understand what you intend to do. The best way to check the clarity of your writing is to ask someone to read your proposal to see if that person has any difficulty understanding your writing. You may also team up with a classmate and read each other's proposal so that you and your classmate may comment on them.

Logically means that you organize your writing with a clear sense of order and structure. Sentences in a paragraph should relate to each other and contribute to the theme of the paragraph. Similarly, each paragraph under one subtitle should clearly connect to the theme of the subtitle and the transitions from one paragraph to the next should make sense. While the overall outlines would give the proposal a well-organized structure, each part of the proposal should also have self-contained structures.

Formally means that you use formal language and avoid slang, colloquial expressions, or professional jargon which others cannot easily understand. One way to write formally is to use the passive voice in quantitative studies. But for qualitative research, you may need to use the active voice. As in the case of any professional writing, careful proofreading is necessary. Do not simply rely on computerized spelling and grammar checks; take the time to proofread your proposal, or ask a trained person to proofread your writing. Finally, maintain consistent formatting, including consistent first and second level subheadings and uniform font size and style. Also, the document should have numbered pages.

Incorporating Feedback from Faculty Supervisors

After your project supervisor, faculty mentor, or thesis committee members review your research proposal, they will provide you with helpful comments and suggestions. Take good notes about their comments, and think about how to incorporate them to revise your research plan. Do not hesitate to ask questions, if any of the comments is unclear. This should be a productive dialogue and a good opportunity to improve your proposal and research.

Your thesis committee or your research project supervisor will approve your proposal when your research plans meet scientific and ethical standards. This means that they support your research questions and the means by which you intend to answer those questions. When you carry out your research, you are expected to execute it according to the approved proposal. However, also keep in mind that sometimes you may not be able to do your research exactly as your research proposal stated. As we indicated in this chapter, unexpected things occur during research, which require you to make adjustments to your research plans. This is quite common. But if you need to make significant changes to your research plans either theoretically or methodologically, or you see your research deviating considerably from your original proposal, you need to consult your supervisor or professor for further guidance or approval.

References

American Psychological Association. 2014. *Publication Manual of the American Psychological Association*. 6th ed. Washington, DC: American Psychological Association.

American Sociological Association. 2014. *American Sociological Association Style Guide*. 5th ed. Washington DC: American Sociological Association.

Galvan, Jose L. 1999. *Writing Literature Reviews: A Guide for Students of the Social and Behavioral Sciences*. Los Angeles, CA: Pyrczak Publishing.

Galvan, Jose L. 2013. *Writing Literature Reviews: A Guide for Students of the Social and Behavioral Sciences*. Los Angeles, CA: Pyrczak Publishing.

Wang, Gabe T. 1996. *A Comparative Study of Extrinsic and Intrinsic Work Values of Employees in the United States and Japan*. Lewiston, NY: The Edwin Mellen Press.

Further Reading

Locke, Lawrence F, Waneen Wyrick Spirduso, and Stephen Silverman. 2013. *Proposals That Work: A Guide for Planning Dissertations and Grant Proposals*. 3rd ed. Thousand Oaks, CA: Sage.

Ogden, Thomas E., and Israel A. Goldberg, eds. 2002. *Research Proposals: A Guide to Success*. 3rd ed. Academic Press.

Patten, Milfred L. 2014. *Proposing Empirical Research: A Guide to the Fundamentals*. 5th ed. Glendale, CA: Pyrczak Publishing.

Internet Resources

Online Writing Lab (OWL) at Purdue University has guidelines for various citation styles including APA, ASA, and Chicago Manual Style: https://owl.english.purdue.edu/owl/

University of Southern California Library's research proposal writing guides: http://libguides.usc.edu/content.php?pid=83009&sid=2319840

The University of Edinburgh Business School's website has a link to a document about how to write a postgraduate research proposal and a sample student proposal. http://www.business-school.ed.ac.uk/phd/how-to-apply/your-research-proposal

Exercises for Chapter 7

There are three exercises for this chapter. In Exercise 7.1, you will outline your research proposal. An outline is always helpful to researchers, including you. Exercise 7.2 helps you evaluate your written proposal to see if you have included the most important parts in your proposal. Your research proposal can be written differently depending on the requirements of your assignment. The second exercise asks you to evaluate the parts of a proposal that most researchers would agree are important. Exercise 7.3 provides sample templates for constructing time management plan for your research.

Exercise 7.1 Proposal Outline Check List

Use below outlines to structure your research proposal, if there is no required format for your assignment.

1   Title of research project

2   Introduction

3   Literature Reviews

4   Research Methods

    a. Sample size and sampling methods

    b. Measures (if your study is a quantitative study)

    c. Data Collection Strategies

    d. Site information (if your study is done at a particular site or at a community)

    e. Ethical concerns and ethical safeguards

    f. Methods of data analysis

5   Significance of the Current Study

6   Research Timeline

7   Potential Problems and Remedies

8   References

9   Appendix (e.g., survey instrument, interview schedules)

Exercise 7.2 Evaluation of Your Research Proposal

After completing the proposal, you want to evaluate whether your research is ready to take off. You can use the following rubric for self-evaluation, or, better yet, ask a peer to review your proposal. Or, your project supervisor or professor may give you feedback using this rubric.

	Criteria	✓ Self-evaluation			Notes/ Feedback
		Good	Fair	Revise	
1	Direct, concise and descriptive topic				
2	Clearly stated research objective or objectives				
3	Sufficient background information for the research project				
4	Significance of the study				
5	Adequate literature review and justification for the research				
6	Specific and clearly stated research questions or hypotheses				
7	Specific and clearly stated study population and sampling				
8	Specific and clearly stated data collection procedures				
9	Assessment of potential problems and proposal of remedies				
10	A well-planned timeline for carrying out the research project				
11	A complete reference list in appropriate format				
12	Survey instrument, interview guides, and/or site information				

Exercise 7.3 Constructing a Table-format Research Timeline

Meeting the deadlines for the completion of your research is an important part of your goals. Creating a timeline at the proposal stage is essential for a balanced allocation of time for each phase of the research process. Below are two models for timeline for a 16-week semester project. Choose one of them to construct your own timeline table.

Model A

Use shaded blocks, as shown below, to mark how many weeks you plan to allocate for each stage of the research. Example shown below is based on two weeks allocated for topic selection, one week for compiling a working bibliography, and three weeks for the literature review. Continue to mark the time allocation for each phase using shaded blocks.

Month and Week	Fall / Autumn Semester September				October				November				December			
Tasks	W 1	W 2	W 3	W 4	W 5	W 6	W 7	W 8	W 9	W 10	W 11	W 12	W 13	W 14	W 15	W 16
Topic Selection	▓	▓														
Literature Search			▓													
Literature Reviews				▓												
Methods Design																
Proposal Writing and Approval																
Data collection																
Data Analysis																
Report Writing																

Model B

As shown below, write in the tasks you plan to complete for each of the week during the research period. Below is our suggestion for a 16-week semester project. But you can modify the time allocation to fit your schedule and needs.

Month	Week Number	Task	Note
September	Week 1	*Topic selection*	
	Week 2	*Information search*	Topic approval by supervisor
	Week 3	*Reading/literature review*	
	Week 4	*Literature review*	
October	Week 5	*Literature review*	
	Week 6	*Methodological design*	
	Week 7	*Proposal writing*	

(continued)

	Week 8	*Proposal-completion*	Ethics approval and Supervisor approval
November	Week 9	*Data collection/Field research*	(If qualitative study) Transcription
	Week 10	*Data collection/Field research*	(If qualitative study) Transcription
	Week 11	*Data collection/Field research*	(If qualitative study) Transcription
	Week 12	*Data collection/Field research*	(If qualitative study) Transcription
December	Week 13	*Analysis of data*	
	Week 14	*Analysis of data*	
	Week 15	*Report-writing*	
	Week 16	*Report-writing*	

Your Project Outcome after Chapter 7

At this point:

- You have a complete research proposal which has been evaluated by yourself, or by a peer.
- You have obtained the approval for your research from the ethics committee or the IRB of your university.
- You have fully discussed your proposal with your project supervisor and have obtained an approval for the proposed research methods.

Chapter 8

Practical Issues While Carrying Out Research

Even when you go on a journey with a well-prepared map, you sometimes run into unexpected obstacles. Some roads are blocked by construction. Bumper-to-bumper traffic jams highways. Or you make a wrong turn by accident and are late to your destination. Likewise, when you carry out research and collect data in the field, you face unexpected problems. For example, your surveys could have a low response rate. Funding cuts closed down the community center where you had planned to conduct client focus groups. Or the parents of middle school students whom you want to interview do not send the informed consent forms on time. Sometimes, you face an ethical dilemma while collecting or handling the data. You may fall behind schedule and cannot complete your research on time. These are quite probable scenarios, even if you have a solid research proposal. Here are some questions that students ask frequently when carrying out their research project or writing their theses:

- Do I have to get my research project approved by the university?
- How do I carry out my data collection effectively?
- What problems will I encounter in data collection?
- How do I appropriately handle ethical issues?
- How do I maintain good communications with my project supervisors?
- How do I complete my research project on time?

These questions are not always a basic part of your research design or research report writing, but they are practical issues that you need to handle and resolve. In this chapter, we discuss these issues and provide you with some practical suggestions.

Student Research and Report Writing: From Topic Selection to the Complete Paper, First Edition. Gabe T. Wang and Keumjae Park. © and Published 2016 by John Wiley & Sons, Ltd.

Do You Have to Get Your Research Project Approved by Your University?

What types of approval you need to obtain from your university will vary by institution, but, at the minimum, you are likely to need an ethics clearance and an approval from your project supervisor on your readiness for the field research project. At this time, you should check what the official requirements are for the project you are working on. If this is a term project required for a class, you should revisit the assignment requirements. Most of you who are using this book are likely to be working on more substantial projects, such as Bachelors theses, honors papers, postgraduate research reports, or Master's theses. Typically, your university has format requirements and/or templates for these types of research papers. There may be pages of required front matters (such as an official title and signature page, an ethics statement, a copyright page, an abstract, and so on). More importantly, there may be required sections, and particular citations styles requirements for your report. It is very helpful to clearly understand these guidelines before embarking on your field research.

Before you start collecting information through interviews or questionnaire surveys, also check the procedure for a research ethics review. They may be called institutional review boards or IRBs (in the United States), or research ethics committees (in the United Kingdom). These groups of specialists will review your research proposal to make sure that your protocol follows the important ethical standards we discussed in Chapter 5. The procedures and timeline for ethics reviews differ from one institution to another, and in different countries. In the United States, for example, both biomedical and behavioral research protocols are reviewed by your university's IRB. Information on the forms and procedures for student research is usually specified on your university's IRB website.

In the United Kingdom, depending upon your type of research, you may need to obtain an approval from a research ethics committee under the UK Health Department's Research Ethics Service or from your institution's ethics committee through your department. You should consult your project supervisor or professor about the procedures, forms, and documents required at your institution and apply for the ethics review. For postgraduate research, you may be required to complete a research ethics training program before you receive the ethics approval on your research project. Keep in mind that you should not begin your data collection until you receive approval from your IRB or ethics committee.

The most important requirement for ethics approval is to make sure that the human rights of your research participants are being respected and that they will not be harmed physically, psychologically, or socially. If there is a potential risk for your research subjects, you must take steps to minimize or avoid the risks to your research subjects. At the same time, the researchers must follow relevant policies and regulations and do their research according to the professional ethics standards.

For example, when you use a questionnaire or other research instruments to collect data from your participants, you must inform them of the purpose of your research and that their participation is voluntary. If any participants refuse to participate in your research, or refuse to participate in parts of your research, or refuse to answer some of your questions, you should always respect their decisions. Additionally, you must tell your participants how you are going to use the data you collect from them. The participants should know that the information you collect from them will remain confidential and for research purposes only. Whenever possible, you need to make sure that respondents' participation in your research remains anonymous. These can be made aware by including informed consent statements in the introduction of your survey questionnaire. In qualitative studies, obtaining signatures from the participants is often necessary.

How Can You Carry Out Your Data Collection Effectively?

Starting your field research or interviews and being effective, like anything else in life, requires a management plan. "Successful" field research means that you are able to collect sufficient amount of relevant data within the projected time frame. In addition, you should pace yourself appropriately, maintain your health, and avoid emotional burn-out. But, even if you have a sound methodological design, things do not always go as planned. You need to remain flexible enough to handle unexpected developments during field research but focused enough to continue with the data collection despite distracting circumstances. Here are a few important things you need for an effective field research.

Time Management Plan
Time management is an essential skill in today's professional life that we probably do not need to explain it twice here. Constructing a realistic timeline for field research and remaining close to your timeline is one of the most important determinants of well-managed field research. Do some mathematics; calculate the time you need to spend on each case and multiply that number by your sample size. This is the approximate number of hours you need to spend on your field research. In addition to the time spent on data collection, you also need to add to your calculation the time you need to spend on making arrangements for site visits, travel, and contacting and recruiting participants. Keep in mind that gaining access to your field research site (e.g., getting approval from organizational leaders, establishing relationships with people who are willing to talk to you) can take several weeks or even months before you can actually begin data collection. In qualitative research, you should allow sufficient time to introduce your research to your informants.

Find out the maximum number of hours you can realistically set aside for your field data collection. It will vary depending on your individual situation; some of you may have most of the day available for research while others can set aside only a few hours a week because of demanding responsibilities such as work and family. Consider the time you can reasonably allocate for your research per week, and estimate the weeks or months you will have to spend on data collection. If you plan to complete your research project within a semester, setting up a realistic timeline is extremely important.

We recommend marking weekly schedules on your calendar. Make a reasonable goal about how much progress (e.g., number of interviews or visits to research sites) you want to make each week. Your reasonable goal may be to complete two interviews per week because you can only set aside weekends. If you can dedicate more time, set a goal to complete five to eight interviews per week. You should pace yourself considering the general routine of your life. Pushing yourself is not a bad thing, but setting an overly ambitious goal may end up producing a feeling of defeat. The key is to set realistic goals and meet those goals each week. Box 8.1 illustrates a sample schedule for data collection for in-depth interviews.

Consider ways to save time. If you have to visit different sites for your research, you should map out your route ahead of time and consolidate nearby site visits or interviews, for instance, visiting two sites in neighboring towns on one weekend. If your surveys are out in the mail and you are waiting for the responses to come in, spend the waiting time preparing follow-up letters, organizing a system for the returned responses, or another task. If you need to contact individuals for interviews, use small slots of free time during your day for phone calls so that you do not cut into larger chunks of time dedicated to research.

Small Steps, Specific Targets, and "Chipping Away"
When we ask our most productive researcher colleagues about the secret of their academic success, the most common answer we get is "making small goals and meeting them." You might have also heard from your supervisor or faculty mentor the importance of "baby steps." To carry out your research effectively, it is important that you make specific goals in terms of timelines, objectives, and outcomes. Break down your goals into specific daily, weekly, and monthly targets and record them in a table, on a calendar, or onto an organizer app on your smartphone. Even more important is to achieve those goals as planned. Focus on the specific day's or week's goals rather than thinking about the entirety of work waiting to be done. Assess each day whether you met the goals for the day and record your reflections. If you missed a goal one day under unexpected circumstances, think of a way to make up for it soon. If you are able to meet the small goals each day, you will maintain a sense of accomplishment and make steady progress without overwhelming yourself.

Keeping in Contact with Site Personnel
If your research occurs at particular sites (e.g., within an organization, a school, a government agency, or a community), your communication and relationship with people at the site will affect your research greatly. Usually, before you construct your research design, you will need to contact the leader(s) or key informants at

Box 8.1 Sample Time Management Planner.

Sample Time Management Plan for Data Collection
Data Collection Goals: 15 Interviews and transcribing of the interviews
Time Period: 6 Weeks
Time Allocated Each Week: 12–15 Hours

	Mon.	Tue.	Wed.	Thur.	Fri.	Sat.	Sun.
Week 1 Goals: 3 Interviews 4 hour Transcribing Total: 12 hours	Interview 1 1½ hours plus Travel 2 hours	Transcribing 2 hours		Interview 2 1½ hours Travel 1 hour	Arrange Interviews 5 and 6	Interview 3 1½ hours Travel 1 hour	Transcribing 2 hours
Week 2 Goals: 2 Interviews 8 hour Transcribing Total: 14 hours	Transcribing 2 hours Arrange Interviews 7, 8, 9	Transcribing 3 hours	Interview 5 and 6 3 hours Travel 3 hours		Transcribing 3 hours Arrange Interviews 10, 11		
Week 3 Goals: 3 Interviews 4 hour Transcribing Total: 12 hours		Interview 7 1 ½ hours Travel 1 hour	Interview 8 1½ hours Travel 1 hour	Transcribing 2 hours Arranger Interviews 12, 13	Interview 9 1½ hours Travel 1½ hours	Transcribing 2 hours Email/phone contact with project supervisor	

Week 4 Goals: 3 Interviews 4 hour Transcribing Total: 13 hours			Transcribing 2 hours Arrange Interviews 14, 15	Transcribing 2 hours	Interview 10 and 11 3 hours Travel 4 hours	Interview 12 1½ hour Travel 40 minutes
Week 5 Goals: 3 Interviews 6 hour Transcribing Total: 13 hours	Transcribing 3 hours	Transcribing 3 hours	Interview 13 1½ hours Travel 1½ hour	Interview 14 and15 3 hours Travel 2 hours		
Week 6 Goals: 15 hour Transcribing Total: 15 hours	Transcribing 3 hours	Transcribing 3 hours	Transcribing 3 hours		Transcribing 3 hours Email/phone contact with supervisor	

155

a site to gain access. We advise that you have an open and honest discussion with these people about your research. You probably do not need to tell them details about your hypotheses and research questions. But you should at least clearly disclose your identity and your purpose and explain what you will ask participants to do. Risks and benefits for participation should also be explained up front.

Ethnographic researchers typically receive help from particular contacts, or "key informants," at the sites or in the community. During your research, keep a list of the contact information of the site leaders and key informants and any emergency numbers you need to know. Make your contact information (e.g., emails, phones) and your research schedules available to them and keep communication channels open at all times. Their cooperation is likely to be critical for your research, and it is best if you keep amicable and collaborative relationships with them.

Keeping Records Using Field Notes and Journals

Field notes and field journals can be the same documents, but for the purpose of clarification, we will make a distinction here. **Field notes** are the notes of your observations, questions, and theoretical thoughts during your data collection activities. For example, while you are conducting tape-recorded interviews, you may take notes on the interviewee's observable characteristics, facial expressions, gestures, interview surroundings, and the interviewee's reactions to unexpected comments or situations during the interview. Any theoretical questions or thoughts you have can also be recorded in the field notes. Bear in mind that it is most often impossible to take detailed notes on the spot. Many researchers initially "jot down" some short notes and elaborate them into longer notes as soon as they have a chance to be away from activities. Diamond, for example, during his research in nursing homes, wrote that he took notes "on scraps of paper, in the bathroom or otherwise out of sight, jotting down what someone had said or done" (Diamond 1992: 6–7).

Research logs or journals are daily records of your research activities, assessment of your activities in light of your management plans, "to do" lists, problems and your handling of them, and your daily reflections. Like a diary, this could be a space for your personal thoughts and sometimes emotional reactions to the daily happenings. Theoretical ideas and questions can also be a part of your research journal. As you can see, there is an overlap between field notes and research journals, and we are making the distinction for a heuristic purpose. Some of you may want to keep the log or journal as personal narratives, while others may decide to use one document to record all of these. We think this is fine as long as you have solid records of all of the elements discussed above.

Here is why notes and journals are important for you. First, as a scientific researcher, you need to keep a chronicle of the research process, as you would do when doing experiments in a science lab. These records will be useful in examining the scientific validity of your research, gaining feedback from your supervisor and collaborators, and allowing later researchers to replicate your study, if needed. Second, you need to keep a record of issues and problems during the actual research and how you respond to these problems. This is a natural aspect of conducting research in the real world, especially if you are conducting qualitative research. Keeping notes on how you resolve unanticipated problems will allow you to develop consistent responses to repeated issues, and assess what principles you apply to unexpected problems. Third, if your research is a qualitative study, your reflections on the daily situations and people you encounter are a part of your data. Thus, you need to record your thoughts and reflections as much as possible.

We suggest you develop a disciplined habit of writing, recording, and even photographing. You should include several relevant items in your field notes and journals. See Exercise 8.2 for a list of recommended items in your field journal.

What Are Common Practical Problems in Qualitative Research?

It is difficult to predict the full range of practical problems that you may run into during your data collection. Here are some of the more frequently encountered problems:

Gaining Access to Study Sites

Catherine was a student who wanted to conduct an interview-based study of domestic violence victims. She contacted a few shelters but the shelter directors were reluctant to have an inexperienced student researcher conduct interviews at their sites. She then turned to her personal network to find anyone who knew any domestic violence victims. Through a friend of hers, she connected with a young woman who goes to a local support group. The woman told her that her group meets about twice a month. After establishing a relationship with her, Catherine was introduced to the participants of the support group and was able to conduct her study.

When you are going into a community to conduct your study, gaining an introduction to the community or the group can be difficult. Gaining entry into the community is not only a challenge but also a critical factor that can shape your research outcomes. There are a few different ways in which you can make your entry into the field. Find someone in the community who can introduce you to the community. For example, in his classic ethnographic study, *Street Corner Society* (1955), William Foote Whyte, needed the help of a respected figure in the community, "Doc," to gain entry into Boston's Italian neighborhood after he failed on his own to make contacts on the streets (Schutt 2009: 329).

Some researchers apply for positions or sign up as volunteers to gain entry into an organization or a community. If you intend to take a job or work as a volunteer at your study site for your participant observation, you may need to obtain some qualifications. For example, volunteering at an afterschool program as a care-taker to observe the dynamics between children may require some type of certification as a teacher's assistant or some basic training as a childcare worker.

When you go into a community other than your own, acculturating yourself to the subcultures may be necessary. Without familiarizing yourself with the subcultures, you may experience a "culture shock," and find yourself standing out awkwardly in the community. If you intend to study rave culture in clandestine rave parties, for instance, you need to dress and conduct yourself in a manner that will allow you to blend in with its members.

Recruiting Participants

If you select your sample from the sampling frame (i.e., the list of everyone in your study population) and have a list of their contact information (e.g., addresses, email directory, phone directory, etc.), reaching out to your participants is straightforward. But very often, student researchers do not have access to the sampling frame. If you are using an availability sample, or snowball sample designs, you may face difficulties recruiting participants during your research. One difficulty is finding willing participants. When using these non-probability sampling strategies, you may use a variety of methods to find available participants, including approaching people in a public space, using your social networks to find potential participants who fit your sampling criteria, or asking previous participants to refer you to additional participants. Keep in mind that if you are relying on the above methods, your sample is not considered a random sample (i.e., probability sample). Your ability to generalize your findings from this type of sample to the target population is highly limited. Thus, you will need to specify the limitations of your study when you write your report.

If you are working with a population that is not clearly defined or identifiable, you may have a research design based on snowball sampling methods. Examples of such populations include homeless people, undocumented immigrants, members of secret organizations, drug dealers, or sex workers. When you conduct a study on this type of population, you are likely to rely on the help of your participants to recruit additional participants, which is the case with snowball sampling methods. A frequent challenge with the snowball sampling method is when the chain of referral breaks because a participant refuses to introduce an additional contact. This happened to one of us during field research on immigrant women (Park 2009). After about the eighth or ninth interview, she could not obtain any additional contacts from a working mother who thought that her friends were all too busy to meet with an unknown researcher to talk about their lives. She went back to her other participants to ask for more contacts and started a new chain of referrals. Another helpful tip when you use snowball sampling methods is to mobilize multiple chains of referrals. Instead of starting with one person, start with two people in two different geographical locations or two different groups. Since people in the same social network tend to share some commonalities, recruiting participants belonging to different social networks has the added benefit of increasing the heterogeneity of the sample.

Making Cultural Adjustments

You should be prepared to make cultural adjustments when you conduct interviews with people from different backgrounds. You will often learn that norms of personal interaction are quite different. For instance, in reflecting on her interview research experiences in Malaysia, Sharan B. Merriam discusses how in a culture that values and emphasizes relationships she spent substantial time in personal conversation before she asked interview questions. Furthermore, in most interviews, family members and her contacts were present, and she had to get used to conducting interviews more publicly, instead of the one-on-one interactions she was used to in the United States (Merriam 2002: 58–61). She also learned that she needed to allocate a lot more time for an interview, considering the socializing before the interview. Respecting the values and norms of the interviewee's culture is not only an important element of ethical research, but it also helps you establish trust and comfort with your interviewee.

Facilitating Focus Group Discussions
Focus group discussions are group discussions facilitated by the researcher on topics that are relevant to the study (Morgan 2004: 264). Common problems in focus group research include facilitating discussions, mediating relations between group members, and note-taking while facilitating discussions. If you have multiple focus group discussions planned for your study, standardization of questions and facilitation of discussions need to be considered for consistency (see Morgan 2004: 274–275 for more detailed discussions on standardizing questions and procedures for multiple focus groups).

In facilitating focus group discussions, pay attention to allowing all participants to voice their ideas and opinions. As is the case in most group dynamics, there may be people who are marginalized in focus group discussions for various reasons (e.g., gender, race, age, or language barriers). While emerging interactional dynamics are a natural part of focus group data, you can play a role as the facilitator in giving opportunities for quieter members of the focus group to speak their thoughts. Though focus group styles vary tremendously, you are likely to want to maintain some level of control over discussions rather than surrender completely to developing group dynamics. For instance, suppose you are conducting a focus group study on mothers' ideas on healthy school lunch menus. When you ask a question about what the mothers think about the current menu offered at their children's schools, the conversations can easily get bogged down in children's unhealthful eating habits and idiosyncratic food choices. Participants can become passionate about what their children do with food. In this case, you will need to decide whether to intervene and bring the conversation to the original topic of school menus or to let the conversation evolve for a while to gain insights about children's food-related habits.

Another challenge in focus groups is to take notes while facilitating discussions. You want to follow the flow of the conversation without interrupting it to write notes; it is best if you quickly jot down shorthand notes and elaborate them into longer notes later. If you have received informed consent forms from the participants, record the discussions using a voice-recording device. You will later transcribe the recording and add your notes to it. Consider having another note-taker/observer in the room. You will then have a second set of notes to compare and supplement yours.

Bear in mind that voice-recorders can malfunction more often than you think. It may not record at all, or the sound quality may be too poor to understand. Make sure you test your recording device before you start the discussions. In focus group discussions where you place the voice-recorder will matter for capturing everyone's voice.

Sources of Stress

Data gathering in the field can be exciting and stressful at the same time. A major source of stress is the difficulties and problems you encounter during research, which you need to resolve within a relatively short amount of time. Before you begin your data gathering, prepare yourself for a bumpy ride. Be open to the possibility that you will experience trouble so that you do not panic, should you encounter it. Have alternative plans built into your research design. When you face difficult problems, you have at least two ways to proceed. One, seek advice from your supervisors, professors, teachers, or colleagues. Two, revisit the principles of your research design and ethical standards and consider how to apply them to the situation you encounter.

Other sources of stress include juggling research with your routine life responsibilities and isolation from your peers and research colleagues. As we explained above, have a clear and reasonable time management plan, especially if you have other demanding life responsibilities in addition to your research. Look at your time management plan with family and others involved in your life and see if it is reasonable and allows personal time to decompress and relax. You should have regular time for rest and enjoyment.

As a student researcher, field research moves you away from a collaborative class environment to a more isolated and autonomous work space. You may develop relationships during data collection, especially if you are doing qualitative research, but you may feel that none of the participants can truly identify with what you experience as a researcher. We recommend that you have a support group or a "buddy" among your peer student researchers who understands your perspective and experience as a student researcher. We strongly recommend having a support system along with regular communications with your mentor or supervisor. They will help you greatly in easing the stress and make your field research a more enjoyable and productive experience.

What Ethical Dilemmas Will You Encounter in the Field Research Process?

Even if you have an approved research design that meets the ethical standards, you still may encounter unexpected problems in the field. In the example of the Stanford Prison Experiment discussed in an earlier chapter, researchers were unable to anticipate that the research situation would develop so quickly into a stressful and volatile environment. Even with the best intentions, it is difficult to foresee potential risks and problems in a research plan. Potential ethical dilemmas may come from different sources.

Ethical dilemmas can arise because of a blurred line between the researcher-participant relationship and personal relationships you may develop in your sustained interactions. For instance, many ethnographic researchers form personal ties in the communities in which they work and study. You may become friends with community members. Imagine someone at your research site confided in you, as a friend, with damaging gossip about another person at the research site. What if the gossip is relevant to what you were studying? Can you use this information as research data? Probably not. It is a piece of information shared with you as a friend, and not as a researcher.

You often have great leverage in a research situation either due to community respect given to the researcher or due to your power to control the research environment. Because of this power, it is often very easy to slip into a situation where you misuse or overuse your power as a researcher to extract information from participants. For example, suppose you were interviewing a teenager about the use of contraceptives and the student was reluctant to reveal details about how she negotiates contraceptive use with her boyfriend. In this situation, you cannot use your position as researcher to coerce the story out of her. She must volunteer it.

Conflicts of interest are a more obvious source of ethical concern. If there is personal gain to you, other than the scientific value of the data, from collecting information or treating participants (in the case of experimental research), then you should avoid the situation. In biomedical research, for instance, it would be unethical for a researcher to use a particular experimental drug, if he is a stockholder of the company which sells the drug.

Another possible scenario is becoming aware of information about illegal activities or activities that could hurt someone. For example, sociologist Sudhir Venkatesh conducted ethnographic research on urban gangs in a Chicago public housing project (Venkatesh 2008). During his participant observation, he learned, among many other things, of a plan for a drive-by shooting, an act of violence that can potentially harm someone. What should he do with this information? Does he alert law enforcement so that they can stop this plan? By doing this, he is likely to lose the trust of the gang members and may be unable to continue his research with this group. Obviously, this is an extreme case. On the other end of the spectrum, you may become aware of an illegal activity that has no immediate threat to others, for example, a confession of steroid use by a football player in a professional league, whom you interviewed. In encountering these instances, you will constantly measure the risks for people involved and the benefit of continuing data collection for the participants, their communities or for the field of knowledge. In short, ethical concern is not a one-time issue that can be "cleared" once and for all by obtaining approval from an ethics committee. Research ethics are an on-going process you will have to negotiate throughout the research process.

What Should You Do When You Face Ethical Dilemmas?

There are no set answers to many different types of ethical problems. You need to approach them case by case, making judgments based on the ethical principles you have established. Consult your supervisor, mentor, or ethics committee when you face difficult ethical dilemmas. Otherwise, you have to make informed and conscious decisions on your own to sustain ethical research. There is no cure-all remedy for this, but we would like to suggest a few "bottom line" issues to keep in mind:

- Always disclose your identity as a researcher up front and obtain informed consent from participants. Informed consent may be obtained orally, if obtaining it in writing is difficult.
- "Do no harm" is an important rule to remember at all times. If you think that participants may be harmed in any way by being a part of your research or your writing about them, you should avoid the situation.
- Your standards should go beyond simply "doing no harm." The principle of beneficence requires you to do your best to secure the well-being of participants.
- Carefully safeguard participants' identities by using pseudonyms at all times, not only in your submitted reports but in your field notes as well.
- Prepare contact numbers for emergency hotlines or help centers when you conduct research on sensitive issues.
- Take the most conservative approach possible in deciding what to do with ethical dilemmas. If you are unsure if it is ethical to write about something, it is best to leave it out of your report.
- Always remember that participants are your collaborators and not "subjects." Treat them with respect. It is ethical to consult and negotiate with participants what information you should have access to and what information you should make public. Imagine what your collaborators (participants) will think when they see what you write about them. In fact, many researchers show participants what they write and ask them for feedback so that the representation of their stories is accurate and not harmful to them.
- Once again, seek advice from your faculty supervisor, department chair, or from a contact person in your school's Institutional Research Board or ethics committee, if you are unsure of the right action to take.

What Problems Are Common in Questionnaire Surveys?

In conducting questionnaire surveys or interviews, you may encounter methodological problems which compromise validity and reliability of your research or even derail your research project. Problems frequently encountered by student researchers follow.

Low Return Rates

For questionnaire surveys, a major problem is low return rates. For mail-in surveys, the return rate can be extremely low. One of us worked on a mail-in survey project about families in a large city in the United States. Three weeks after mailing out 3,000 questionnaires, only 250 were returned. The same questionnaires were re-mailed to the 2,750 selected respondents who had not returned their questionnaires. Another three weeks after the second mailing, only 110 came back filled out. The third mailing of 2,640 questionnaires only got about 50 returns. Such a low return rate may considerably jeopardize the representativeness of the data.

Sometimes, a student may want to distribute his/her questionnaires to a specific group of respondents and collect them personally. This may increase the returning rate but it can go wrong, too. For example, one of our students wanted to conduct a questionnaire survey on family and religion among his church members. He distributed 300 copies of his survey questionnaire to the congregation of a large church and instructed them to answer the questions and bring them back the following Sunday. When he placed a large box at the entrance of the church to collect his surveys the following week, however, fewer than ten were returned. The number of questionnaires returned was simply too few for an analysis.

Nowadays, online surveys are becoming more popularized. Online surveys can be a convenient and efficient tool. Nevertheless, it also needs to be done properly. A student, John, wanted to conduct an online survey on university students' diet, exercise, and sleep habits. He randomly selected 500 student email addresses from the university's student email directory and sent the online survey link to them. John thought that if half of the contacted students would respond to his surveys, he would have enough number of responses for his study. Three days after he sent the surveys links using emails, John checked his online surveys and was dismayed that only seven students participated in the survey. He waited another week, but only to add 11 participants. He had only 18 surveys returned, which was much lower than what he had anticipated.

Then, John sent the email one more time to all 500 participants, but only a handful more students took the survey after the second email. He had to revise his email introduction to make it more appealing and had to add additional participants into the sample to reach out to a larger pool of potential respondents. John also realized that he should reach students at the right time; they were unlikely to respond to surveys if they read the email in the morning when they were about to go to classes. He sent emails at various time during the day, including late evening hours when university students were most likely to be online. Eventually, he was able to collect enough surveys to complete the study.

Invalid Answers

Even when you have designed your survey questionnaire carefully, you may receive invalid answers to your questions. For example, one of the authors conducted an interview survey that studied parental supervision and juvenile delinquent behaviors. To get information about parental supervision of the juveniles, one of the questions asked the juveniles if they told their parents where they were going during the weekend. During the interviews, the young respondents almost always responded to the question with a "Yes" and some smiled. The interviewee's smile made the researchers and interviewers suspicious of their responses. Later, the interviewers were instructed to probe more deeply for the truth by asking again if the juveniles really tell their parents where they were going during the weekend. This time, many juveniles said "No." Some replied that had they told their mothers where they were really going, they would not let them out of the house. Without further probing, the interviewers would not have gotten honest responses and the research on the issue could be misleading.

Sometimes, survey respondents may either over or under report their behaviors in responding to survey questions. One of us conducted a survey on juvenile drug use. To verify the reported information, the author's questionnaire asked the juveniles how frequently they used a non-existent drug during the previous month. After the survey was completed, the author found that about 1% of the juveniles reported that they had used the non-existent substance. Sometimes, respondents may also under report their deviant behavior. Either way, the information collected through survey questionnaires may not be accurate.

How Can You Conduct Your Questionnaire Surveys Effectively?

To administer your surveys effectively, consider the following issues. First, schedule your surveys appropriately. If you plan to mail out your questionnaires, you may need to consider how many waves of mailing you plan to do and think about possible return rates. Before you start, consider how you will space out the various stages of contacts with the participants; keep in mind that you will need to contact the participants multiple times to raise response rates. You should space out the initial contacts (for introduction letters, emails, or calls), the actual surveys (e.g., calls, online, mail-in), the waiting period for surveys to return, any follow-up contacts, and additional rounds of surveys, as needed. Plan out the intervals between these phases and calculate how much time you will need for the data collection.

Since low survey return rates are a common problem, make your introduction convincing and send it at the most appropriate time, if you do it online. It is our experience that the return rates for mail and email surveys are usually low. As you can imagine, it is very easy for people to dismiss emails from a stranger. Also, people are reluctant to open links or file attachments from a stranger in fear of computer viruses. A few things can make a difference in improving response rates. Your introduction letter should be professional and convincing, and you need a follow-up plan because few people will respond to your initial contact. In case of email surveys, you may even consider sending emails at different times of the day as John did since respondents are more likely to answer an email when they are not busy. The lesson is that you should prepare back-up plans in anticipation of low response rates.

Collecting reliable and valid information is important when you conduct surveys or interviews. One step is to add questions at different points to verify the information collected by other questions. For example, if you ask your respondents to tell you how they feel about a sensitive social issue at the earlier part of your survey, ask a similar question in the latter part of your survey to verify the respondent's earlier answers. If answers to similar questions are quite different, you may need to be cautious. If you conduct questionnaire interviews, you should also pay attention to the body language in addition to interviewees' words. An unusual facial expression or gesture may reveal something important to your research.

When you design your questionnaire, it is appropriate to ask a little more than you may eventually use. Similarly, when you conduct highly structured interviews, you may probe further when you notice something unexpected. After you have collected your data, you may fully utilize it to improve the quality of your research project. Do not sacrifice the quality of your research project simply because you are under the pressure of time or you do not know how to analyze data. If you need help, do not hesitate to ask for help, either from your professor or from your university's academic support center.

Maintaining Good Communications with Your Supervisor

You probably have a project supervisor or a faculty mentor. They have different titles (e.g., supervisors, professors, tutors, committee chairs, advisors), but their role is usually to guide you throughout your research. In some schools, you may participate in regular seminars as a part of your research course; in other schools, you are expected to arrange individual meetings with your supervisor or tutor. In most cases, it is understood that you will take the initiative in your own research. You are expected to play the active role in coming up with ideas, constructing a plan and a schedule for your data collection or field research. Your research supervisor or mentor will assist you in making decisions on what literature to review, what methods to use, and what approaches are appropriate for your research project. We assume that at this point you have been closely working with your project supervisor or mentor.

When and how you meet with your project supervisor will depend on the institutional setting. If you have regularly scheduled class meetings, then you will have that time to communicate with your supervisor. In some schools, you have to initiate and arrange individual meetings as needed. If this is the case, there are a few points in your research process where you may particularly want to communicate with your supervisor. These include discussions on topics, literature reviews, research designs, data collection, and analysis. You can greatly benefit from your supervisor's feedback at different phases of your research. Professors, especially those with research expertise in your topic area, have a great breadth and depth of knowledge in this area, and are much more experienced in doing research in general. They are wonderful resources and support systems for you, and will be able to help you substantially. If you have already designed your research plans in close collaboration with your project supervisor, you are likely to have a solid blueprint for your field research.

You should provide your supervisor with a copy of your research proposal when it is ready. We strongly recommend you to prepare in writing your time management plan, site information, and other organizational plans and share them with your supervisor. If you have a thesis committee, you should give all of them copies of your proposal. Routine and open communication with your supervisor should continue throughout the field research process regardless of what type of data collection you are doing. Keep your supervisor or mentor informed about weekly or bi-weekly progress of your data collection, even if s/he did not require you to do so. We notice that students, when they feel they are not making efficient progress, tend to stay away from their supervisors or mentors, perhaps out of embarrassment or even a feeling of guilt. We want to remind you that this usually makes the situation worse. Give him/her updates on how you are doing and what you have been able to (and unable to) accomplish. Do not hesitate to ask questions and ask for help and advice whenever you encounter problems, including the problem of slow progress. Supervisors and mentors are there to support you. During the data collection phase, your supervisor or mentor can advise you on strategies for effective data collection, on the quality of data collected, and on any ethical questions you may have. Do not forget expressing your gratitude for their help.

Weekly emails can be a great way to give your supervisor or committee members updates on your progress. Some committee members may regularly reply to you with feedback, while others may not feel the need to send responses if you seem to be doing well with your research on your own. In either case, you will stay on the same page with your supervisor or mentor throughout the research process by providing periodic updates. Then, your supervisor can help you effectively when you need his or her assistance. If there are potential problems in your research project, your supervisor who is much more experienced in doing research, is likely to be able to point them out.

How to Complete Your Research Project on Time

A problem that students commonly have in doing research or writing a thesis is finishing on time. Many students either cannot complete their project on time or rush the last part of their work. When a student submits a research report or thesis in a hurry, the quality of the paper is compromised. Some have to rework their papers considerably to meet their professor's requirements.

Generally speaking, there are three reasons for such a problem. First, many students do not realize that doing research and writing a research report is as time-consuming as it is. They often underestimate how demanding the work is. Second, some students do not plan their research work or have an unrealistic timeline. Some students simply do not adhere to their schedule even if they had a good timeline for the research project. Third, many students unconsciously give other classes priority. When deadlines and exams in other classes press on, their research work tends to be pushed aside by the urgent demands of their other classes. It is generally not a good idea take many other demanding courses at the same time, when you have to dedicate yourself to a research project.

To complete your research and finish writing on time, you should realize that a research project is time-consuming and demands a substantial work schedule. While giving yourself some leeway in completing your research and writing your final report, you should do your best to follow your self-imposed research schedules.

References

Diamond, Timothy. 1992. *Making Grey Gold: Narratives of Nursing Home Care*. Chicago: University of Chicago Press.

Merriam, Sharan B. 2002. "'Do All These People Have to Be There?' Reflections on Collecting Data in Another Culture. " Pp. 58–61 in *Qualitative Research in Practice: Examples for Discussion and Analysis*, edited by Sharan B. Merriam and Associates. San Francisco, CA: Jossey-Bass.

Morgan, David. L. 2004. "Focus Groups." Pp 263–285 in *Approaches to Qualitative Research: A Reader on Theory and Practice*, edited by Sharlene Nagy Hesse-Biber and Patricia Leavy. New York and Oxford: Oxford University Press.

Park, Keumjae. 2009. *Korean Immigrant Women and the Renegotiation of Identity: Class, Gender, and the Politics of Identity*. El Paso, TX: LFB Scholarly Publishing LLC.

Schutt, Russell K. 2009. *Investigating the Social World: The Process and Practice of Research*. Thousand Oaks, CA: Pine Forge Press.

Venkatesh, Sudhir. 2008. *Gang Leader for a Day: A Rogue Sociologist Takes to the Street*. London: Penguin.

Whyte, William Foote. 1955. *Street Corner Society*. Chicago: University of Chicago Press.

Further Reading

Boellstorff, Tom, and Bonnie Nardi, Celia Pearce and T. L. Taylor. 2012. *Ethnography and Virtual Worlds: A Handbook of Method*. Princeton, NJ: Princeton University Press.

Emerson, Robert M., Rachel I. Fretz, Linda L. Shaw. 2011. *Writing Ethnographic Fieldnotes*. 2nd ed. Chicago, IL: University of Chicago Press.

Fink, Arlene G. 2012. *How to Conduct Surveys: A Step-by-Step Guide*. Thousand Oaks, CA: Sage.

Guest, Gregory Stephen, Emily E. Namey, and Marilyn L. Mitchell. 2012. *Collecting Qualitative Data: A Field Manual for Applied Research*. Thousand Oaks, CA: Sage.

Rossman, Gretchen B., and Sharon F Rallis. 2011. *Learning in the Field: An Introduction to Qualitative Research*. Thousand Oaks, CA: Sage.

Sunstein, Bonnie Stone, and Elizabeth Chiseri-Strater. 2011. *Field Working: Reading and Writing Research*. 4th ed. Upper Saddle River, NJ: Prentice Hall.

Internet Resources

Duke University Global Health Institute's Research Tool-kit. http://globalhealth.duke.edu/research-toolkit

Field Studies Council (UK). http://www.geography-fieldwork.org/

Social Science Research Council (SSRC) Research Matters website provides several first-hand reflection essays from the fields. http://www.ssrc.org/pages/research-matters/

The Writing Studio at Colorado State University (Writing@CSU). http://writing.colostate.edu/guides/guide.cfm

Exercises for Chapter 8

Exercises in this chapter are sample templates for time management planning and research journals, which are essential for a successful execution of data collection. Use Exercise 8.1 to lay out a time management plan and weekly schedules for your field research. You may modify it to fit your own needs. Exercise 8.2 provides a list of standard items you should include in your field research journal, as discussed in this chapter. Exercise 8.3 is a sample template for managing survey research.

Exercise 8.1 Constructing a Schedule for Your Research

Time management is an important key to a successful completion of research. Create a schedule according to your needs.

Data Collection Goals: Total _____ Surveys, Interviews, or Focus Groups

Time Period: From _____ till _____ (_____ Weeks)

Total Research Time Needed: _____ Hours

Time Allocated for Each Week: _____ Hours

Weekly Schedules

	Mon.	Tue.	Wed.	Thur.	Fri.	Sat.	Sun.
Week 1 Goals: Total: _____ hours	Tasks: Hours:	Tasks: Hours:	Tasks: Hours:	Tasks: Hours:	Tasks: Hours:	Tasks: Hours:	Tasks: Hours:

(continued)

Week 2 Goals: Total: _____ hours	Tasks: Hours:	Tasks: Hours:	Tasks: Hours:	Tasks: Hours:	Tasks: Hours:	Tasks: Hours:	Tasks: Hours:
Week 3 Goals: Total: _____ hours	Tasks: Hours:	Tasks: Hours:	Tasks: Hours:	Tasks: Hours:	Tasks: Hours:	Tasks: Hours:	Tasks: Hours:
Week 4 Goals: Total: _____ hours	Tasks: Hours:	Tasks: Hours:	Tasks: Hours:	Tasks: Hours:	Tasks: Hours:	Tasks: Hours:	Tasks: Hours:
Add additional weeks as needed							

Exercise 8.2　Field Research Journal Template for Qualitative Research

A field research journal is important for various reasons. First, as a scientific researcher, you need to keep a chronicle of your research procedures. Second, you need to keep a record of any unexpected issues or concerns and how you responded to these problems. This is a natural aspect of conducting scientific research in the real world. You should document whether you are able to handle them consistently and what principles you apply in responding to unexpected problems. The following items are recommended for inclusion in your daily research journal. More items can be added according to the particular research activities that occur in a given day and the research goals for the day.

1 Date:

2 Site:

3 List and description of research activities:

4 How long you were in the field:

5 People involved in today's activities:

6 List of respondents interviewed, or events observed (if applicable):

7 Additional contacts recruited (if applicable):

8 Problems encountered:

9 How I handled the problems:

10 Items on which I spent research funds (if applicable):

11 Reflections:

12 Attach any field notes written during the day:

Exercise 8.3 Management Plan for Survey Research

Use the template below to plan for and record progress of survey distributions.

Planned Timeframe: _____ Weeks

Population and Sample Size: _____

Survey distribution methods (e.g., online, in-person, mail-in): _____

Target response rate: _____ %

Procedure	Start and End Dates	Planning Questions	Notes on Progress
Introductory contacts		• Will it be necessary to make introductory contacts before distributing surveys? • Will a written introduction be integrated into the survey questionnaire?	
Informed consent		• Is participation voluntary? • Are the surveys anonymous? • Is the collected information confidential? • Will separate contacts for the informed consent be necessary? • Can the informed consent statement be written on the questionnaire as introduction?	
First round surveys		• How will the surveys distributed (e.g., online, mail-in, in-person distribution)? • What is the expected response rate? • How long is the wait period before the follow-up contacts?	
Follow-up contacts		• What is the method of follow-up contacts (e.g., emails, phone calls, and letters)? • Will the follow-up correspondence be sent to only non-respondents? Is there a way to identify non-respondents?	
Second round surveys		• Will the same methods of distribution be used as the first round of survey? • Will the surveys be sent to the non-respondents?	

(continued)

Procedure	Start and End Dates	Planning Questions	Notes on Progress
Follow-up contacts		• Will the follow-up correspondence be exactly the same and the first one, or will a different method be used? • What is the target response rate? • Will another round of distribution be necessary?	
Post-survey contacts		• Will post-survey contacts be needed (e.g., "thank you," additional information, etc.)? • What is the method of contacting?	

Your Project Outcome after Chapter 8

At this point:

- You have collected sufficient amount of data for the study.
- You have a secure place for the storage of the data.
- You have addressed any ethical concern raised during the data collection process (e.g., debriefing, assigning pseudonyms, disclosure of your researcher identity).
- You have prepared for proper existing processes from the data collection sites (if applicable).
- You are in the process of transcribing voice-recorded data.
- You have maintained good communication with your project supervisor or professor.

Chapter 9

Quantitative Data Analysis

Quantitative data analyses are very useful in student research. Although you might have been required to take statistics, research methods, or computer data analysis classes, doing quantitative data analysis in your own research may still pose a great challenge. The following are some frequently asked questions by students who are expected to undertake computer data analysis in their empirical research. Let's take a look to see if any of these questions are yours.

- I conducted my questionnaire survey; now, how do I do data entry?
- Why do I have to know the levels of measurement in my data analysis?
- I learned different procedures of data analyses, but which ones are most appropriate for my research?
- What do I do, if I just want basic descriptive analyses of my data?
- Which procedure should I perform to determine whether two variables are related to each other?
- Which analysis procedure should I use to see how several variables are related?
- Which analysis procedure should I use to compare different groups of people?
- How do I use my data to explain the causal relationships between my independent and dependent variables?
- How do I use several independent variables to explain or predict a dependent variable?
- How do I interpret the data after my data analysis?
- What should I include in my paper when reporting the findings of my data analysis?

This chapter answers these questions and shows you how to start your data entry, select appropriate procedures for your specific data analysis, and report findings in your final report or thesis. Although there are different kinds of computer

Student Research and Report Writing: From Topic Selection to the Complete Paper, First Edition. Gabe T. Wang and Keumjae Park. © and Published 2016 by John Wiley & Sons, Ltd.

software available for data analysis, this chapter will show you how to use IBM SPSS Statistics software version 22 for computer data analysis. The basics in earlier versions are similar to this version. SPSS stands for Statistical Package for the Social Sciences and it is powerful and the most frequently used computer data analysis software for social science research.

This chapter is written with the perspective that you have studied statistics and have done some practice in data analysis but may need to refresh your skills or need more help with your specific research. If you have never learned statistics or how to use SPSS to do computer data analysis, then you may need to read more systematic textbooks on statistics and computer data analysis. This chapter does not attempt to give you a comprehensive training in computer data analyses; instead, it focuses on guiding student researchers, as they try to conduct quantitative data analyses using actual research projects.

Students who are interested in learning systematic data analysis may want to consult *How to Use SPSS, Eighth Edition: A Step-by-Step Guide to Analysis and Interpretation* by Brian Cronk (2014). Another textbook, *PASW Statistics 18 Guide to Data Analysis* by Marija J. Norusis (2010) may be helpful for students who need more detailed instructions.

How Do You Start Entering Data From Your Survey or Interview Questionnaire?

Coding

After completing your questionnaire survey or structured questionnaire interviews, you are ready to use SPSS (or other software) to do data entry and data analysis. If you did not assign a number to each of the values in your survey questions, you need to code your questions first because the computer software mostly analyzes numbers but not words. What we mean by coding is to change respondents' answers into numbers and enter the numbers into the SPSS program so that you can analyze them. For example, if you asked your respondents the following question about gender without assigning a number to the two possible answers:

What is your gender? ___ male _____female

Then, you will need to assign a number to each of the two options, for example:

What is your gender? *0*___male *1*___female

In this way, the number 0 stands for males and the number 1 stands for females. This is the task of coding. In other words, if one respondent checked "male," you will code it as "0" for a male respondent. If the respondent checked "female," you will use the number 1 for a female respondent.

Here is an example of coding that has already been built into the question. You may have asked how frequently your respondents go to the university library:

How often do you go to the university library?

1   Very often
2   Often
3   Sometimes
4   Seldom
5   Never
6   I do not know

In this case, you already have a number code for each answer your respondent may have checked off. The number 1 stands for those who go to the university library *very often*, 2 stands for those who go to the university *often*, 5 stands for those who *never* visit, and 6 stands for those who do not want to tell you how often they visit or who simply do not want to answer the question. After you have coded your surveys or structured interview questionnaires, you may assign a case number to each of your respondents and start entering the data into the SPSS software.

Starting SPSS Software

After you started the IBM SPSS Statistics (Version 22) software, your computer screen looks like Figure 9.1. Two windows are now available: a **Data View** and **Variable View** window. Both are indicated at the lower left-hand corner of the

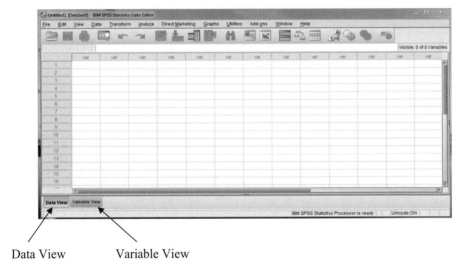

Data View   Variable View

Figure 9.1   SPSS Window. *Source:* IBM SPSS Statistics Software (SPSS), version 22. Reproduced with permission of International Business Machines Corporation.

screen. Select either by clicking on the tab. By default, the Data View window is activated and the computer software is ready for data entry.

The Data View window allows you to enter the number codes for the answers the respondent selected and the Variable View window allows you to define your variables, including variable names, value labels, missing values, data measurement levels, and other data specifications such as decimals. There is a **tutorial**, if you need to refresh your memory about how to use the software. The helpful tutorial is usually available when you first start the SPSS program on your computer. If it is not readily available, you may click on **Help** and then click on **Tutorial** to start the tutorial program.

Defining Your Variables

We recommend that you begin your data entry by setting up your variables in the SPSS first. To do this, click on the **Variable View** tab and switch to the variable view window so that you can start to define and enter information about your variables. In this **Variable View** screen, each row represents all the information about one variable and each column is for one kind of information about all of the variables. For example, the first column automatically provides you with a serial number for each variable. The second column is to enter the variable names. In the sample survey illustrated below, the first variable is *gender*; to enter this information to SPSS, you can type in *gender* in the first cell in the second column. For the second row, you may type in the second variable in the survey, which is *age*. For the third row, you may type in the third variable, which is university status or year of study at a university. Since SPSS only allows you to enter one word for your variable name, you will need to use abbreviations or acronyms for your variable if one word is not appropriate for your variable. As for the third variable, you may use *ustatus* as your variable name instead of *university status*. Then later on, you may use a more descriptive variable label to inform you what the variable is. You can continue until you type in all the names of your variables in the second column.

The purpose of this survey is to understand your experiences on campus at the university. There is no right or wrong answer to the questions. We would appreciate your giving us the most truthful and accurate answers possible. This questionnaire survey is anonymous and your name is not needed. All data collected from this survey will remain strictly confidential and only be used for computer data analysis. Participation in this survey is voluntary, but any information you can provide will be helpful and appreciated. You may refuse to participate or stop answering questions at any time. It should take approximately 5 minutes to complete the survey.

PLEASE DO NOT WRITE YOUR NAME ON THIS QUESTIONNAIRE

First of all, please tell us something about yourself.

1   What is your gender? Are you 0 <u>X</u> Male 1 _____ Female?

2   What is your age? <u>26</u>.

3   What is your university status?
    1 _____ Freshman
    2 _____ Sophomore
    3 <u>X</u>____ Junior
    4 _____ Senior
    5 _____ Graduate
    6 _____ Other

4   What is your racial background?
    1 _____ Caucasian
    2 _____ African
    3 _____ Asian
    4 <u>X</u>____ Hispanic
    5 _____ Native
    6 _____ Other

5   What is your current marital status?
    1 _____ Married
    2 _____ Living together as an unmarried couple
    3 _____ Divorced
    4 _____ Separated
    5 <u>X</u>____ Never married
    6 _____ Widowed
    7 _____ Other

6   What is your father's education?
    1 _____ Less than high school
    2 _____ High school
    3 <u>X</u>____ Two-year college
    4 _____ Four-year university
    5 _____ Graduate school or more
    6 _____ I do not know

The third column is for the **Type** of data, which includes numeric, string, and so on. If you only have numeric data, keep **Numeric** in the cells of the column. The fourth column, **Width**, indicates how many digits will be displayed for your variable value. The fifth column, **Decimals,** indicates how many places your values will have after the decimal point. Usually, you do not need to make any changes for the fourth and the fifth columns. The default number for displayed digits (fourth-column) is eight, and the default number of decimal places is two. Both should be sufficient for your data analysis. If you want to make nominal level variables easy to recognize in data analysis, change the decimals for nominal variables into 0.

The sixth column, **Label**, is for variable labels. In this column, you can type in the labels for each of the variables. If you used abbreviations or acronyms for your variable names in Column 2, you may want to enter longer variable descriptions. For example, for the third variable, you may type in *university status* to indicate what *ustatus* in the second column stands for.

The seventh column, **Values**, is for value labels. This is where you enter the information about what numeric code is given for each answer in your questionnaire. Before you start, place the cursor in the cell and click on it. The **Value Label** window will open and you can type in a value in the **Value** box and an associated label in the **Value Label** box. For example, for the first variable, enter the value "0" in the **Value** box and "male" in the **Value Label** box. After you enter each value and associated label, click **Add** and the newly typed value and label will be shown in the lower window. After you enter all the values and labels for a variable, click *OK* and return to the **Variable View** window. Then move on to the next column.

The eighth column, **Missing,** is for missing values. When a respondent did not answer a question, or provided an invalid answer, you will need to assign a special number code that will not be confused with other numeric codes used in the dataset. The convention is to use the number 9, 99, or 999 to indicate missing values. The key is to designate an impossible value as a missing value on each variable. If a variable has one digit, you may use 9 as your missing value. If a variable has two digits, you may use 99 as your missing value. Similarly, if a variable has three digits, you may use 999 as your missing value. However, if your one digit variable values may go all the way to 9, you may also use 99 as your missing value for the variable. Similarly, if your two digit variable values (like age) may go up to 99 or more than 100, you may use 999 as your missing value for the variable.

If you have set a value such as 9, 99, or 999 for the missing value, click the cell, click on **Discrete missing values**, and enter the missing value in the first box and click on **OK** at the bottom to return to your **Variable View** window. Late on, when you enter your data, you will use this code for missing values (i.e., 9 or 99) whenever you have an invalid answer or a missing answer in the surveys. For the ninth columns, **Columns**, and tenth columns, **Align**, you may just use the default form.

The eleventh column, **Measure**, is for the level of measurement of your variables. In this column, click the cell, then click the down-pointing arrow, and select the level of the measurement for each of your variables. You should have learned in your research methods or data analysis class that there are four levels of measurement. As we reviewed in Chapter 5, they are nominal, ordinal, interval and ratio levels. Since SPSS does not differentiate between the interval and ratio level of measurement, only three levels of measurement are provided: **scale, ordinal and nominal.** When you have a nominal level of measurement for a variable, click "**Nominal**." When you have an ordinal level of measurement for a variable, select it by clicking on "**Ordinal**." When you have an interval or ratio level of measurement, however, select "**Scale**." As for the twelfth column, **Role**, it is beyond this book and you do not need to worry about it now.

When you complete entering the information for the first variable on the first row, you move to the second row and start to enter information for the second variable. If you have a total of six variables, you should complete entering your variable information in six rows. For example, if your returned questionnaire looks like the previous example, your complete variable information entry in the **Variable View** window should look like Figure 9.2.

After defining all your variables, you may switch to the **Data View** window by clicking on the **Data View** tab. Figure 9.3 shows the data view screen which is ready to accept your raw data.

The structure of the **Data View** window is different from that of the **Variable View** window. Each column is for a distinct variable and each row is for one case (one questionnaire or one interview) of your research project. All the information from one questionnaire or one interview should be entered in one row and the information on a variable from all respondents or interviewees should be entered in the same column. In other words, each row contains information from one respondent, or a case. Each column contains information for all respondents for a variable. For example, if your returned questionnaire looks like the example on the previous page, your first questionnaire data entry should look like Figure 9.4.

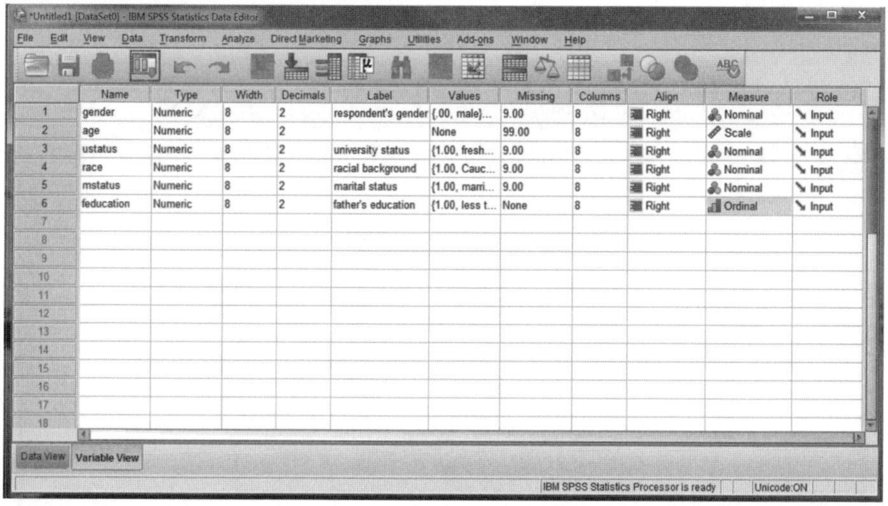

	Name	Type	Width	Decimals	Label	Values	Missing	Columns	Align	Measure	Role
1	gender	Numeric	8	2	respondent's gender	{.00, male}...	9.00	8	Right	Nominal	Input
2	age	Numeric	8	2		None	99.00	8	Right	Scale	Input
3	ustatus	Numeric	8	2	university status	{1.00, fresh...	9.00	8	Right	Nominal	Input
4	race	Numeric	8	2	racial background	{1.00, Cauc...	9.00	8	Right	Nominal	Input
5	mstatus	Numeric	8	2	marital status	{1.00, marri...	9.00	8	Right	Nominal	Input
6	feducation	Numeric	8	2	father's education	{1.00, less t...	None	8	Right	Ordinal	Input

Figure 9.2 Variable View Window. *Source:* data input into IBM SPSS Statistics Software (SPSS), version 22. Reproduced with permission of International Business Machines Corporation.

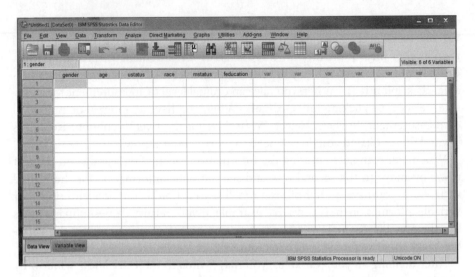

Figure 9.3 Data View Window. *Source:* IBM SPSS Statistics Software (SPSS), version 22. Reproduced with permission of International Business Machines Corporation.

After you complete your raw data entry for the first respondent, start the second case beginning at the first cell on the second row. You may continue your data entry until you complete all the cases in your questionnaire survey. Suppose you have interviewed 200 students and asked 30 questions. After you complete your data entry, your **Data View** window should show 200 rows (each a case) with 30 columns (each a variable), not including the case id number column. During data entry, you should save your data frequently so that you will not lose data should something go wrong with your computer.

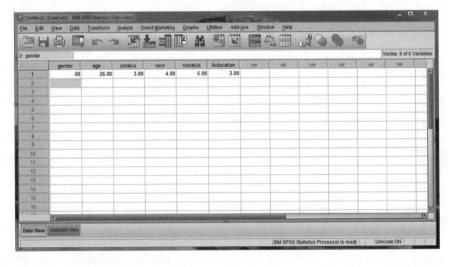

Figure 9.4 Data View Window with Data. *Source:* data input into IBM SPSS Statistics Software (SPSS), version 22. Reproduced with permission of International Business Machines Corporation.

After you complete data entry, including every variable, for your respondents or interviewees, edit and correct any errors that occur. This is called "**data cleaning**." Data cleaning is an important process for accurate statistical analyses. Check if you have entered the numeric codes accurately; for example, if you have a value "3" under variable gender which has only two values, 0 for male and 1 for female, you will notice that this is an error. Another type of error could be when a respondent provided an invalid answer. For example, if a respondent checked off two answers for the "race" question, then you should have entered "9" for the respondent to mark it as a missing value and not any of the valid answers the respondent provided. (The book, *IBM SPSS Statistics 21 Step by Step: A Simple Guide and Reference* (13th Edition) by Darren George and Paul Mallery (2013) provides more details for data entry and editing). After you enter your data, correct data entry errors, and save your data, then your SPSS data are ready for data analysis.

To save your data file, you may click on **File** at the top left corner of your screen; and then click on **Save** or **Save As** to specify a file name for your data. If you are using a computer in your university, you should save your data file on your movable USB drive or internet storage so that you can take the data with you. It is always a good idea to save your data file on your USB drive and save a second copy on an internet storage service or in your own personal computer. When you save your data file, SPSS will automatically add a ".sav" extension to the end of the file name. When you retrieve your file later, the added extension should help you recognize your SPSS data file.

Why Do You Need to Know the Levels of Your Measurement?

In computer data analysis, the selection of analysis procedures is not only related to the purpose of your research but also closely related to the measurement level of your variables. In many circumstances, the level of your measurement will determine the procedures you use in data analysis. For example, if you want to do a regression analysis to find out how an independent variable may explain or predict a dependent variable, your independent and dependent variable cannot be measured at a nominal level (nominal variables can be used as an independent variable only when they are used as dummy variables). Similarly, if you produce a frequency table, the cumulative percentages are useful and can be interpreted meaningfully when your variable is measured on an ordinal, interval, or ratio level. If your variable is measured on a nominal level, however, the cumulative percentage means very little although it has been produced by a computer.

In computer data analysis, it is always important to know the level of measurement of the independent and dependent variables. For example, when you produce a bar chart, it is appropriate to have nominal or ordinal variables. You can only calculate means, however, when your variables are interval or ratio level variables. When you calculate a median, it is appropriate for ordinal, interval, or ratio variables (Norusis 2012). For correlation data analysis, your variables should be measured on an interval or ratio level.

Obviously, you need to understand the level of measurement clearly so that you know what procedure to use in your data analysis. There are four levels of measurement: **nominal, ordinal, interval, and ratio.** A nominal level of measurement is the lowest level of mathematical precision and a ratio level of measurement is the highest level. The point is that when you know what computer data analysis procedure you are going to use, you can design your measurement accordingly (a detailed discussion of the four levels of measurement can be found in Chapter 6).

What Computer Data Analysis Procedure Should You Use for Your Research?

SPSS provides you with all kinds of procedures for your data analysis: summarizing the distribution or dispersion of one or more variables, analyzing the relationship between two variables, or calculating the causal relationships between independent and dependent variables, for example. You may also compare two or more groups of populations or means to see if they are significantly different. Some of these procedures are simple and some are sophisticated. What data analysis procedure you employ depends on what you want to discover and what level of measurement you used to collect data for your variables.

Table 9.1 provides you with some basic information about how to select appropriate SPSS procedures for your computer data analysis. These data analysis procedures are most frequently used by students. The discussions or introduction of other procedures may be found in *IBM SPSS Statistics 21 Step by Step: A Simple Guide and Reference* (13th Edition) published in 2013 by Darren George and Paul Mallery. Our discussions, while not exhaustive, will provide you with a quick overview of which procedure is appropriate for your research.

To Provide Descriptive Information about Your Respondents, Use Frequency, or Descriptive Analysis

When you conduct a quantitative data analysis and write your research report, you usually need to provide your readers with descriptive information about your sample. You may include the distribution of age, race, and gender of your respondents and the distribution of your major research variables.

For example, if your research project or your thesis examines how university students' gender and age affect the frequency of their party attendance and you collected survey data from 398 students from your university, you may want to inform your readers that among the 398 respondents, 36.7% (146) are males and 63.3% (252) are females. You may also want to inform your readers that 20.1% (80) are freshmen, 14.6% (58) sophomores, 28.6% (114) juniors, 26.1 (104) seniors, and 10.6% (42) are graduate students; and that the average age of respondents is 22.2 with a standard deviation of 5.28. At the same time, you may inform your readers

Table 9.1 Research Purpose, Appropriate Computer Data Analysis Procedures, and Level of Measurement.

Purpose of Your Data Analyses	Data Analysis Procedures	Examples	Level of Measurement of Independent Variable	Level of Measurement of Dependent Variable
1 To provide descriptive information about respondents (distributions, percentages, means, maximum, etc.)	1 Frequency analysis 2 Descriptive analysis of mean, standard deviation, median, mode, etc.	1 The distribution of gender and race among respondents 2 The mean age or median income		Nominal Interval/ratio
2 To find out if two nominal variables are statistically related to each other	Cross tabulation and Chi-square test	If gender is related to occupation	Nominal	Nominal
3 To find out correlations between variables	Pearson's r	If students' frequency of going to parties is related to the frequency of their church attendance		Interval/ratio/dichotomous nominal (with 2 levels)
4 To find out how an independent variable affects a dependent variable	Regression analysis	If students' study time can be used to predict their academic performance (GPA)	Interval/ratio/dummy variables*	Interval/ratio
5 To find out how several independent variables affect a dependent variable	Multiple regression	If students' study time and frequency of drug use affect their academic performance (GPA)	Interval/ratio/dummy variables	Interval/ratio
6 To compare two groups or test if two means are significantly different	1 Independent-samples t-test 2 Paired-samples t-test	1 If male and female employees' salary are significantly different 2 If the patient's temperature is significantly different before and after a treatment. Or if husband's education is significantly different from wife's education	Nominal (2 groups) Nominal (one group at two points of time, or two groups logically related to each other)	Interval/ratio Interval/ratio
To compare one mean with a reference value	3 One-sample t-test	3 If students' average study time is significantly different from professors' expectations	Nominal (one group's score tested against a reference value)	Interval/ratio
7 To compare more than two means	One-way analysis of variance	If university status (freshman, sophomore, juniors, or seniors) or the year of study affects the frequency of students going to parties	Nominal (3 or more groups or categories)	Interval/ratio

* Dummy variables are coded as 0 (normally lack of some characteristic) or 1 (presence of some characteristic). For example, for gender, male is coded 0 and female is coded as 1. Similarly, for race, Caucasians are coded as 0 and non-Caucasians are coded as 1.

that on average, the respondents go to parties 3.6 times each month with a standard deviation of 4.23. Such demographic information on gender, university status, and age, as well as frequency of party attendance may tell your readers whether your respondents are representative of your study population. If your respondents well represent your study population, the results of your research are more likely to be reliable and generalizable to your study population.

Frequency analyses allow you to inform your readers of the distribution of your major study variables such as the monthly frequency of respondent party attendance. When reporting basic information, it is always a good idea to report percentages. Percentages are standardized to the size of the group, and give your readers a better idea about the gender and university status distribution of your respondents than absolute numbers. It is usually the convention to include frequencies or absolute numbers in parentheses after the percentages. In addition, graphs are effective tools to visually represent the distribution of your major variables.

Let's try to use IBM SPSS Statistics 22 to run frequency data analysis of your variables. Here, we use student survey data[1] to run a simple data analysis. The specific steps we took to run the frequency analysis follow.

1 We start the SPSS program and move the cursor over *File => Open => Data* and click on **Data,** then retrieve our Student data (as you normally retrieve your Microsoft files).
2 After the Student data has been retrieved, we move the cursor over *Analyze => Descriptive Statistics => Frequencies*, and then we click on ***Frequencies***.
3 When the **Frequencies** dialogue window opens and all the variables are listed in the left-hand box, we select the variables *gender* and *university status* and move them to the **Variable(s)** box by clicking the arrow between the two boxes. (You may also double click on a variable in the left box and move it over to the **Variable(s)** box on the right. If you have several variables that you want to run frequency analyses simultaneously, move them all over to the **Variable(s)** box).
4 After selecting and moving the variables to the **Variable(s)** box, we click on *OK* at the bottom of the window to run the frequency statistics analysis. In a few seconds, the results of the frequency analyses appear on the screen. Figure 9.5 is the output file of the frequency tables of *gender* and *university status*:

Since frequency analysis is most appropriate for nominal variables but not quite appropriate for interval and ratio variables, now we use descriptive analysis to analyze age and frequency of party attendance. The following are specific steps to do the analysis.

1 We move the cursor again over *Analyze => Descriptive Statistics => Descriptives* and click on **Descriptives**.

---

[1]We collected the student data from a university in the United States in 2005 and will use these data for demonstration purposes in this chapter.

Gender

		Frequency	Percent	Valid Percent	Cumulative Percent
Valid	male	146	36.7	36.7	36.7
	female	252	63.3	63.3	100.0
	Total	398	100.0	100.0	

university status

		Frequency	Percent	Valid Percent	Cumulative Percent
Valid	freshmen	80	20.1	20.1	20.1
	sophomore	58	14.6	14.6	34.7
	junior	114	28.6	28.6	63.3
	senior	104	26.1	26.1	89.4
	graduate	42	10.6	10.6	100.0
	Total	398	100.0	100.0	

Figure 9.5 Frequency Analysis Output File. *Source:* data input into IBM SPSS Statistics Software (SPSS), version 22. Reproduced with permission of International Business Machines Corporation.

2 When the **Descriptives** dialogue window opens and all the variables are listed in the left box, we select the variables, *age*, and *parties* and move them to the **Variable(s)** box by clicking on the arrow between the two boxes after selection.
3 After moving the variables to the **Variable(s)** box, we click on **Options**.
4 When the **Descriptives: Options** dialogue window opens, we check **Mean, Std. Deviation, Minimum, and Maximum** and click on *Continue* to return to the **Descriptives** window.
5 Then we click on *OK* at the bottom of the window to run the Descriptive statistics analysis. Figure 9.6 is the output file of the descriptive statistics for *age and parties*:

Either print a copy of the output file or directly cite the numbers when you write your research report. When you report on such information, it is necessary

Descriptive Statistics

	N	Minimum	Maximum	Mean	Std. Deviation
age	394	17.00	50.00	22.2234	5.28196
parties	384	.00	20.00	3.5859	4.23206
Valid N (listwise)	380				

Figure 9.6 Descriptive Analysis Output File. *Source:* data input into IBM SPSS Statistics Software (SPSS), version 22. Reproduced with permission of International Business Machines Corporation.

to remember that some statistics are inappropriate depending on the level of measurement of your variables. For example, mean, valid percent, or cumulative percent are all useful statistics to show the distribution of the variable *age* which is a ratio level measure. You may also use valid percent to indicate the gender distribution of your respondents. The mean score of *gender*, however, is not really meaningful since it is a nominal level measure.

To Determine If Two Variables Are Related to Each Other, Use Cross Tabulations and Chi-square Analysis

If you want to test whether two variables measured on a nominal level are related to each other, run a cross tabulation. Use percentages to describe how the two variables are related. In addition, an inferential statistics technique called "Chi-square" will further allow you to assess whether the two variables are statistically related to each other. For example, you may want to test if gender is statistically associated with marital status among university students. You may also use this method to examine if occupation is related to race, or if occupation is related to gender, or if political affiliation is related to occupation, or if political affiliation is related to gender.

Here are the steps we took to produce crosstabs of the two variables (gender and marital status) and calculate the Chi-square value. The output file is shown in Figure 9.7.

1 After starting the IBM SPSS Statistics software and retrieving our Student data, we move the cursor over *Analyze => Descriptive Statistics => Crosstabs* and click on **Crosstabs**.
2 When the **Crosstabs** dialogue window opens, we select an independent variable (*gender*) from the variables list in the left-hand box, move it into the upper right-hand box under **Row(s)** by clicking the arrow between the variable box and the box under **Row(s)**.
3 We next select a dependent variable (*marital status*) from the variable list in the left box and move it into the middle right box under **Column(s)** by clicking the arrow between the two boxes.
4 Then, we click the **Cells** on the right side of the window and check *Row, Column,* and *Total* in the middle of the left side under **Percentages**. These selections will provide us with row, column and total percentages of each variable and each value. Then we click *Continue* to return to the **Crosstabs** dialogue window.
5 Next, we click on **Statistics** on the right side of the window and check *Chi-square* at the upper left to get the Chi-square value.
6 After we click **Continue** to get back to the **Crosstabs** dialogue window and then click **OK** to run the analysis. Figure 9.7 shows the results of our data analysis.

Case Processing Summary

	Cases					
	Valid		Missing		Total	
	N	Percent	N	Percent	N	Percent
gender * marital status	398	100.0%	0	0.0%	398	100.0%

gender * marital status Crosstabulation

		marital status						
		married	living together as an unmarried couple	divorced	separated	never married	other	Total
gender	male							
	Count	2	6	6	5	118	9	146
	% within gender	1.4%	4.1%	4.1%	3.4%	80.8%	6.2%	100.0%
	% within marital status	4.0%	28.6%	46.2%	45.5%	42.0%	40.9%	36.7%
	% of Total	0.5%	1.5%	1.5%	1.3%	29.6%	2.3%	36.7%
	female							
	Count	48	15	7	6	163	13	252
	% within gender	19.0%	6.0%	2.8%	2.4%	64.7%	5.2%	100.0%
	% within marital status	96.0%	71.4%	53.8%	54.5%	58.0%	59.1%	63.3%
	% of Total	12.1%	3.8%	1.8%	1.5%	41.0%	3.3%	63.3%
Total	Count	50	21	13	11	281	22	398
	% within gender	12.6%	5.3%	3.3%	2.8%	70.6%	5.5%	100.0%
	% within marital status	100.0%	100.0%	100.0%	100.0%	100.0%	100.0%	100.0%
	% of Total	12.6%	5.3%	3.3%	2.8%	70.6%	5.5%	100.0%

Chi-Square Tests

	Value	df	Asymp. Sig. (2-sided)
Pearson Chi-Square	28.036[a]	5	.000
Likelihood Ratio	36.067	5	.000
Linear-by-Linear Association	20.909	1	.000
N of Valid Cases	398		

[a] 2 cells (16.7%) have expected count less than 5. The minimum expected count is 4.04.

Figure 9.7 Cross Tabulation and Chi-square Test Output File. *Source:* data input into IBM SPSS Statistics Software (SPSS), version 22. Reproduced with permission of International Business Machines Corporation.

You may also want to calculate the strength of the relations between the two variables. If the two variables are measured on a nominal level, select the contingency coefficient, Phi and Cramer's V, Lambda, or Uncertainty coefficient value to indicate the association between the two variables. The Phi coefficient can be used as a measure of the relationship for a contingency table where at least one of the two variables is measured on a nominal level when the Chi-square is calculated for a 2×2 table. If the two variables are ordinal level variables, you may select Gamma, Somers' D, Kendall's tau-b or Kendall's tau-c to measure the association between your two variables. If one of the variables is measured at the nominal level and the other is measured at the interval level, use eta to indicate their relationship.

Our cross-tabulation and Chi-square test produced three tables. The first shows that all 398 respondents answered the two questions on their gender and marital status. The second table indicates how the distribution of marital status is related to the distribution of gender. The first column of the second table indicates what each value is (i.e., male and female). There are four values in each cell. To understand the second table, you can read across or read down the table. For example, you may read across the table to find the numbers and the percentage distribution of marital status among the male and female respondents. For male respondents, you read the first and the second values in each cell in the second row. It shows that, among the male respondents, 2 or 1.4% are married, 6 or 4.1% are living together as unmarried couples, 6 or 4.1% are divorced, 5 or 3.4% are separated, 118 or 80.8% have never married, and 9 or 6.2% indicate other marital status. The total number of the males is 146 and all the percentages add up to 100%.

Among the females (the first and the second values in the third row), and you get the information that 48 or 19.0% are married, 15 or 6.0% are living together as unmarried couples, 7 or 2.8% are divorced, 6 or 2.4% are separated, 163 or 64.7% have never married, and 13 or 5.2% have other marital statuses. The total number of females is 252 and the percentages add up to 100%.

Next, you may read down the table to understand how different marital statuses are distributed between male and female respondents. When you read down the table, you read the first and the third values in each cell in each column. For example, the values in the second column tell you that, among married respondents, 2 or 4.0% are males and 48 or 96.4% are females. The total number of respondents who are married is 50, which are shown by the first number in the second column and in the last row. Similarly, the third column indicates that among respondents, who are living together as unmarried couples, 6 or 28.6% are males and 15 or 71.4% are females. The total number in this group of respondents is 21 which is the first number in the third column on the last row. You may continue to read the table in this way and get more information about the relationships between marital status and gender. So far, each of the values gives you an impression that there is some connection between marital status and gender among students. Let's check if the Chi-square test will confirm your impression.

After you perform a Chi-square test, check if the test is statistically significant. First, you need to see if each cell in the cross tabulation table has sufficient number of cases. What percentage of the cells has expected counts of less than 5? In calculating the Chi-square value, if some of the expected frequencies in a table are less than 5, the observed significance level based on the Chi-square distribution may be inaccurate. Generally speaking, if 25% of the cells have expected values less than 5, you should not trust the result of the Chi-square test. Therefore, sample size is important in a Chi-square test because Chi-square value increases in direct proportion to sample size, if the strength of the relationship remains the same. That means that a large sample size will find small differences to be significant, and a small sample size will find large differences not significant.

If fewer than 25% of the cells have counts of less than 5 (in this example, there are 2 cells or 16.7% which have expected count less than 5), check the level of significance for the Pearson Chi-square value (which is usually used to indicate the relationship between the two variables), if the significance level is equal to or smaller than .05, the two variables are not independent of each other. In other words, the variation of the dependent variable is related to the variation of the independent variable. When reporting the result of the Chi-square analysis in your paper, you need to report the **Pearson Chi-square value** and **the significance level**. Generally speaking, when the significance value is small and when the Chi-square value is large, the relationship between the two variables is stronger. In this example, you will report that a Chi-square test of the relationship between gender and marital status indicates that the two variables are not independent of each other ($\chi^2 = 28.036$, p < .001). In other words, university students' marital status is related to their gender.

To Calculate Correlations between Two Variables That Are Measured at Interval or Ratio Level, Use Pearson's r

If you want to know the correlations between two variables when both are measured at an interval or ratio level, calculate Pearson's r. For example, if you want to discover whether the frequency of college students' party attendance is related to the frequency of their church attendance, you may calculate Pearson's r to indicate the correlation. A correlation is designated by the lower-case letter r. The value of r ranges from −1 to +1. When we consider the strength of the correlation, we consider absolute value between 0 and 1. The larger the absolute value of r is, the stronger the statistical association is between two interval/ratio variables. If Pearson's r is 0, it means the two variables are not associated. If Pearson's r is .8, the two variables are strongly associated. A correlation is also frequently referred to as the Pearson product-moment correlation or Pearson's r. This correlation analysis may also be used to calculate the relations between age and salary, between salary and the years of education completed, between church attendance and illegal drug use, between study time and final examination scores when they are measured on an interval or ratio level.

When calculating correlations between two variables, both of your variables should be interval or ratio level variables (nominal level variables can be used if they are dichotomous or with only two values coded as 0 and 1) that are normally distributed. If you have variables measured at the ordinal level or if your variables are not normally distributed, use Spearman's rho to measure their correlations. Pearson's r measures linear relationships.

Now we would like to use the Student data to show you, step by step, how to produce the correlation table and calculate Pearson's r using SPSS.

1   After starting the SPSS program and retrieving our Student data, we move the cursor over *Analyze => Correlate => Bivariate* and click on **Bivariate**.
2   When the **Bivariate Correlations** dialogue window opens, we select the variables from the variable list in the left-hand box by highlighting them and moving them to the right-hand box by clicking the arrow between the two boxes. For this analysis, we select three variables: university students' party attendance frequency, their frequency of church attendance, and their frequency of getting drunk (you can also move the variables over by double clicking on a variable). You must have at least two variables for this analysis. You may also analyze several variable correlations simultaneously.
3   Then we check **Pearson** and **Flag Significant Correlations**, then click *OK* to calculate the correlations.

In a few seconds, a correlation matrix is shown on the screen. Figure 9.8 shows the results of our correlation analysis. Pearson's Correlation is an indicator of an association between two variables; when you select more than two variables, SPSS output will give you correlation statistics for all possible pairs among your selected variables as shown below.

Correlations

		parties	church attendance	drunk times
parties	Pearson Correlation	1	−.108[*]	.547[**]
	Sig. (2-tailed)		.036	.000
	N	384	380	376
church attendance	Pearson Correlation	−.108[*]	1	−.147[**]
	Sig. (2-tailed)	.036		.004
	N	380	382	376
drunk times	Pearson Correlation	.547[**]	−.147[**]	1
	Sig. (2-tailed)	.000	.004	
	N	376	376	384

[*]. Correlation is significant at the 0.05 level (2-tailed).
[**]. Correlation is significant at the 0.01 level (2-tailed).

Figure 9.8   Correlation Analysis Output File. *Source:* data input into IBM SPSS Statistics Software (SPSS), version 22. Reproduced with permission of International Business Machines Corporation.

Before you read this correlation matrix, draw a line from the upper left corner where the first variable, *parties*, is listed to the bottom right corner of the table to separate the matrix into two triangles. The two triangles are symmetrical and each demonstrates the same correlations as the other. When you read the information in either triangle, you get the same information because SPSS generates two statistics for the same pair. For example, the correlation for the pair, church attendance and parties, is generated for 1) parties and church attendance (first row second column), and 2) for church attendance and parties (second row first column). Notice here that Pearson's Correlation is the same, no matter which of the two variables comes first.

From this output matrix, you can see how one variable is correlated to another. Since we have analyzed three variables, there are three rows and three columns indicating the correlations between each pair of the three variables (Columns 2, 3, 4 and Rows 2, 3, 4). Each cell has three numbers and the first number is the Pearson's r value that indicates the relationship between two variables. The second number indicates the significance level, and the third number indicates the number of respondents included in the analysis.

For example, the three numbers in the third row and in the second column are the Pearson's r value of −.108*, the significance level of .036, and the number of cases, 380. Pearson's r indicates how strongly the two variables are correlated; the value −.108 means that party attendance is slightly and negatively related to church attendance. A "negative" statistical relationship means that the value of church attendance and that of party attendance change in the opposite direction, which means students who go to parties more frequently are slightly less likely to attend church activities and vice versa. This correlation is statistically significant because the significance value .036 is < .05. There are 380 respondents who answered the two questions that asked information about these two variables.

Similarly, the three numbers on the fourth row in the second column are the result of the correlation analysis between student party attendance frequency and frequency of getting drunk. Pearson's r value is .547**, the significant level is .000 (which really means <.001 as statistical probability can never be a zero) and the number of respondents included in the analysis is 376. That means 376 respondents answered the questions on party attendance and frequency of getting drunk. The significance level of .000 means it is smaller than .001 and it is statistically signifi-cant. This is also indicated with a double-asterisk on the Pearson's r. The Pearson's r value of .547 indicates that these two variables have a moderately strong positive relationship, which means those students who go to parties more frequently are much more likely to get drunk.

A positive correlation means that as one variable increases in value, the other variable also increases in value, or when one variable decreases in value, the other variable also decreases in value. In contrast, a negative correlation means that when one variable increases its value, the other variable decreases in value and vice versa.

Either positive or negative, the closer the absolute value of a correlation to 1, the stronger the relationship between the two variables. On the other hand, the closer the correlation value is to 0, the weaker the relationship between the two variables will be. In social sciences, a perfect correlation between two variables is very unlikely. For many social scientists, a correlation from .3 to .5 between two variables, either negative or positive, is considered moderate while a relationship from .6 to .9 between two variables is considered strong. A correlation value that is smaller than .3 is considered weak. A significant correlation (a significance level smaller than .05) indicates a statistically significant relationship, meaning that the likelihood that there is a correlation is high. A significant correlation, however, does not always accurately reflect the strength of the relationship because significance level is affected also by sample size. A weak relationship may be statistically significant, if the sample size is large.

As for the significance level of the test, a two-tailed significance level is normally used. When the significance level is equal to or smaller than .05, asterisks will be printed after the correlation value to flag the significance level. One asterisk * typically indicates that the correlation is significant at the .05 level and two asterisks ** indicates that the correlation is significant at the .01 level. If you are clear about the direction of your correlations, select the one-tailed significance level. In this case, a significance level of .10 may be considered statistically significant.

When you conduct correlation analysis, you may select different ways to address missing values. You may exclude cases **pairwise or listwise**. When you exclude missing cases pairwise, a respondent's missing value on a specific variable will be excluded when the computer calculates particular correlations between this specific variable and other variables, but the respondent will still be included when calculating correlations between other variables. In this way, you may have different numbers of subjects determining different correlations. When you exclude missing cases listwise, respondents with missing values for any variables included in the analysis will be excluded from any correlation analysis.

To Know Whether an Independent Variable Predicts or Explains an Effect on a Dependent Variable, Use Regression Analysis

A correlation between two variables may indicate a potential causal relationship between the two variables. It may not be clear, however, which of the two variables is the independent variable and which is the dependent variable. When you assume that a correlation between two variables indicates a causal relationship, one of the two variables is an independent (the cause) and the other is a dependent variable (the outcome). In a causal relationship, the independent variable has an impact on the dependent variable. To discover whether a causal relationship exists, conduct a simple linear regression analysis.

Examples of bivariate relationships that can be examined using regression analyses include whether university students' study time explains their GPA, whether students' GPA may be a predictor for illegal drug use, whether father's education can affect children's level of education, or if people's education may predict or explain their income. Linear regression analyses require that both variables are measured at the interval or ratio level and the dependent variable is normally distributed around the prediction line. Nominal level variables that have two values (i.e., dichotomous variable) may also be used as independent variables in regression analysis. For example, if male is coded as 0 and female is coded as 1, the variable of gender can be used as the independent variable in a regression analysis. Similarly, if Caucasians are coded as 0 and all other races are coded as 1, race can also be used as the independent variable in a regression analysis.

Using our Student data, we will demonstrate how to run a regression analysis. In this analysis, we are interested in finding out whether the hours university students spend studying predict their academic performance as measured by grade point average (GPA). The steps for doing such a data analysis follow.

1 After starting the SPSS program and retrieving the Student data, we move the cursor over *Analyze => Regression => Linear*. Then, we click **Linear** and the **Linear Regression** dialogue window opens.
2 We highlight the dependent variable (GPA) from the variable list in the left-hand box and move it to the upper **Dependent** variable box in the middle. Then we select our independent variable (study hours per week) from the variable list on the left-hand box by highlighting it and moving it to the **Independent** variable box below the dependent variable box.
3 Finally, we click *OK* to run the analysis. Figure 9.9 shows you the result of the regression analysis.

The output files include four tables. The first table indicates the independent and dependent variable included in the analysis and the method used to include the independent variable. The R Square, .016 in the **Model Summary** table, is the proportion of the variance of your dependent variable, *GPA* that can be predicted by the variation of your independent variable, *study hours*. In this analysis, only 1.6% of the variation in GPA can be predicted by differences in study hours. The more hours a university student spends on studying, the higher GPA she will earn. The significance level, .015, of the F-value shown in the right cell of the **ANOVA** (analysis of variance) table indicates that there is a linear relationship between the two variables, although the relationship seems weak. If the significance level is larger than .05, then you cannot say that there is a linear relationship between the two variables.

You probably have learned in your statistics class that the regression equation is $y = a + bx$. When y is your dependent variable, x is your independent variable. a is the value of y when x is 0, and b tells how much y increases or decreases for a one-unit change in x.

According to the output file of this SPSS regression analysis, the constant value of 2.824 under the column with a "B" in the **Coefficients** table is the value of a

Variables Entered/Removed[a]

Model	Variables Entered	Variables Removed	Method
1	study hours[b]	.	Enter

[a] Dependent Variable: GPA
[b] All requested variables entered.

Model Summary

Model	R	R Square	Adjusted R Square	Std. Error of the Estimate
1	.126[a]	.016	.013	1.53732

[a] Predictors: (Constant), study hours

ANOVA[a]

Model		Sum of Squares	Df	Mean Square	F	Sig.
1	Regression	14.215	1	1 14.215	6.015	.015[b]
	Residual	874.444	370	2.363		
	Total	888.659	371			

[a] Dependent Variable: GPA
[b] Predictors: (Constant), study hours

Coefficients[a]

Model		Unstandardized Coefficients		Standardized Coefficients	t	Sig.
		B	Std. Error	Beta		
1	(Constant)	2.824	.129		21.844	.000
	study hours	.035	.014	.126	2.453	.015

[a] Dependent Variable: GPA

Figure 9.9   Regression Analysis Output File. *Source:* data input into IBM SPSS Statistics Software (SPSS), version 22. Reproduced with permission of International Business Machines Corporation.

(labeled as Constant). The second value *.035*, or the independent variable, *study hours*, is the value of *b* (labeled with the name of the independent variable). There-fore, the prediction equation for the analysis is: *GPA (y) =2.824 + .035(study hours)*. What this means is that for each hour a student spends studying, her GPA increases *.035*. For a student who spends five hours on study per week, her GPA is likely to be *2.284 + .035(5)=2.459*.

How do you report these findings? When you report your data analysis, explain that you conducted a linear regression analysis to predict university student GPAs based on the hours they spend on study each week. A significant regression equa-tion was found (F=6.015, p=.015) with an R^2 of .016. Students' predicted GPA equals 2.824 + .035 × study hours. For each hour students spend studying per week, their GPA increases by 0.035 points.

If you run the regression analysis but find the F-value is not significant, then, you may indicate the regression equation is not significant and university student study hours cannot be used to predict their GPAs.

To Predict or Explain the Effects of Several Independent Variables on a Dependent Variable, Use Multiple Regression Analysis

When you have not one but multiple independent variables potentially influencing one dependent variable, use Multiple Regression procedures. For instance, you may have a hypothesis that more study hours positively affects grades but frequent drug use negatively affects students' grades. If you want to know how these two factors affect GPAs, run a multiple linear regression analysis. Similarly, if you want to find out whether employees' salary, benefit, and working environment may predict or explain their productivity, you may run a multiple regression analysis. If you want to test if new immigrants' language ability, number of relatives, number of friends in the society and education may predict or explain their levels of integration into the society, you may run a multiple regression analysis.

For multiple linear regression analysis, the dependent variable should be an interval or ratio level variable that is normally distributed. The independent variables should all be interval or ratio level variables. But you can also use dichotomous variables, which are often called dummy variables, as your independent variables. Dummy variables are often nominal categories that are given numerical codes, usually 0 and 1 (for example, when gender is coded 0 for males and 1 for females).

We use our Student dataset to run the multiple regression analysis to demonstrate how you can do the analysis.

1   After starting the SPSS program and retrieving the Student data, we move the cursor over *Analyze => Regression => Linear,* and then click **Linear** to open the **Linear Regression** dialogue window.
2   Then, we select the dependent variable (*GPA*) and move it to the middle upper box under **Dependent** by clicking on the top arrow between the variables box and the **Dependent** box.
3   Next, we move the two independent variables (*study hours* and *drug use*) to the second box in the middle under **Independent(s)** by clicking the second arrow between the **Independent(s)** box and the variables box on the left.
4   After we select variables, we click *Statistics* on the right to open the **Linear Regression Statistics** window and check **Estimates** and **Model fit**. Then, we click *Continue* at the bottom to return to the **Linear Regression** dialogue window and click on *OK* at the bottom to run the analysis.

In a few seconds, the results of this analysis appear. Figure 9.10 is the result of the multiple regression analysis.

The output file includes four tables; the first table shows you what independent variables are entered in the analysis. The second table shows you the model summary. The third table shows you the results of the analysis of variance, and the fourth table provides you with the coefficients of the regression analysis.

As in the output file of the regression analysis discussed earlier, you need to know that the R Square, .045, in the **Model Summary** is the proportion of the

Variables Entered/Removed[a]

Model	Variables Entered	Variables Removed	Method
1	drug use, study hours[b]	.	Enter

[a] Dependent Variable: GPA
[b] All requested variables entered.

Model Summary

Model	R	R Square	Adjusted R Square	Std. Error of the Estimate
1	.212[a]	.045	.039	.47258

[a] Predictors: (Constant), drug use, study hours

ANOVA[a]

Model		Sum of Squares	Df	Mean Square	F	Sig.
1	Regression	3.650	2	1.825	8.172	.000[b]
	Residual	77.498	347	.223		
	Total	81.148	349			

[a] Dependent Variable: GPA
[b] Predictors: (Constant), drug use, study hours

Coefficients[a]

Model		Unstandardized Coefficients		Standardized Coefficients		
		B	Std. Error	Beta	t	Sig.
1	(Constant)	2.875	.043		67.205	.000
	study hours	.014	.005	.156	2.972	.003
	drug use	−.009	.004	−.136	−2.582	.010

[a] Dependent Variable: GPA

Figure 9.10   Multiple Regression Analysis Output File. *Source:* data input into IBM SPSS Statistics Software (SPSS), version 22. Reproduced with permission of International Business Machines Corporation.

variance of the dependent variable, *GPA* that can be explained or predicted by the variation of the independent variables, including the frequency of student drug use and study hours. In this analysis, only 4.5% of the students' GPA can be explained or predicted by the combined effects of frequency of drug use and study hours. The more hours a university student spends on study the higher will his/her GPA be. But drug use has a negative impact on student GPA. The more frequently a student uses drugs, the lower his/her GPA will be. The significance level, .000 that is shown in the right cell of the **ANOVA** table indicates that there is a linear relationship between the dependent and the two independent variables. If the significance level is larger than .05, then you cannot say that there is a linear relationship between the dependent variable and the two independent variables.

The multiple regression equation is $y = a + b1x1 + b2x2$, where y is your dependent variable, and $x1$ and $x2$ are your independent variables. In the SPSS multiple regression analysis output, the constant value of 2.875 under column "B" in the **Coefficients** table is the value of a. The second value in the same column, or the independent variable, *study hours*, is the value of b1 (.014). The third value in the column, or the second independent variable, *drug use* is the value of b2 (-.009). Therefore, the prediction equation for the multiple regression analysis is: *GPA=2.875 + 0.014(study hour) −0.009(drug use)*, which means for every hour a student spends studying, her GPA is likely to increase by 0.014 points. When a student uses drugs once, her GPA is likely to decrease by 0.009 points. For a student who spends ten hours studying and uses drugs three times, the predicted value of her GPA = 2.875 + 0.014(10) −.009(3) = 2.988.

When reporting your findings, use the adjusted R Square, which is most useful when you have a model with several independent variables. This statistic adjusts the value of R Square to take into account that a regression model always fits the particular data on which it was developed better than it will fit the population. When there is only one independent variable and a reasonably large number of cases, the adjusted R Square will be close to the unadjusted value. When you have several independent variables, it is better to report the adjusted R Square.

For multiple linear regressions, when the F-value (in the ANOVA table) is significant, it usually indicates that one or more of the independent variables are significant predictors of the dependent variable. An F-value is usually significant, if any of the correlations are statistically significant. The t-value for each variable in the Coefficients table, on the other hand, indicates whether the variable will make a significant addition to the prediction of the dependent variable. In this example, you will find that the F-value is significant (F=8.172, p<.001) and the two t-values are significant for both variables (the t-value for *study hours* is 2.972, p=.003 and the t-value for *drug use* is -2.582, p=.010). Therefore, you can assume that both variables, *study hours* and *drug use,* are significant predictors of student GPAs. Between the two independent variables, *study hours* is a slightly better predictor than student *drug use* on students' GPAs.

To Test If Two Means Are Significantly Different, Use the t-test

If you want to compare two groups of people or know if two average values are significantly different, use the t-test, or the test of comparison of means. There are three kinds of t-tests used for data analysis.

First, you may conduct a two independent-samples t-test to find out if the average values of two independent groups are significantly different; independent groups mean groups with no overlapping members. For example, you may compare the average salary of males and females to see if they are significantly different. You may also compare if the average final exam scores of male and female students are significantly different. Or you may compare if average annual production of steel in two nations are significantly different. If you are interested in studying the family income of majority and minority population in a society, you may also conduct a two independent means t-test.

Second, you may conduct a paired-samples t-test compare the average values from two groups of people that are logically related. For example, you can compare fathers' level of education with mothers' level of education. This is also useful when you want to compare two average values that are collected from one group of people but at different points in time. For example, you may conduct a paired-samples t-test to compare the average weight of a group of patients before and after they receive a special treatment.

Third, you may conduct a one-sample t-test to compare the average value of one group of people or value against a set value or a population parameter. For example, you may compare the average study time of university students against their professors' expected study time to see if they are significantly different. Or you may compare the average study time of the students in a department against the average study time of students from an entire university.

Independent-Samples t-test
To illustrate the t-tests above, we, once again, use the Student data to run those t-tests with SPSS. Here, we are comparing whether male students and female students in this dataset come from families with different income levels. First, we conduct a t-test on two independent samples.

1   After starting the SPSS program and retrieving the Student data, we move the cursor over *Analyze => Compare Means => Independent-Samples T Test*, and then click **Independent-Samples T Test.**
2   After the **Independent-Samples T Test** dialogue window opens, we move the test variable (the dependent variable *family income*) from the left variables box into the **Test Variable(s)** box on the right.
3   The Grouping Variable box is where we need to indicate which groups we are comparing. Since we want to compare males and females, we will select

our independent variable, *gender*, as the grouping variable and move it to the **Grouping Variable** box.

4　When we move the independent variable in the **Grouping Variable** box, SPSS provides parentheses with two question marks inside; we click the ***Define Group*** and type in the first group's value, *0*, in the Group 1 box and type in the second group's value, *1*, in the Group 2 box. (In our data, we coded males as 0 and females as 1. Check your original survey questionnaire to ensure that you entered the correct numbers for the groups that you want to compare. If you have more than two groups, select any of the two groups to make comparisons).

5　After entering the group values, we click ***Continue*** to return to the **Independent-Samples T Test** window and click ***OK*** to run the data analysis. Figure 9.11 shows you the result of the t-test.

The output file includes two tables. The **Group Statistics** table provides you with the basic descriptive statistics for the independent variable for each value of the variables, including the number of respondents in each group, means, and standard deviations. From this table you can see that among the respondents, there are 130 male students and their average family income value is 6.9692 and 226 female students and their average family income value is 6.3637. Keep in mind that

Group Statistics

	gender	N	Mean	Std. Deviation	Std. Error Mean
Family income	male	130	6.9692	2.21320	.19411
	female	226	6.3637	2.25775	.15018

Independent Samples Test

		Levene's Test for Equality of Variances		t-test for Equality of Means						
									95% Confidence Interval of the Difference	
		F	Sig.	t	df	Sig. (2-tailed)	Mean Difference	Std. Error Difference	Lower	Upper
Family income	Equal variances assumed	.048	.827	2.454	354	.015	.60551	.24675	.12023	1.09080
	Equal variances not assumed			2.467	273.481	.014	.60551	.24543	.12235	1.08868

Figure 9.11　Independent-Samples t-test Output File. *Source:* data input into IBM SPSS Statistics Software (SPSS), version 22. Reproduced with permission of International Business Machines Corporation.

these numbers represent the number codes we had assigned during the data entry and we need to check what these numbers mean in actual dollars. (Family income was measured on an interval level and the difference between each two values is $10,000. Our original questionnaire indicates that the value of 6 of family income is between $50,001 and $60,000.) After checking our family income variable, we find that the average family income for the male students is close to $60,000 and the average family income for the female students is approximately $53,000.

As shown in Figure 9.11, the **Independent-Samples Test** table provides you with the F-value for the Levene's test for Equality of Variances, the t-value, and the significance levels for the t-test for Equality of Means. Independent-Samples t-test scores are affected by the variance within each group. If the variance in income is far greater or smaller among males compared to among females, the t-statistics will be computed slightly differently from when you have equal variance in both groups.

Therefore, first, you need to examine the F-value for the Levene's test for Equality of Variance and its significant levels. The F-value and its significance level will tell you whether the two groups have similar within-group variances, and let you choose which of the two t-statistics (in the column labeled "t") in this table you should use. If the F-value is not significant (Sig.> .05), you can assume that the variance within the male students' family income and the variance with the female students' family income are equal. Then, you read the t-value in the first row ("Equal variances assumed"). If the F-value is significant (Sig. < .05), it means that equal variance is not assumed. Then, you read the t-value in the second row, "Equal variances not assumed."

If the t-value is significant (Sig. < .05), then you conclude that the two groups are significantly different. If the t-value is not significant (Sig. > .05), the two groups are not significantly different. In our example above, equal variances are assumed (F=.048, Sig. =.827). Thus, we use the first t-value which is 2.454, with the significance level of .015. When the t-value is significant, the two groups' mean scores are considered significantly different. Therefore, in our example, we can conclude that the family incomes of the male and female students are significantly different.

Paired-Samples t-test

So far, we have used the Student data for our data analysis. To illustrate a pared samples t-test, we now use 2012 General Social Survey (GSS) data for the United States because our Student dataset does not have an appropriate pair of variables for this test.

1 After starting the SPSS program and retrieving 2012 GSS data, we move the cursor over *Analyze => Compare Means => Paired-Samples T Test*, and click on **Paired-Samples T Test**.
2 After the **Paired-Samples T Test** dialogue window opens, we select *paeduc* (highest year of school completed by father) and *maeduc* (highest year of school

completed by mother) from the variable box on the left and move them to the **Paired Variables** box on the right.

3   Then, we click *OK* to run the test. Figure 9.12 shows the result of this paired t-test.

The output file for the paired variables t-test includes three tables. The **Paired Sample Statistics** table provides the average values of the paired variables, the number of total respondents, and the standard deviation. According to the table, 1,344 respondents provided information about their fathers' education and 1,344 people gave information on their mothers' education. The average values of fathers' education is 11.74 years and the average value of mothers' education

Paired Samples Statistics

		Mean	N	Std. Deviation	Std. Error Mean
Pair 1	HIGHEST YEAR SCHOOL COMPLETED, FATHER	11.74	1344	4.307	.117
	HIGHEST YEAR SCHOOL COMPLETED, MOTHER	11.80	1344	3.812	.104

Paired Samples Correlations

		N	Correlation	Sig.
Pair 1	HIGHEST YEAR SCHOOL COMPLETED, FATHER and HIGHEST YEAR SCHOOL COMPLETED, MOTHER	1344	.706	.000

Paired Samples Test

		Paired Differences							
					95% Confidence Interval of the Difference				
		Mean	Std. Deviation	Std. Error Mean	Lower	Upper	t	df	Sig. (2-tailed)
Pair 1	HIGHEST YEAR SCHOOL COMPLETED, FATHER – HIGHEST YEAR SCHOOL COMPLETED, MOTHER	−.065	3.144	.086	−.233	.103	−.755	1343	.450

Figure 9.12 Paired Variables t-test Output File. *Source:* data input into IBM SPSS Statistics Software (SPSS), version 22. Reproduced with permission of International Business Machines Corporation.

is 11.80 years. The **Paired Samples Correlations** table indicates that fathers' education and mothers' education are strongly and positively related (R=.706, Sig. < .001). That means when someone's father's education is high, his mother's education is likely to be high. The **Paired Samples Test** table indicates that the mean scores for fathers' education and mothers' education are not significantly different (t=.755, Sig. =.450). This means that people tend to have parents whose education levels are not significantly different.

One-Sample t-test

Using the Student dataset, we conducted a one-sample t-test to determine whether university students spend significantly different amounts of time studying outside of class than we expected. We expect our students to spend about two hours of studying for each hour of classroom time. That means for students who normally take about 12 hours of classes they should spend about 24 hours studying outside of the classes each week. We conducted a one-sample t-test to learn whether students' average hours spent on study each week are significantly different from our expected 24 hours.

Here are the specific steps to run the analysis.

1   After starting the SPSS program and retrieving the Student data, we move the cursor over *Analyze => Compare Means => One Sample T Test*, and then click on **One Sample T Test**.
2   After the **One-Sample T Test** dialogue window opens, we move the test variable (*study hours*) to the **Test Variable(s)** box by double clicking on it and type in the value of 24 to be tested in the **Test Value** box at the bottom.
3   Then, we click **OK** to run the test. Figure 9.13 shows the results of the one-sample t-test.

One-Sample Statistics

	N	Mean	Std. Deviation	Std. Error Mean
study hours	378	7.1667	5.60738	.28841

One-Sample Test

			Test Value = 24			
					95% Confidence Interval of the Difference	
	t	*df*	*Sig. (2-tailed)*	*Mean Difference*	*Lower*	*Upper*
study hours	−58.365	377	.000	−16.83332	−17.4004	−16.2662

Figure 9.13   One-Sample t-test Output File. *Source:* data input into IBM SPSS Statistics Software (SPSS), version 22. Reproduced with permission of International Business Machines Corporation.

The output file includes two tables. The **One-Sample Statistics** table indicates that 378 cases have been included in the test, the average hours that university students spend each week in this dataset is about 7.17 hours, and the standard deviation is 5.6. The **One-Sample Test** table indicates that the average difference between the time students study and our expected study time is 16.8 hours. The t-value is −58.365 and the significance level is smaller than .001. Therefore, the average hours which university students spend studying outside of class each week are significantly different from the study hours we expected. In other words, university students spend much less time on study outside of class than we expected.

To Determine Whether More Than Two Means Are Significantly Different, Use Analysis of Variance (ANOVA)

When you compare two groups of people or test if two means are significantly different, use a t-test. If, however, you want to compare more than two groups of people or want to test if three or more means are significantly different, use analysis of variance (ANOVA). In other words, when the independent variable has two categories, use a t-test. When you have an independent variable that has more than two categories, use a one-way analysis of variance. For example, you may want to compare if five ethnic groups of students have significantly different test scores, or if people in five countries have the same life expectancy. You may also compare the average salary of the employees from four different occupations to find out if they are significantly different.

Analysis of variance is used to compare sample means to determine if there is sufficient evidence to assume that the means of the corresponding population distributions are significantly different. An F-value ratio is the ratio of two estimates of the population variances: the between-groups and the within-groups variances. A one-way analysis of variance is used when you have one dependent variable measured continuously (i.e., interval and ratio level variables) and one independent variable measured categorically (i.e., nominal level variables). For example, to compare whether freshmen, sophomores, juniors and seniors in a university are equally likely to go to parties, use a one-way analysis of variance.

To do the test, you must assume that each of the groups must be a random sample from a normally distributed population, and in the population, the variances in all groups must be equal. Therefore, before proceeding with your statistical analysis, you look at the means and standard deviations for each of the groups and find out how different the observed means are and how much the observations in the groups vary. The normality of the data distribution should be checked before data analysis. One way to check the differences is to run a frequency of the variable and have a histogram for each group.

In a one-way analysis of variance, the variances within each group and between groups are compared with each other. The analysis will generate a significance value indicating whether there are significant differences within the comparisons being made. For example, if you conduct a one-way analysis of variance to see if university students attending parties is significantly different among freshmen, sophomore, juniors, and seniors, run a one-way analysis of variance. Your one-way analysis of variance makes the following comparisons:

1   Compares freshmen with sophomore
2   Compares freshmen with juniors
3   Compares freshmen with seniors
4   Compares sophomore with juniors
5   Compares sophomore with seniors
6   Compares juniors with seniors

Here are the specific steps to conduct the one-way analysis of variance.

1   After starting the SPSS program and retrieving the Student data, we move the cursor over *Analyze => Compare Means => One-Way ANOVA*, and then we click **One-Way ANOVA**.
2   After the **One-Way ANOVA** dialogue window opens, we move the dependent variable (*parties*) from the left variables box into the **Dependent List** box and the independent variable (*university status*) to the **Factor** box.
3   Then, we click **Options** to open the **One-Way ANOVA Options** window and check **Descriptive** to get the means for the dependent variable at each level of the independent variable. We then click *Continue* to return to the **One-Way ANOVA** dialogue window.
4   Since the analysis of variance F test does not pinpoint which pairs of means are significantly different from each other, we need to conduct a **Post Hoc** test to make comparisons between each pair of the groups being tested. Therefore, we click **Post Hoc** to open the **One-Way ANOVA Post Hoc Multiple Comparisons** window and check **Scheffe** to get comparisons between pairs of means. Then, we click *Continue* to return to the **One-Way ANOVA** dialogue window and click *OK* to run the analysis. Figure 9.14 is the result of the analysis.

The output file includes three tables. The **Descriptives** table lists each group of students' monthly average frequency of party attendance. Among the 348 undergraduate students who participated in the survey, freshmen go to parties most frequently (4.7 times a month) and sophomores go to parties least frequently (2.4 times a month). Juniors go to parties 4.1 times, and seniors attend parties 3.6 times a month.

The **ANOVA** table indicates that at least two of the four student groups' mean number of their party attendance is significantly different (F=3.494, Sig.=.016). When the F test is statistically significant, it does not indicate that the mean number

Descriptives

Parties

	N	Mean	Std. Deviation	Std. Error	95% Confidence Interval for Mean		Minimum	Maximum
					Lower Bound	Upper Bound		
freshmen	80	4.7000	5.05263	.56490	3.5756	5.8244	.00	15.00
sophomore	58	2.3966	2.94803	.38709	1.6214	3.1717	.00	10.00
junior	112	4.1161	4.26487	.40299	3.3175	4.9146	.00	20.00
senior	98	3.5612	4.41837	.44632	2.6754	4.4471	.00	20.00
Total	348	3.8075	4.36801	.23415	3.3469	4.2680	.00	20.00

ANOVA

Parties

	Sum of Squares	Df	Mean Square	F	Sig.
Between Groups	195.798	3	65.266	3.494	.016
Within Groups	6424.803	344	18.677		
Total	6620.601	347			

Multiple Comparisons

Dependent Variable: parties

Scheffe

(I) university status	(J) university status	Mean Difference (I-J)	Std. Error	Sig.	95% Confidence Interval	
					Lower Bound	Upper Bound
freshmen	sophomore	2.30345*	.74530	.024	.2096	4.3973
	junior	.58393	.63263	.837	−1.1934	2.3612
	senior	1.13878	.65118	.384	−.6906	2.9682
sophomore	freshmen	−2.30345*	.74530	.024	−4.3973	−.2096
	junior	−1.71952	.69912	.111	−3.6836	.2446
	senior	−1.16467	.71596	.451	−3.1761	.8467
junior	freshmen	−.58393	.63263	.837	−2.3612	1.1934
	sophomore	1.71952	.69912	.111	−.2446	3.6836
	senior	.55485	.59778	.835	−1.1245	2.2342
senior	freshmen	−1.13878	.65118	.384	−2.9682	.6906
	sophomore	1.16467	.71596	.451	−.8467	3.1761
	junior	−.55485	.59778	.835	−2.2342	1.1245

* The mean difference is significant at the 0.05 level.

Figure 9.14 One-Way Analysis of Variance Output File. *Source:* data input into IBM SPSS Statistics Software (SPSS), version 22. Reproduced with permission of International Business Machines Corporation.

of party attendance of the four groups are all significantly different; instead, it only indicates that at least two of the four groups are significantly different in their party attendance.

The **Multiple Comparison** table produced by **Post Hoc Tests** indicates that only two groups, freshmen and sophomores, with a mean difference of 2.30345, are significantly different in the frequency of going to parties (Sig.=.024). The differences between all other groups are not significant. Specifically, the mean difference between freshmen and juniors is 0.58393 (Sig. =0.837), the mean difference between freshmen and seniors is 1.13878 (Sig. =.384), the mean difference between the sophomores and juniors is −1.71952 (Sig. =.111), the mean difference between the sophomores and seniors is −1.16467 (Sig. =.451), and the mean difference between juniors and seniors is .55485 (Sig. =0.835). In reading this **Multiple Comparisons** table, you will find there are repeated reports. What you need to do is to find the comparisons you intended to make and find the related information for your report.

There are still many more procedures in data analysis that you can use with SPSS software. This chapter has provided shorthand reviews of the most frequently used procedures in undergraduate and postgraduate level student research. It assumes that you already have learned a wider range of data analysis procedures in your previous coursework. If you are interested in using procedures that are not covered in this chapter, consult other books, including those in this chapter's reference list, that provide more systematic introductions.

References

Cronk, Brian. 2014. *How to Use SPSS: A Step-by-Step Guide to Analysis and Interpretation*. 8th ed. Glendale, CA: Pyrczak Publishing.

George, Darren and Paul Mallery. 2013. *IBM SPSS Statistics 21 Step by Step: A Simple Guide and Reference*. 13th ed. Boston, MA: Allyn and Bacon.

Norusis, Marija J. 2010. *PASW Statistics 18 Guide to Data Analysis*. Upper Saddle River, NJ: Prentice Hall.

Norusis, Marija J. 2012. *IBM SPSS Statistics 19 Guide to Data Analysis*. Upper Saddle River, NJ: Prentice Hall.

Further Reading

Abbott, Martin Lee. 2011. *Understanding Educational Statistics Using Microsoft Excel and SPSS*. Hoboken, NJ: John Wiley & Sons, Inc.

Field, Andy. 2013. *Discovering Statistics Using IBM SPSS Statistics*. 4th ed. London: Sage.

Quirk, Thomas J. 2012. *Excel 2010 for Social Science Statistics: A Guide to Solving Practical Problems*. New York: Springer.

Pallant, Julie. 2013. *SPSS Survival Manual*. 5th ed. Victoria, Australia: Allen and Unwin.

Petscher, Yaacov, Christopher Schatschneider, and Donald L. Compton, eds. 2013. *Applied Quantitative Analysis in Education and the Social Sciences*. New York and London: Routledge.

Internet Resources

ICPSR (Inter-university Consortium for Political and Social Research) at the University of Michigan provides links for useful resources for students. The ICPSR YouTube Channel offers Webinars and tutorials on data analysis. http://www.icpsr.umich.edu/icpsrweb/ICPSR/support/students

The Nature Conservancy's (nature.org) Conservation Gateway website offers Webinars on quantitative analyses for social sciences. https://www.conservationgateway.org/ConservationPractices/PeopleConservation/SocialScience/QuantitativeDataAnalysisI/Pages/quantitative-data-analysi.aspx

Yale University library provides links to various international data sources (by country and region) for social sciences. http://guides.library.yale.edu/content.php?pid=14700&sid=1145844

Exercises for Chapter 9

Choosing the right statistical procedure for quantitative data analysis is always a challenge for student researchers. We designed Exercise 9.1 to help you identify the right statistical procedure for your computer data analysis. Exercise 9.2 is a template to create a summary of the results you obtained in the statistical analysis.

Exercise 9.1 Determining the Right Procedures

Use this exercise to determine which statistical analysis procedure you need to choose. Circle your answers for question 1 and 2 for each of your research questions or hypotheses; the last row of the table will tell you which statistical procedure may be appropriate for this hypothesis.

Hypothesis/Research Question	(Write down your hypothesis)
1. What do you intend to find out? (Circle your answer)	1-a. Statistical association between two variables
	1-b. Impact of an independent variable on a dependent variable
	1-c. Impact of multiple independent variables on a dependent variable
	1-d. Comparing means of different groups

(continued)

Hypothesis / Research Question	(Write down your hypothesis)
2. What level measures are the variables in this hypothesis? (Circle your answer)	2-a. Both are nominal or ordinal level variables 2-b. Both are interval-ratio level variables 2-c. The independent variable is a nominal or ordinal level and the dependent variable is interval-ratio level
If your answers to the above questions are...	**(1-a and 2-a)** => Perform **Cross tabulation and Chi-square test** **(1-a and 2-b)** => Perform **Correlation** analysis **(1-b and 2-b)** => Perform **Regression** analysis **(1-c and 2-b)** => Perform **Multiple Regression** analysis **(1-d and 2-c)** => • Perform **t-test**, if the independent variable has only *two groups.* • Perform One-way **ANOVA**, if the independent variable has *more than two groups.*

Exercise 9.2 Summary Notes for Statistical Results

Having a summary sheet can be handy when you begin to write your statistical findings into a report. Below is a table format sample for the summary overview of all statistical findings from your data analyses. In each row, record your hypothesis, statistical technique performed for the hypothesis, test statistics, and your interpretation of the statistics.

Hypotheses or Research Questions	Statistical Procedure Used	Test Statistics and Significance Levels (For example, $\chi2 = 12.207$, Sig.= 0.0432)	Interpretations and Conclusions
1			
2			
3			
4			
5			

Student Research and Report Writing

Your Project Outcome after Chapter 9

At this point:

- You have your quantitative data stored in a computer file.
- You have performed all statistical analyses necessary to answer your research questions, or to test your hypotheses. You have saved the output files from the statistical analyses.
- You have interpreted the statistical results and made notes on the findings.
- You have discussed the findings with your project supervisor. You have examined whether there are anomalies or questions emerged in the findings, and determined whether additional analyses are needed.

Chapter 10

Qualitative Data Analysis

If you have conducted a qualitative research, you should have a set of non-numeric data such as texts, images, observational notes, and voice-recording. Summarizing and analyzing them can be challenging because there is no one standard procedure that fits all types of data. When you are ready to analyze and interpret your qualitative data you might ask:

- What is the purpose of qualitative data analysis?
- Do I need to transcribe all my interviews?
- Where do I start?
- How do I conduct an inductive analysis?
- What is the process of analysis when I use deductive coding?
- What tools do I use to organize and summarize the codes?
- How do I write about my findings from qualitative data?

What Is the Purpose of Qualitative Data Analysis?

Qualitative data analysis shares some similarities with quantitative data analysis (Neuman 2011). Both methods systematically summarize and compare data to obtain theoretical ideas from empirical data. There are key differences, however, in the purpose and procedure of qualitative data analysis that distinguishes it from quantitative data analysis. Unlike quantitative data analysis which follows standardized procedures and techniques, qualitative analysis uses a variety of creative techniques that require open and flexible approaches. While the purpose of quantitative data analysis is to test already established theories, qualitative data analysis is most often used to "conceptualize and build a new theory" (Neuman 2011: 509). For this reason, qualitative data analysis is most often inductive or "bottom-up,"

Student Research and Report Writing: From Topic Selection to the Complete Paper, First Edition. Gabe T. Wang and Keumjae Park. © and Published 2016 by John Wiley & Sons, Ltd.

starting from concrete data to extract more generalizable theoretical ideas embedded in the data.

There is truly a wide range of techniques for qualitative data analysis. Although we cannot cover all of them here, we will describe some of the more popular techniques in this chapter. But no matter which technique you use, there are principles common to various qualitative data analysis strategies which you can keep in mind before reviewing the different analytic techniques.

Interpreting
The foundation of analyzing non-numeric data is finding *meanings* implied in the data. Regardless of the type of qualitative data you work with, your analysis is based on the principle of interpretation. Suppose your interviewee stated:

> I had a lot of difficulty juggling work and the family; finding someone on a short notice when my regular childcare arrangement falls through was a nightmare.

You will need to figure out the meaning of this statement (i.e., interpret it). Does it mean that this person wants to spend more time with the child but cannot because of work? Why is it so difficult to balance work and childcare? Is it due to particular circumstances, or is it an experience common to most workers? Is childcare the only challenge this person feels as a working parent? What is her "regular childcare arrangement" and why it would not work sometimes? By considering these questions, you are beginning to interpret the meaning of the data. Obviously, thinking about contexts is an important part of interpreting your data.

Coding or Identifying Themes
Analyzing qualitative data frequently requires reducing long texts, video footage, and complex images into shorter and simpler labels that capture the idea. We call these "codes." Codes represent units of meaning. For example, you may use the code "work-family balance" for the above quotation. In other parts of the interviews, you may find other codes and themes such as "career disadvantages," or "unable to do everything," "feeling torn," and so on. Coding is a process to identify small and large units of meaning, which is to be done throughout the analysis process.

Establishing Relationships between Codes / Themes
Codes or units of meaning by themselves do not really tell a whole story. To truly interpret the meaning of the data you gathered, you will engage in layers of analysis about how each code or theme is related to another. What codes / themes seem to cause the others? What comes first and what comes later? What codes / themes are conflicting? Which are supplementing one another? What are the broader historical, cultural, and social contexts of the relationships? You should keep writing notes and memos on these questions and integrate them into your analysis. In a sense, theorizing and analyzing progress simultaneously during a qualitative data analysis.

Back-and-Forth Processes

As you can imagine, qualitative data analysis is, in no way, a straightforward process; in the process of coding, you will go back and forth to your data and may re-code and re-classify codes numerous times. It is quite probable that in the process of coding you will have new questions that had not been a part of your original research questions. You may have changed your initial assumptions. Often, the first stage of coding makes you feel that your data have become even more complicated. Do not worry, for almost everyone runs into this situation. While staying focused is important, it does not mean that you ignore when you find something unexpected or something new in the process of analysis. Remember that being able to immerse yourself deeply into the data and find emerging stories in them are the benefits of qualitative research.

Constructing a Theoretical Story with Your Data

In the end, the goal of qualitative analysis is to tell the story of your data. Regardless of which analytic route you decide to take, you will report the prevailing patterns, claims, and ideas about your topic. It is through the process of constructing concepts and telling the story of your data that you will find answers to your initial research questions. Let's consider some more questions you might have when you analyze qualitative data.

Do You Need to Transcribe All Your Interviews?

Since interviews and focus groups are common data collection methods many students use, we most often encounter questions such as "Do I need to tape-record my interviews?" or "Do I need to transcribe everything?" The clear answer to these questions is "yes." The reasons are: 1) no matter how fast you write, it is simply impossible to take field notes in complete detail during interviews and in focus group discussions; 2) your field notes already reflect your immediate interpretation of the situation and are not objective records of exactly what is said. In short, tape-recording and transcribing is critical to having a record of the full range of data collected during your field research.

There are a variety of recording devices today. You may use your smartphone apps, tablet devices, or a digital recorder. In case one device malfunctions, it is not a bad idea to have a back-up device when you record. We would like to remind you one more time that tape-recording requires informed consent by the participant prior to the interview. At the time of recording, you should have informed the participants that the conversation will be recorded and transcribed for the analysis. Interview recordings obtained through this proper procedure should be transcribed before you begin coding. If you were unable to obtain the informed consent, the recording cannot be used.

There are times when an interviewee does not want the interview to be recorded. If this is the case, you will have to rely on taking notes during the interview. You may have to pause from time to time to write notes. You should tell the participant up front that you may go slow and may pause from time to time to write notes. Use shorthand notes during the interview, and immediately after the interview, find a quiet place to extend your notes while your memory is still fresh. As we discussed in Chapter 8, you may have to do this frequently if you are conducting ethnographic research.

Transcribing is straightforward. You will simply play the recorded interviews and type them onto a word processing program. Transcribing is a time-consuming work, taking longer than the interviews themselves. You will probably have to allocate about three to five hours to transcribe a one-hour interview, for instance. Your university libraries may have transcribing machines which you can borrow. This will help you with the tedious task of listening to the recorded interviews, stopping, and typing. The machine allows you to use a convenient pedal to stop the recording and restart as you transcribe.

Once fully transcribed, the voice data become text which you can analyze. You may also have taken field notes about the settings, and any non-verbal cues such as gestures, smiles, laughs, and facial expressions during the interviews and any group dynamics you observed during focus group discussions. These written notes should also be included in the transcribed data. If you conducted interviews in languages other than the language in which you will write your analysis, you may need to translate the transcribed interviews. For instance, if you conducted interviews with immigrants in their native languages but wish to write the report in English, you will need translated interview transcripts.

Where Do You Start?

Students who have spent several weeks or sometimes months transcribing their interviews come to us and say, "Here are my data, but I don't know what to do with these!" Unlike the answer choices in surveys which can be easily converted into numbers, qualitative data, such as images and transcribed conversations, do not readily lend themselves to a systematic analysis. You need to develop systematic yet flexible ways to summarize them. How do you do this? First, think about a few things in order to find the starting point for your analysis.

- Different types of qualitative data
- Deductive and inductive coding
- Manual coding and computerized coding
- Units of analysis in qualitative coding

Different Types of Qualitative Data
Qualitative data include but are not limited to transcribed interviews, printed texts (e.g., archival records, diaries, letters, emails, speech scripts, and newspaper stories), images (e.g., photographs, magazine ads, children's drawings), video-recordings (e.g., TV show segments, documentary video footage, music videos), or your own field notes made from observations. You may consider them as two broad categories: texts and images.

In-depth interviewing is perhaps the most widely used qualitative method. Transcribed interviews are treated as text data, similar to archival data or other document-type data. When your data are texts, you are likely to follow multiple stages of analysis to find first small units of meaning and then gradually merge and group them into a few broader themes. This is the case with the grounded theory (Glaser and Strauss 1967), a popular technique in sociology, anthropology, and related disciplines for analyzing and theorizing text data. We will explain this technique in greater detail below.

When you are working with images, you may treat them as symbols or signs for certain meanings; examining closely each piece of image data, you first assign a code or codes based on your interpretation of the image and, in a later stage, merge and group similar codes to construct broader themes and categories of the meaning embedded in the images. But for visual data, we frequently find studies using pre-constructed coding schemes; in this case, codes are predetermined and the researcher identify and count the images in the data, which correspond to the coding scheme. This is a common strategy in content analysis. For example, if your research investigates racial stereotypes in magazine advertisements, you may first construct, based on previous literature, categories of stereotypes on which you want to focus (e.g., Black athletes, White nuclear families, Asian women in service roles, and so on). Then, you can systematically examine the advertisements in your data to identify the images which contain the different stereotypes in your coding scheme. Content analyses report the counts and percentages of each of the thematic codes and interpret what those statistics tell us about the research topic at hand.

Coding: Deductive or Inductive Approach

In quantitative analysis, the primary goal is to reduce data into numbers that can be manipulated and computed mathematically. The goal of qualitative coding is very different. The primary goal of qualitative coding is "to focus on the potential meanings of your data" (Esterberg 2002: 158). Qualitative coding will eventually allow you to systematically summarize scattered and seemingly episodic stories and images into patterns of themes and emerging theoretical stories. Keep in mind, however, that the primary focus of coding is not reducing the complexity of the data, but identifying and interpreting meaningful patterns in the data.

The vast majority of qualitative researchers identify themes in the data through what we call "inductive coding procedures" – that is, to first approach the data without pre-conceived ideas, pay attention to *emerging* themes, and gradually classify them into a handful of recurring concepts to generate a theoretical story by linking these themes. This bottom-up approach is most common in published qualitative studies.

Qualitative data coding can be done in a top-down fashion as well. When conducting content analyses, for instance, researchers often construct coding schemes first, and then sort the data according to the coding scheme. For example, a researcher who is interested in studying whether editors assign male and female reporters to different types of news stories may start with a pre-constructed typology of news stories, such as "crime," "entertainment," "children," "leisure and lifestyle," and "politics," and assign these codes to each news story in the collected data. In this case, the codes are initially derived deductively from existing theories, and the corresponding contents are extracted from the raw data. This process is sometimes called directed content analysis (Berg and Lune 2011). Even in a directed analysis, however, you should be open to the possibility of new codes and themes emerging from the data itself; we advise that you include these emerging themes in your analysis as new codes. Table 10.1 illustrates how inductive and deductive coding processes may differ from each other.

Understanding these two types of analytic approaches and considering which may best fit your research will be a useful first step when you do not know where to begin. You should make a decision on which approach is suitable for your research questions. There is no set rule for choosing either approach. By and large, we would recommend that if your study is based on a clearly established theoretical framework and has a relatively specific set of research questions, a deductive approach may be effective. If your study is an exploratory study on a relatively new topic or your research questions tend to be broad and open-ended, an inductive approach will allow you to extract a wider range of theoretical ideas from your data. Since coding is unique to each research project, consult your project supervisor and faculty mentor about your ideas on coding for your project. Remember that qualitative data analysis is a flexible process. Even if you choose to take a deductive approach, you should keep your eyes open for unexpected patterns and themes in your data and find ways to integrate them into your analysis as they surface. Likewise, during an inductive coding, you will frequently go back to the previous stage and re-code the data based on some new themes you develop while summarizing.

Manual Coding and Computerized Coding
While many researchers still rely on manual coding, there are a growing number of researchers and students who have begun to explore the option of using

Table 10.1 Which Approach Is Suitable for Your Analysis?

	Deductive Coding (Top-down Approach)	Inductive Coding (Bottom-up Approach)
Definition	Pre-constructed coding scheme to apply to data	Gradual formation and emergence of coding scheme from the examination of data
Procedures	Codes (based on theories) => Identifying parts of data corresponding to codes => Summary of coded themes/ concepts in the data	Data => Codes/Themes => Broader Categories of Themes => Summary of themes => Development of a theory
Popular Technique	Content Analysis	Grounded Theory

computer software for coding. There are a number of computer software pro-grams for qualitative coding. Some have been around for a number of years (e.g., NUD*IST and NVivo, ATLAS.ti). But there are many others, including newer web-based programs. Each computer application works differently, and your data should be prepared according to the program's specifications. Thus, it requires some knowledge and familiarity before you decide to use a computer application.

Demonstrating how to use computerized coding software is beyond the scope of this book; however, we want to discuss briefly some pros and cons about using computerized coding to illustrate different ways of qualitative data analysis. Because coding your data is mechanized, using computer procedures allows you to conduct more standardized and uniform coding. In addition, since you will have a stored record of the coding process, any modification done on the coding process can easily be traced. If you have to repeat the coding process for any reason, it will take much less time than recoding the data manually. Many applications also allow you to organize your data, your notes, and even related external sources together. It can be advantageous for data storage, retrieval, and even making connections between different types of data and contextual materials for your analyses. These are important advantages in qualitative analysis. If you have multiple research-ers involved in coding, you can improve the inter-coder reliability or consistency across different coders, by using a uniform computerized coding system.

But there are also good reasons why so many researchers still choose to code their qualitative data manually. Qualitative analysis is a process of interpretation, and multiple interpretations of the same text can easily emerge in different con-texts. For instance, if someone said "I was thirsty," this could mean a number of things. This person may have really needed hydration, or have been extremely nervous, or have been "thirsty" metaphorically for more information, or sim-ply have said this as an excuse to get out of a situation. While today's software may be able to capture a few different meanings, it can only capture the set of meanings you had programmed into the computer application. In other words, the way computerized coding works is still essentially by way of sophisticated "matching," rather than "interpreting" the way human minds do. While some programs are available free-of charge, others can also be expensive. For most student researchers, especially for undergraduate students with little experience doing independent research, we highly recommend trying manual coding first, as it offers good learning experiences. The "arts" of qualitative coding can be best learned by practicing.

If you and your supervisor agree to use a computer program, consider differ-ent options depending on the types and amount of data as well as your research objectives. Weighing the advantages and disadvantages of manual and computer-ized coding, however, may actually help you clarify your research goals. Visit some websites about coding software such as the ones listed in Box 10.1 for more infor-mation. You should find out whether your university has licenses for any software you might want to use, as purchasing an individual license on your own could be quite expensive.

Box 10.1   Web Resources for Qualitative Software Programs.

ATLAS.ti Qualitative Data Analysis
http://atlasti.com/video-tutorials/

CAQDAS Network Project
(General online resources for qualitative analysis software programs)
http://www.surrey.ac.uk/sociology/research/researchcentres/caqdas/index.htm

Qualitative Data Analysis Program (QDAP) at the University of Massachusetts Amherst
http://www.umass.edu/qdap/

QSR International (Producer of NVivo)
http://www.qsrinternational.com/solutions_education.aspx

Unit of Analysis in Qualitative Coding

Before you actually start the coding process, determine the unit of analysis you will focus on. This is a very important and helpful thing to consider. We are borrowing this term from the standard quantitative research methods. The term "unit of analysis" in quantitative research refers to the unit from which information is collected, or the unit that is the analytic focus of your research (Schutt 2011: 191–194). In quantitative research, a unit of analysis may be individuals, groups, cities, or states. In qualitative research, units of analysis are diverse. We can apply this concept to qualitative analysis and consider the basic unit of data we need to focus on. In analyzing text data, the units of analysis can be phrases, sentences, paragraphs, entries of blogs, or whole stories. Likewise, when you work with visual data, your unit of analysis may be scenes, magazine pages, whole images, segments of images, or entire episodes of TV shows.

Appropriate units of analysis will depend on the purpose of your research and how detailed you wish your analysis to be. Words or terms are usually the smallest of the units in text analysis. You may analyze the frequency of particular words related to the research focus. For example, if you wish to study gender biases by comparing the use of gendered pronouns in science textbooks and social science textbooks, you may use the word "he," "she" or "he or she" as units of coding and highlight these pronouns in the two groups of textbook. In reporting the results, you may provide counts and percentages of gendered and gender-neutral pronouns in the two groups.

It is also possible to work with more than one unit of analysis at different stages of coding. For example, when Park (2014) conducted a content analysis of Korean press media on immigrants, she used paragraphs within a news story to extract themes in her first stage of coding. At a later stage, she took an entire news story and coded it based on the prevailing themes of the story, so as to develop a typology of media discourses on immigrants.

In fact, with inductive coding strategies such as grounded theory, you are likely to pay attention to all units of analysis in the text, such as words/terms, phrases, sentences, and paragraphs. That is, as you read through the texts carefully, you will identify strings of words that carry a theme, regardless of their length. You may highlight a word, a phrase, or a paragraph of any length and label it with a code during the first-stage coding process.

If you focus only on larger units, such as paragraphs or an entire story/episode, be mindful of the information you may lose. Paragraphs can contain complex thoughts; even though each paragraph is supposed to have a "thesis," or a predominant theme, you may still be suppressing other themes in the paragraph by labeling it with one code. If your data are formal documents with clearly organized paragraphs (such as laws), you may consider using paragraphs as the unit of analysis. With in-depth interview data, we recommend zooming into smaller units such as words and phrases, since interviews, like conversations, do not follow the organized structure of paragraphs.

Sometimes, a part of a document can be coded as one theme. In an analysis of newspaper article perspectives on immigrants in the U.S., Keogan (2002) coded the central theme of each article in the sample by reviewing their abstracts. In this case, abstracts were the units of analysis. Or you may code an entire piece of a document. If you are analyzing life stories of successful business executives to investigate the role of mentors, you may treat one person's whole narratives as a unit, and code the type of relationships this person has with his or her mentors. Using the entire piece of data as a unit is a strategy often found in analyzing images. For example, a page of advertisement can be coded into a theme based on the gender presentation of the scene as a whole. Which of these units will be your unit of analysis in the first stage of coding depends on your research questions, the purpose of your analysis, and the types of data you have.

Once you have some ideas about which coding approach to take, discuss them with your project supervisor or faculty mentor. Another important task before you begin the coding procedure is to give identification numbers to your cases and organize them into groups. Label your data and put them into folders. Your data can be classified by the date collected, by the type of data, or by the demographic characteristics of the interviewees.

What Is the Process of Inductive Analysis? Steps of Grounded Theory

When you first look at your data, you may be overwhelmed by the sheer amount of text or images you have collected. Data seem chaotic, dispersed, and without order. Take a deep breath. In fact, it is precisely your job to create a sense of order with your data, by discovering patterns and developing thematic summaries. How do you achieve this? You *do it step-by-step*.

You must understand that coding qualitative data is a multi-level process, especially if you choose an inductive analysis approach. Since inductive coding is most often used in student research, we will focus on the steps of grounded theory (Glaser and Strauss 1967) as a popular example of inductive coding strategy. This strategy can be similarly adopted in interpretive analysis, and discourse analysis (for more details on interpretive analysis and discourse analysis, see Bernard 2002).

Grounded theory methods develop a theory grounded in the data by way of a multi-level coding and summary procedure. In this method, you first read your text data several times to become familiar with the overall themes of the narratives. Then, as you start the coding process, you carefully read the texts line by line while identifying any embedded theme in any part of the text ("open coding"). The units of analysis here can be a word, a phrase, a few sentences, or paragraphs; any small unit that carries a theme should be identified and labeled with a code at this stage (see Box 10.2).

Box 10.2   Open Coding: An Example.

Below is an excerpt of an interview Park conducted in 2003 for a research on immigrant women's adaptation to the United States. We used the "Add comments" function in the computer word processor program to show an open coding process.

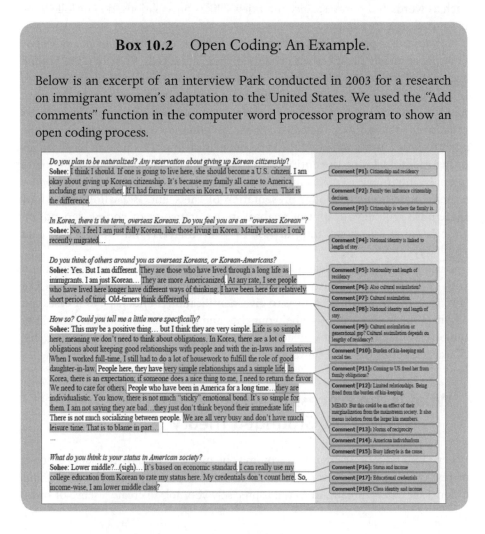

In the second stage of coding, you will read through your data again, while re-examining the themes identified in the open-coding stage, and merge and group similar themes into broader *categories of themes*. If necessary, you will merge and group similar categories into even broader *classes of themes* in a subsequent step ("selective coding"). It may take more than one or two steps to come up with the broadest classes of themes in your data. Once you have summarized your data into a few classes of themes, you will have extracted theoretical concepts. Box 10.3 shows a sample illustration of the second-level coding for the example in Box 10.2. You will see that, in this stage, we attempted to merge some themes into a broader label/code and also wrote memo notes on our reflections and theoretical questions which will later help to build a theoretical story.

Box 10.3   Second-Level Coding: Merging Codes.

A sample illustration of **Selective Coding** using the example from Box 10.2.

First Stage Code	Relation to other codes	Merging (Second-level Codes)
"citizenship"	"family": Presence of family is said to influence decision on naturalization. There was an indication that the family influences the participants' sense of belonging. "national identity": In most interviews, national identity was separate from legal citizenship. Naturalized citizens still maintained a sense of allegiance to the country of origin. MEMO: What is the relation to "Americanization"? Does cultural assimilation go hand-in-hand with national identity or motivations for naturalization?	Merged and recoded into *"Belonging"* MEMO: The notion of citizenship was considered as more legal/technical label. Women considered national identity or sense of belonging more important. The sense of belonging was shaped by presence of the family, and cultural assimilation. This was often believed to be proportional to the length in the U.S.
"national identity"	"length of residency": National identity was shaped by participants' length of residency. Recent immigrants tend to see themselves as "Korean" regardless of the visa statuses. "cultural assimilation": There were remarks indicating that culturally assimilated immigrants were not considered authentic.	Merged and recoded into *"Belonging"*

First Stage Code	Relation to other codes	Merging (Second-level Codes)
"length of residency"	"cultural assimilation": Participants considered "length of residency" as the proxy for cultural assimilation. MEMO: I wonder if there is a difference between people in ethnic enclaves and people who live in integrated communities.	Merged and recoded into *"cultural assimilation"*
"cultural assimilation"	"Americanization": Americanization meant culturally assimilated to the US culture. This was considered as having a strong component of "individualism." Recent immigrants used this term negatively.	Recoded into *"cultural assimilation"*
"individualism"	"cultural assimilation": Individualism was identified as the primary characteristics of Americanized immigrants. "length of residency": Participants believed that the longer U.S. residency is, the more Americanized one is. MEMO: Recent literature on transnationalism disputes this correlation. Need to look into the theory.	Merged under *"cultural assimilation"*
"Americanization"	"cultural assimilation": These two terms were interchangeable in most interviews. "length of residency": Participants believed that length of residency increased Americanization. "old-timer" vs. "recent arrival": This may be an oppositional internal segregation among immigrants. The criterion for the segregation was considered the degree of Americanization.	Merged and recoded into *"cultural assimilation"*

First Stage Code	Relation to other codes	Merging (Second-level Codes)
"old-timer" and "recent arrival"	"length of residency": Is there a segregation among immigrants by the length of residency? "cultural assimilation": The oppositional identity was constructed in relation to the degree of cultural assimilation.	Is there an oppositional identity among immigrants? Recoded into *"Internal segregation"*

In the final stages of your inductive coding, you examine the relationship between these concepts which you have extracted from your data and develop logical statements about their relationships ("theoretical coding"). Here, you will re-examine your narrative data again to understand how themes are connected to one another. Which issue, according to the interviewees, happens before the other? Which one is the cause and which one is the effect? Which theme is the condition and which is the outcome? Do themes contradict one another or are they related? What are the broader social contexts that give rise to these patterns? Considering these questions and ordering your thematic classes and concepts into a set of logical statements requires *theorizing*. Use a concept-mapping (Figure 10.1), or paragraphs of

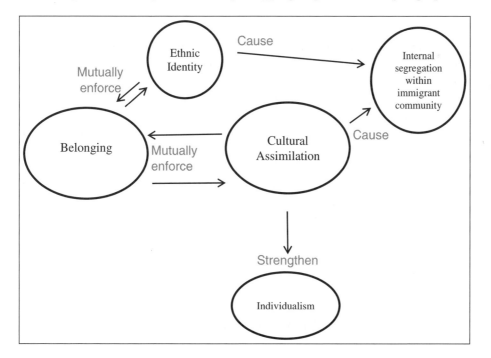

Figure 10.1   Sample Concept-mapping Using the Example from Box 10.3.

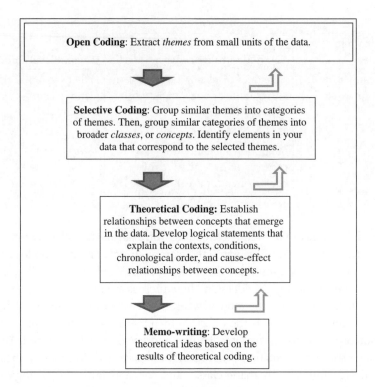

Figure 10.2   Process of Qualitative Coding.

free-writing to summarize what you discovered as a result of your theorizing. Then write your thoughts into paragraphs of memos that describe the emerging concepts as well as the theoretical relationships between the concepts ("memo-writing").

In summary, Figure 10.2 illustrates the general stages of coding in an inductive approach. The upward arrows indicate that you often need to go back to the previous stage and re-code, re-read, or add notes to the data. As indicated in this diagram, dispersed data will become organized into a handful of conceptual ideas and put into theoretical stories. Throughout the process, revisiting the raw data may become necessary. After narrowing down your themes to the most important ones, you should go back to the original data and re-capture parts that are relevant to the theoretical concepts you eventually develop. As we emphasized before, qualitative coding is a "messy" and circular process because you want to decipher the complexity in the data and be able to draw conclusions which reflect that complexity.

What Is the Process of Deductive Coding in Content Analysis?

When you have a set of very specific and focused research questions, you may be inclined to take a more "top-down" approach. If you take this strategy, you will construct a coding scheme first and then go to your data to find the parts that correspond to the pre-constructed codes.

How do you know what codes to use for your analysis? A few things will give you some ideas about coding schemes. The first is theory. If your project is based on a particular theoretical framework, you will have some expectations about what common patterns exist in your data. For instance, if your project is a study of suicide among students in highly competitive universities based on Agnew's general strain theory (1992), you may anticipate accounts of strain in your data, such as poor grades, academic pressure, peer pressure, troubles in the family, and so on. If these are targeted variables in your study, you may use these as your coding scheme and identify parts of the transcribed interviews containing these thematic codes.

Second, you may use coding schemes developed in another published study. In his seminal work, *Gender Advertisements* (1979), Erving Goffman analyzed the way advertisements portray women's subordination. Goffman's study used a 5-category coding scheme as visual signs of subordination: relative size, feminine touch, function ranking, ritualization of subordination, and licensed withdrawal. If you are doing a project on gendered images in different communication media (e.g., newspaper photos, Instagram posts), you can utilize Goffman's coding scheme for the analysis of your own data. In fact, Goffman's coding scheme is often adopted by student research on gendered images in media data.

Third, your research questions may be used as the coding scheme to classify the information in your data. For example, suppose a student focused on the following questions in her study of victims of intimate partner violence: 1) who is most instrumental to finding support services for victims?; 2) what/who encourage victims to separate from the violent partners?; 3) what are victims' most immediate concerns when they escape home? These questions are relatively specific, and therefore the researcher can use these categories as the pre-constructed codes: "helpers," "motivations," and "concerns." For example, consider the following passages from a student interview transcript:

> One morning, after my husband left for work, I sat on kitchen floor and just broke into tears. I didn't realize that my front door was not completely shut. Nancy, my neighbor, happened to drop by to ask if I can pick up her mail for a couple of days while she is gone for a work trip. She saw me and froze. I had big bruises on my arms, which I would normally cover with long sleeves when I go out. We talked and cried the whole morning. About a couple of days later, she brought this woman who was a part of a support group for survivors. She gave me the contact information for a women's shelter.

This passage provides some answers to question 1) above, and therefore can be coded as "helpers." If there are narratives about worrying about money or safety in other parts of this interview, those contents could be coded as "concerns."

Keep in mind that any qualitative analysis will involve switching back and forth between inductive and deductive modes of coding. Even if you are taking a deductive approach, you may need to modify the pre-constructed coding scheme in light of some emerging patterns you find in your coding process.

What Tools Can You Use to Organize and Summarize Codes?

Coding is a complicated process, and you cannot conduct coding in a haphazard manner. During your first stage of coding, you will have a large number of different codes. In addition, you are likely to make some reflections and notes to yourself as you proceed with your coding. This is a lot of information to keep track of. Therefore, it is critical that you find a system to keep your codes and notes organized.

A simple way to differentiate themes and mark them on the data is to use color coding. Our students often use this method. In the first stage of coding, read the text carefully and code any theme present in the text data. Then, review the codes and highlight or underline the same code dispersed in the data with a color. For instance, a code for "work and family balance" may come up several times in an interview with a working mother; you may use a yellow marker to highlight wherever this theme is present in the data. Use another color for a different theme (for example, blue for "career disadvantage" or green for "the supermom syndrome") and highlight again all the passages relevant to this theme throughout the text. Repeat the process for other themes using different color markers each time. Keep a record of what color represents what theme. Also write reflection notes, summaries, and comments about this theme on matching color paper. For instance, after reading the narrative data, if you had additional thoughts about work and family balance, write them down on yellow paper or an index card. That way, you know everything in yellow in your data shares the same group of themes or ideas.

One of our colleagues uses the "Comments" feature in her word processor to organize her notes. She reads through her narrative data on the computer screen carefully and clicks on the "Add New Comments" function to insert a keyword/ code and any notes she want to make. She uses the code as the heading for each comments box. That way, you can later pull out the comments that have the same code/heading and group them together. For example, every time narratives of a struggle with the "work and family balance" come up, you will highlight the text and add a new comments box, and write something like "Work-Family Balance." At the following stage of coding, you can use the "find" function of the word processor to find the places which you have marked with the code "Work-Family Balance."

After your first stage coding – i.e., identifying small units of a theme and assigning them with initial code labels – construct a grid of themes and sub-themes with notes about where to find those themes in the transcribed interviews. We recommend that you notate case numbers and page numbers in which the themes are found. In this way, it is easy to locate the sections to use as block quotes when you write your analysis. You can use Exercise 10.1 at the end of this chapter or any modified version of it as your model.

Finally, when you have narrowed down the themes into a handful of broader concepts, "map" them. What we mean by "map" is to consider the relationship between the concepts and the hierarchies between them and create a "map-like" diagram on a piece of paper as we showed in Figure 10.1.

How Do You Write about Findings from a Qualitative Analysis?

When you finish summarizing your data, you are ready to write the results of your analysis. The goal of your qualitative analysis is to address your initial research questions by presenting what you have found through your multi-level analysis. The following issues should be considered in writing your analysis.

Theorizing with Qualitative Data

Theorizing is the process of extracting a set of concepts which various cases in your data illustrate and articulating how they are related to one another. In fact, this task should be carried out throughout the multi-phased coding process itself. Once you have categorized, compared, and synthesized the codes and themes, you will have already exercised theoretical thinking and have some ideas about the relationships between concepts. At this stage of writing, you will focus on how to organize various theoretical ideas found in your data, elaborate them, and create an *analytic* summary of these ideas.

An analytic summary is different from a descriptive summary. A descriptive summary focuses on stating what happens in the data you collected and makes little attempt at broader generalizations. A descriptive summary simply addresses the question, "what stories have I collected?" An analytic summary, on the other hand, *interprets* the meaning of your findings in terms of a theory or in relation to a broader context. An analytic summary attempts to address the "how" and the "why" questions; to do this, you need to make connections between themes. By linking the findings from your study to the findings from other studies and making connections to various contextual factors, you will *explore possible causes, conditions, contexts, and outcomes* of the patterns and themes in your data.

To achieve this, an analytic summary requires comparing, generalizing, sequencing/ordering, and making inferences. A popular method used in analytic strategies is the "illustrative method" (Neuman 2011: 519). Illustrative methods apply a theory or theoretical concept to specific settings or examples in the data; the points derived from the data serve as "illustrations" or examples of the theory. You may use a single case to illustrate a theoretical idea or several cases (sometimes cross-cultural cases) to illustrate it.

Negative Cases

Not every case in your data will illustrate expected theoretical outcomes. Sometimes, you have to pay attention to what are called "negative cases." Negative cases refer to instances when you did not find what you had expected based on knowledge obtained from existing studies or theories. Neuman uses the example of Sir Arthur Conan Doyle's story, "Silver Blaze," in which Sherlock Holmes paid attention to a guard dog that did not bark during a theft and concluded that the dog knew the thief (Neuman 2011: 529). Likewise, when what is commonly found in other cases does not occur in your data, it may be worthwhile to think about why the pattern did not occur in these particular cases. If you have a group of women who only have one or two children in a high fertility area in Nigeria, for example, you may be able to learn about factors leading to lower fertility rates by studying this group of women. The lesson is not to simply dismiss negative cases. Instead, examine them in comparison with positive cases. Then, you may find something exciting.

Organizing Theoretical Ideas into Sections
When the analysis is complete, you will have a "theoretical story" about your data. What is the best way to present this story in a research paper? The most common format used in published research is to organize the findings into sections and sub-sections using the themes/concepts as headings. By the time your multi-stage analysis is complete, you will have a few broad conceptual themes generated from your data. Using these themes, patterns, or concepts as headings is particularly effective when your research is an exploratory study the purpose of which is to provide an overview of the themes and initiate some discussions around potential theoretical issues.

If you choose to do this, a good way to start is to write short paragraph memos for each of the conceptual themes or your sub-sections. Then organize an outline of the sub-sections and place the paragraph memos in the appropriate sub-sections. Later, you can revise the sections by elaborating your paragraphs and adding details. You also should find some block quotes from your data which support and illustrate the themes you are presenting.

Use of Block Quotes and Examples
Consider the following passages from Rhacel Salazar Parreñas' book (2001) on Filipino domestic workers.

> In Rome, providers of elderly care agree that their duties require more skills than do other domestic jobs. In contrast to their counterparts in Los Angeles, however, they believe that they, along with other domestics, still occupy a low position in society because of their segregation from the formal labor market. For example, Lorna Fernandez, not unlike other care providers in Rome, is keenly aware of her subordinate status. "They still see me as a maid. There is no improvement. You make good money, but they still call you a *ragazza* [girl]. When you are a *ragazza*, you are a maid."
> (2001: 157)

Here, the author used a block quote from her interview data to illustrate the perceived low status of elder care workers, despite their income and skills level. Here, the quotes provide illustrations, or a vivid example – i.e., being called by a belittling term – of the author's argument about the contradictory statuses of educated Filipina domestic workers. In qualitative analysis, evidence is most often presented in form of quotes from the data as in this example.

Identify which quotes are appropriate for what themes throughout your analysis. When you begin to theorize (selective coding), you should mark passages in the text data that are supportive of the emerging theoretical themes. Do this by keeping a note of case numbers and page numbers in a coding summary table (see Exercise 10.1), or use color coded highlights as explained above. Since qualitative analysis requires constant feedback between the data and the emerging thematic patterns, keeping track of quotes will be an integral part of your coding procedures.

When you insert block quotes, remember to provide information on the interviewee you have quoted. In the above example, Parreñas identified the interviewee by a pseudonym in the passages preceding the quotes; this is a common practice. Another way is to provide the interviewee's pseudonym in parentheses at the end of the quotes. Using a collection of block quotes from several interviews as evidence supporting each point you make is a popular strategy in many published studies. To ensure anonymity, you should use pseudonyms or the interviewees' initials only in your paper.

Case Studies

Another common technique of data presentation is to use a more detailed and holistic story about a single case as an illustration of your arguments. In this strategy, you are describing one element in your sample as "a case" of the general theme you would like to discuss. For example, a researcher who studies different paths of recovery among alcoholics may collect life history data through interviews and identify three or four different types of turning-points that led interviewees to become sober. These may include catastrophic experiences of "hitting bottom," a positive relationship with someone, or finding an effective treatment. In writing the results, the researcher can describe a case that best illustrates each of the different kinds of turning-point.

The benefit of a case study is that it can present more complex details involved in a single scenario. Whereas use of block quotes can support your points by providing snap-shots of the pattern you are describing, a case study can provide the holistic development of the contexts in which such patterns occur.

Visual Data

The above principles of qualitative data analysis can be adopted to analyze different types of data including visual data. Visual data, images such as photographs, magazine advertisements, or video footage, are understood as *symbols* or signs which contain particular messages and meanings about social issues.

Visual data can be grouped and categorized into thematic categories in a similar inductive process as used in the grounded theory; in this method, you will first identify the message/meaning embedded in each of the images and then classify images with the same message/meaning into a broader group until you merge them into a few meaningful conceptual categories. Similar to text analysis, you can present these thematic groups of images using sub-headings. In the example of research on female reporters and types of the news mentioned earlier, suppose you found that female reports are typically assigned to 1) interviews with women, 2) stories on "feminine" subjects such as food, arts, and fashion, and 3) topics related to "nurturing" roles such as education, animal rescues, or community service. You could create a section dedicated to each of these themes and describe the stories, or provide TV screen shots supporting the theme in each section.

But more frequently, visual data are analyzed using content analysis techniques with pre-constructed coding schemes. First a few categories of themes, based on theories or existing studies, are developed into codes. Then, the images or segments of visual data containing the themes/codes are counted and quantitatively summarized into percentages and frequencies. Whether you will take an inductive or deductive approach will depend on your research questions. Whichever approach you take, you may still use selected images to support the arguments of your paper as you would with block quotes.

References

Agnew, Robert. 1992. "Foundation for General Strain Theory of Crime and Delinquency." *Criminology* 30: 47–87.

Berg, Bruce, and Howard Lune. 2011. *Qualitative Research Methods for the Social Sciences.* 8th ed. Upper Saddle River, NJ: Pearson.

Esterberg, Kristin G. 2002. *Qualitative Methods in Social Research.* Boston, MA: McGraw-Hill Companies.

Glaser, Barney and Anselm Strauss. 1967. *The Discovery of Grounded Theory: Strategies for Qualitative Research.* Hawthorne, NY: Aldine de Gruyter.

Goffman, Erving. 1979. *Gender Advertisements.* New York: Harper & Row.

Keogan, Kevin. 2002. "A Sense of Place: the Politics of Immigration and the Symbolic Construction of Identity in Southern California and the New York Metropolitan Area." *Sociological Forum* 17(2): 223–253.

Neuman, W. Lawrence. 2011. *Social Research Methods: Qualitative and Quantitative Approaches.* 7th ed. Boston, MA: Allyn and Bacon.

Park, Keumjae. 2014. "Foreigners or Multicultural Citizens? South Korean Press Media's Construction of Asian Immigrants." *Ethnic and Racial Studies* 37(9): 1565–1586.

Parreñas, Rhacel Salazar. 2001. *Servants of Globalization: Women, Migration, and Domestic Work.* Stanford, CA: Stanford University Press.

Schutt, Russell K. 2011. *Investigating the Social World: The Process and Practice of Research.* 7th ed. Thousand Oaks, CA: Pine Forge Press.

Further Reading

Bazeley, Patricia, 2013. *Qualitative Data Analysis: Practical Strategies.* Thousand Oaks, CA: Sage.

Denzin, Norman K., and Yvonna S. Lincoln. 2008. *Collecting and Interpreting Qualitative Materials.* Thousand Oaks, CA: Sage.

Saldaña, Johnny. 2012. *The Coding Manual for Qualitative Researchers.* 2nd ed. Thousand Oaks, CA: Sage.

Schreier, Margrit. 2012. *Qualitative Content Analysis in Practice.* London: Sage, Ltd.

Internet Resources

Coding Analysis Tool-kit (CAT) at University of Pittsburgh, USA. http://cat.ucsur.pitt.edu/

International Visual Sociology Association (IVSA) Showcase of Visual Research. http://visualsociology.org/showcase.html

Online QDA (Learning Qualitative Data Analysis on the web). http://onlineqda.hud.ac.uk/index.php

ReStore (by Economic and Social Research Council, UK) Web Resources. http://www.restore.ac.uk/resources/

Exercises for Chapter 10

Exercises in this chapter provide tools for qualitative coding. Use Exercise 10.1 to organize your notes on codes, reflections on the codes, and the location of corresponding data quotes. Exercise 10.2 is a sample mapping tool to merge and summarize smaller codes into broader themes. Exercise 10.3 provides some guiding questions for theorizing with the themes extracted from the data. Exercise 10.4 is useful for summarizing the results of a content analysis.

Exercise 10.1 Organizing Codes and Notes

The table format can be a useful way to organize codes. Use the table below to keep notes of emerging themes and categories of themes emerging from your data. An example is provided in italics to show what kind of information should be noted in each column.

Theme	Definition/elaboration of the theme	Related themes that can be classified into the same broader theme	Corresponding case and page numbers
Example: "Turning point"	The majority of the sample has memories of a turning point that was critical to their recovery from substance abuse. Turning points included "hitting bottom," intervention, or changes in relationships.	significant relationships, role models, "hitting bottom," "wake-up call" events	#2 (pp. 4–5), #14 (p. 16), #33(pp. 20–25), #34 (pp. 38–40)
1			
2			

(continued)

Theme	Definition/ elaboration of the theme	Related themes that can be classified into the same broader theme	Corresponding case and page numbers
3			
4			
5			

Exercise 10.2 Merging into Broader Themes

The key principle of inductive coding is merging smaller themes into broader categories of themes and establishing order or relationships between them. Use one of the two models in this exercise to merge the first-level codes into broader, second-level codes.

Model A: *Using Diagrams*
Use the diagram below to merge and organize codes and themes in your data. First, write down the names of the codes/themes you found during the first-stage coding in the squares at the bottom (i.e., Code 1, Code 2…).

Second, group similar themes into broader concepts. Write in the concepts in the ovals below.

Third, write notes about the relationships between the concepts. Which one affects the other? How? Is there a hierarchical order or a chronological order between these? Are there any intervening factors or contextual conditions for this relationship? Describe them in the rectangle.

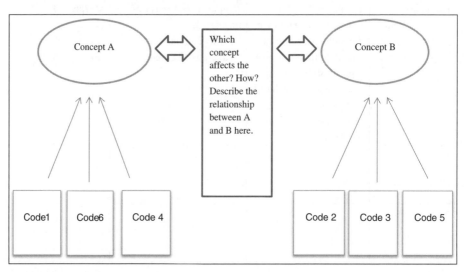

Model B: *Using a Table-format*

Instead of a diagram, you can use a table-format as we did in Box 10.3 in this chapter.

First-level Code labels	Relation to Other Codes	Merging into Second-level Codes
Code label:	List of other related codes: Notes:	New code label (merged into a broader second-level code)
Code label:	List of other related codes: Notes:	New code label (merged into a broader second-level code)
Code label:	List of other related codes: Notes:	New code label (merged into a broader second-level code)
Code label:	List of other related codes: Notes:	New code label (merged into a broader second-level code)
Code label:	List of other related codes: Notes:	New code label (merged into a broader second-level code)
Add more rows as needed.		

Exercise 10.3 Guiding Questions for Memo-writing

When you are able to extract 3–4 classes of themes from your text data, create narrative memos in preparation for the report-writing. For each of the themes, write a few paragraphs of summary memos while thinking about the following issues.

Theme #1
  a. What is it? Describe the theme. Give definitions.

  b. Why is it important? In what ways, does it matter to the participants?

  c. How is this related to other themes in the data? Describe the relationships between this theme and other prevailing themes in the data. Describe whether there is a time order, or possible causal relationships.

  d. What are external influence and conditions? What are the contexts? Describe the people, relationships, cultural norms and expectations, economic and social conditions involved in the theme.

  e. What are the outcomes or consequences of this theme?

  f. How does this theme answer my research question(s)?

Exercise 10.4 Summarizing Content Analysis

Unlike inductive data analysis, content analyses most often use pre-constructed coding scheme and produce statistical summaries of the distribution of the codes in the data. Below is a template for a shorthand summary of your content analysis.

Coding Scheme	Description and Criteria	Statistical Summary
Code Label:	What the code symbolizes:	Raw counts in the data:
	Types of image or narratives to be categorized into this code:	Percentage:
	1	
	2	
	3	
	4	Other relevant statistics:

(continued)

Code Label:	What the code symbolizes: Types of image or narratives to be categorized into this code: 1 2 3 4	Raw counts in the data: Percentage: Other relevant statistics:
Code Label:	What the code symbolizes: Types of image or narratives to be categorized into this code: 1 2 3 4	Raw counts in the data: Percentage: Other relevant statistics:
Add rows as needed		

Your Project Outcome after Chapter 10

At this point:

- You have completed multiple stages of coding and have written theoretical memos and reflections to gradually merge data.
- If you performed a content analysis, you have statistical summary of your coded data.
- You have a good idea about what the "theoretical stories" of your data are, and have paragraphs of written memos and notes of the theoretical ideas and concepts developed from your data.
- You have an outline of the broadest themes, concepts, and theoretical ideas you have developed from the qualitative data analyses you have performed.
- You have identified block quotes to be used in your paper and organized them with the theoretical themes you plan to write about.

Chapter 11

Writing the Final Report

Now that you have completed your data collection and data analysis, it is time to put together a report of your research findings. The final report is the ultimate product of your research. You will share it with others so that they will learn about your discoveries. There are professional standards for research reports in social sciences, which we will discuss in this chapter. We will provide guidance in writing each section of your research paper. In writing the final report, you may have some of these questions.

- What should I include in my final report?
- How is my final report different from my proposal?
- What should I consider before I begin to write the final report?
- What do I write about my research method?
- What should I write about my research findings?
- What should I write for my discussion?
- Do I need to include problems I had in my research?
- Should I use the same outlines for quantitative and qualitative research?
- How many references do I need for my reference list?

In this chapter, we will respond to and discuss these questions which students frequently ask.

What Should You Include in Your Final Report?

If there are specific requirements for your assignment, follow them. If your professor has no specific requirements, use the following general outline:

1   Title
2   Abstract

Student Research and Report Writing: From Topic Selection to the Complete Paper, First Edition. Gabe T. Wang and Keumjae Park. © and Published 2016 by John Wiley & Sons, Ltd.

3   Introduction
4   Literature review
5   Research methods
6   Findings
7   Discussion
8   Conclusions
9   References

How Is Your Final Report Different from Your Proposal?

If you look at the standard outline above, you will realize that it is somewhat similar to the format of the research proposal we discussed in Chapter 7. Since the research proposal is a plan and the final report is the outcome of the plan, you can expect a lot of overlapping contents between the two documents. Before looking at closely how to write each section of the research report, we would like to first discuss how the final report is different from your proposal.

What Should Be in the Final Report?
Since your research report is the description of what you have actually done and found, there are new sections in your final report, which were not in the proposal. They are the sections related to data analysis and the results of your study, including Findings, Discussions, and Conclusions sections. They constitute a substantial part of your final report. In addition, when the research report is complete, you will add an Abstract at the beginning of the report so that the readers will get a quick summary of your research. If you are writing a formal thesis, such as an undergraduate honors thesis or a postgraduate thesis, there may be other required sections by your university, such as an ethics declaration statement, a copyright page, the table of contents, or an acknowledgement section. Carefully consult the guidelines for the final product at your university to include all required sections.

What Should Not Be in the Final Report?
On the other hand, some parts of your research plan, which were included in your proposal, are no longer needed in the final report. The contents related to project management plan need not be included in the final report. For example, the proposed timeline, budget statements, contact information, and potential problems and remedies sections are normally not needed in the final report.

You may also wonder whether you need to include some primary documents from your field research, such as surveys collected, a print out of your raw data, hard copies of SPSS output tables, transcribed interviews, coding sheets, or signed informed consent forms. Normally, none of these should be included in the final report. Occasionally, your supervisor or instructor of your class may wish to see some of these documents for the purpose of evaluating your research process; upon their requests, you may include them as appendices to your final report.

Research ethics standards require that participants' identities should be protected. Thus, no real names of the participants should be in your final report; you will either use their initials only, or use pseudonyms.

Using Revised Contents from your Proposal

We expect that there are overlapping contents between your proposal and the final report. Thus, you can import some contents from your proposal and revise them for your final report. For example, some information you used to write the introduction of your proposal may still be useful for your final report. However, you cannot simply copy it into your final report. Instead, you need to revise it to fit into your final report. You may also need to add something new to your introduction, such as a brief report of the most important findings of your research and a brief description of how your final report will be structured.

The literature review in your proposal is likely to have served as the theoretical foundation for your completed research. In this case, the literature review section of your proposal would be imported and revised into the literature review section of your final report. Keep in mind, however, that you may have to revise it substantially in case there has been a change of theoretical direction during the process of your research. For example, suppose you had proposed a study about parent-child relationship and family bonds in step-families but ended up focusing on the factors at home which affect step-children's academic performances in your analysis; then the literature review in the final paper should include the literature on the linkage between family backgrounds and school grades. On the other hand, if a part of your literature review is no longer relevant to your final report, you should leave it out.

The methods section of your proposal had been the blueprint for your field research. If you were able to collect the data according to the original methodological plan, then the descriptions of methods in your final report will be very similar to the methods section in your proposal, except that you will now write them in the past tense (since you already carried out the research). But it is possible that you had to make methodological changes and adjustments during the data collection stage, either in light of pilot tests, or due to methodological difficulties. If this is the case, make sure your final report reflects what was actually done. It is quite common that a researcher has to make changes to the original methodological plans; avoid copying and pasting the methodology section of your proposal onto your final report when in fact you carried out different research. It is okay if not everything proposed was conducted during the field research, or different analytic techniques were used in your analysis. Simply write in your research report what was actually done.

Writing Styles for the Final Report

You should write your final report in the past tense, as you are describing a completed project. This applies to both the Methods section and the Findings section. If you are "recycling" your methods section from the proposal, make sure you change to the past tense. Literature reviews, Discussions, and Conclusions may be variously written in the past tense or in the present tense.

Students often ask if they should write in passive voice or in active voice. This seems to vary mostly by the research method and the disciplinary tradition. When you report a quantitative research, passive voice seems more common, though there are still a lot of studies using "I find ..." or "we find ..." statements. When you report qualitative research, the active voice may become necessary at times. It is not a matter of right or wrong to use the passive voice or active voice; it is a matter of convention. You may look up articles in a major journal in your discipline for guidance, and also consult your supervisor or mentor for advice.

Social science research papers are usually succinct and to the point. You need to write clearly and unambiguously so that other people can understand your report. A good way to find out whether your writing is clear is to ask a peer or your supervisor to read an early draft. What is clear to you may not be clear to the reader; thus, having someone's input on an earlier draft will be very helpful for your revisions.

Your final report should have an internal logic; the sequence of sentences, paragraphs, and sections should be related to each other logically, and the whole paper should be coherent. Use transitional phrases and sentences enhance the flow greatly. As it is the case with any academic writing, you should avoid slang and colloquialism in your research report.

You must pay more careful attention to citations in your final report. Since research proposals are often considered as "preliminary" documents and are circulated among limited number of people, occasionally missing citations in proposals may not create a huge problem. However, you may be accused of plagiarism when citations are omitted your final research report, especially if it is a thesis or a postgraduate research paper. You may revisit Chapter 4 for more advice on citations.

What Should You Consider Before You Start Writing Your Final Report?

Before you start writing your final report, ask about the length and the format required for your report. If it is a term paper for a course, there may be a format your professor, lecturer, or tutor requires. Undergraduate and Master's theses will follow the standards required by your university. Your program chair or the librarian in charge of thesis collections will let you know what they are. Once you learn about the length and format requirements, you will have a rough idea of how much you should allocate for each section of your paper. You should not write too much for one part or too little for another.

If there is no length requirement, however, you should write as much as you need to give a full report of the research project. Look at a few research articles published in an academic journal that are similar to your research for the length and format. A good model will help you more than anything else. If you are writing a thesis, take a look at a few theses written by students in your department in previous years. They are usually available in your university library.

Prepare an outline, including your topic, main headings, and second level subheadings, with short notes (such as bullet points) about what you would like to write in each section. Having an outline will help you write a well-structured paper. Research reports for quantitative and qualitative research are different in style. Quantitative research reports tend to closely follow a standard format (such as the one above) while qualitative research papers take more diverse forms. We will first discuss quantitative research papers. Report writing for qualitative research will be discussed in a later section of this chapter.

Title of Your Final Report or Thesis

Now that you understand the nature of the final report and have developed an outline, let's go over each section in the outline in greater detail. The title of a research paper sets the tone for the entire paper. A good title tells your readers instantly what you are writing about, grabs their attention, and builds anticipation for further reading. Therefore, the title of your research report should be descriptive and concise. It must effectively and accurately represent the contents of your report. If someone reads your title and understands what your paper is about, then you have a good title. Here are a few tips that can help you think of an effective title.

The title often includes the concepts and variables studied your research project. According to Pyrczak and Bruce (1998), if only a small number of variables are studied, the title of your paper should name those variables. For example, if your research studied how race and gender affect respondents' income, your title can be "Race, Gender and Income." If many variables are studied in your research and they are too many to list in your title, name a broader concept which would include your variables. For example, "A Study of the Relationships between Students' GPA, Class Attendance, Study Time and Marijuana, Cocaine and LSD Use" can be changed to "Student School Performance and Substance Use." Also, your title should be concise; if your title is longer than two lines, make it shorter.

If your research makes unique and significant contributions, such as using an innovative research method or studying a unique population, indicate them in your title. For example, if your research involves military spouses' attitudes towards war, specifying "military spouses" in the title may attract readers who are interested in this population. If your research employs an interesting research method, such as participant observations of police behavior, include this in the title so that readers know you applied uncommon data collection methods. Similarly, you can include in your title your data analysis techniques; for example, if you used structural equation modeling, you can use the title, "A Structural Equation Model for Juvenile Delinquent Behaviors."

We recommend you to create a separate title page. Typical items on the title page include the title of your paper, your name, to whom you are submitting the paper (e.g., the thesis committee, your university, etc.), date of submission, and the supervisor's name. But it is best if you find out exactly what is required for your assignment and follow the required format of your university or your department. The title is usually centered, with the first letter of each word capitalized except for articles, conjunctions, and prepositions (such as *the, a, and, or, at, in,* or *on*). When these words, however, are at the beginning of the title, either on the first line or the second line, the first letter should be capitalized.

Remember, your title page is the first impression you give to your readers and professors about your research. So make it look great.

An Abstract of Your Final Report

It is a common practice that an abstract precedes the contents of the paper. The abstract of your paper is a brief summary which tells the readers the purpose, significance, study population, research methods, and the most important findings of your research. Each of these areas included in the abstract may need one or two sentences. Readers will decide whether or not to read the entire paper after reading the abstract.

The length of the abstract is usually specified as a part of the format requirements. If you are writing a thesis, your school or your program will have some guidelines about the length of the abstract. If you are writing the report as a course project, ask the instructor. When there is no specific guidelines, the general convention is about 150–350 words for an article length paper, that is, about one-fourth to one-half of a page. Abstracts can be longer for theses that are over 40 pages in length. If you are thinking about submitting your paper to an academic journal for publication, check the journal's website; each journal has specific length requirements.

Although the abstract is normally placed at the beginning of your research report, it should be written last, after you completed your final report. Since the abstract should best capture the core contents of the entire paper, you should write it when you know exactly what your paper is about. This is only possible after you have completed the analysis and discussions, and have drawn some conclusions from your research.

A common problem we find in the abstracts of student papers is that too many minor details are included. An abstract is not an executive summary, so it does not have to be a complete summary of your research. Another problem is that students frequently fail to focus on the paper's most important information. Avoid these problems when you write the abstract. Once again, seeing good models is very helpful. Pick up a few published journal articles and look at the abstracts closely to learn what kind of information should be included.

Introduction

The main text of your research report starts with an introduction. The purpose of the introduction is to describe your research topic and tell your readers briefly why you conducted the study, and how the research was carried out. It is similar to the introduction of your proposal but you may add some information about the major findings of your research.

Your introduction should state the topic, provides some background information and justification to your research, raise the research questions your research will answer, and specify the significance and contribution of your research to your academic field and to society.

In addition, your introduction can include description of the methods you employed and your most important findings. If your research paper or thesis is more than 40 pages long, describe in the introduction how your paper is organized. In other words, tell your readers what you are going to tell them. Your introduction should be succinct and clear, but interesting and compelling at the same time.

Literature Reviews

Although you probably had already written your literature reviews before you started your data collection, it is time to revisit and revise your literature reviews. You need to address any changes you made to your research direction and polish the reviews so as to build the argumentation for your final report. Effective literature reviews synthesize previous works, establish a connection between existing studies and the research you just completed, clarify the theoretical foundation, and specify the research questions investigated in your research. Since we have already discussed how to write effective literature reviews in Chapter 4 and Chapter 7, we will now focus on some practical problems students often face in writing the literature review section of the final research report. To recapitulate the points we made in earlier chapters, your literature reviews should include the following two parts: the synthesis of previous studies and your own research questions and hypotheses for your study.

Synthesizing Previous Studies on Your Research Topic
The larger part of your literature review will be dedicated to summarizing and synthesizing existing studies done on your research topic, and discussing different theories relevant to your research topic. What we mean by "synthesizing" is to create an organized summary of the literature as a whole, based on a careful assessment of how different groups of studies fit one another. You may have to revisit Chapter 4 to have a clear understanding of what literature reviews look like. In finalizing your report, pay attention to the following.

First, try to avoid the narrative review style. In other words, the literature should be sorted and grouped by certain characteristics (i.e., variables tested, methodology used, or theoretical approaches) and the ordering of the groups should have a rationale. Clarify the relationships between groups of literature and present them in an organized manner. If a student reviews 15 sources on a topic, and writes 15 paragraphs, each summarizing one source, you can see that there is no synthesizing, nor analysis of the reviewed literature as a whole.

Second, the literature reviews should have a focus. If you summarize everything about an article without specifying how it is relevant to your own study, you are not achieving the main goal of the review. While we do not recommend you take arguments out of context, we advise that you *highlight* the aspects of a study that relate directly to your study. For instance, if you included in your review a study because it was based on a different theory from the prevailing one, highlight how this article fits into the theoretical debates about your topic, and make a theoretical assessment the focus of your review. If this is the case, you do not have to try to report all empirical findings from this study. Or, if the significance of your own research lies in its methodological innovation, you can focus on methodological critique of the existing studies in your review.

Third, use relevant theories. The keyword here is "relevant." Since many professors encourage students to utilize theories in their research, some students discuss any theories in the literature review, even if they are not necessarily related to their research questions. For example, a student of ours was interested in investigating the challenges of raising children as single mothers, such as time constraints, resources, problems with work travels, and finding suitable male role models for their children. In her literature review section, however, she discussed "feminist theory" as the theoretical perspectives and summarized feminist critiques on women's economic dependency and their assignment to reproductive labor. Here, you can see that the particular branch of feminist theory she discussed is not directly related to the specific variables examined her study. She should have focused on theories related to parental resource constraints in a society that assumes two-parent family models. In short, it is a good idea to use a theory to guide your research. But assess whether the theory is directly related to your research questions.

Last but not the least, exercise proper citation and avoid plagiarism. There are several things to watch out for. One of the frequent mistakes students make is an excessive reliance on direct quotes from sources. Is it all right to copy and paste endless quotations from sources as long as they are properly cited? The answer is "no." It is not unheard of that professors receive undergraduate papers with nearly half the contents directly quoted from sources they consulted. In this case, a student may be able to avoid plagiarism by properly citing the sources of the quoted passages, but this is hardly an original work by the student. Moreover, the student is running the risk of misinterpreting the quoted materials, as they are taken out of context. Unless there is a compelling and justifiable reason, it is simply a lazy writing practice to use someone else's words to express your thoughts. In short, your literature reviews cannot be a patchwork of quoted passages, even if the sources are cited.

Needless to say, copying long passages from published articles or internet documents without placing them in quotation marks constitutes plagiarism. When you directly borrow exact wording from a source, you must place the sentences in quotation marks or make them an indented paragraph and clearly cite the author, publication year, and the page numbers of the source at the end. Paraphrasing is recommended whenever possible, and paraphrased passages must be followed by parenthetical citation. You should work on a reference list at the same time as you cite. It will save you a lot of time. Computer word processor programs often have functions which allow you to create a reference list as you add citations in the text.

As we discussed in Chapter 4, citing sources is not only an ethical obligation but also a tool to strengthen your arguments. Citations show that your arguments are built on expert knowledge. In addition, citations enable the readers to look up the original sources and trace back the intellectual roots of your arguments. Keep in mind that the goal of your literature review is to give a sense of where your own study fits within the body of knowledge. If your study examines an understudied sub-topic, or new variables that have not yet been tested, then you are making great contributions to the literature.

In short, good literature reviews will provide a justification for your research questions, and allow readers of your paper to say "Aha, I understand why you are investigating these problems." Generally speaking, your literature reviews should give your readers an impression that you have a good understanding of what has been known on your research topic, what still needs to be investigated, and how your research would do the needed job or a better job. In other words, your literature reviews should justify and give your research a rationale.

Stating Your Research Questions or Hypotheses
The logical ending of the literature review section is (you guessed it!) a set of your own research questions. Conclude the literature review section of your final report with a set of research questions or hypotheses examined in your study. For example, you may write, "In light of the literature review, this research examined how age, gender and race affect college students' drug use." Notice here that we suggested the past tense, since you have already completed the research and examined this topic.

In published journal papers, authors often use bullet points to present the list of specific questions they examined. It is a common practice and one we recommend to student researchers like you. In the above example, you may write "The following relationships are examined in this paper: 1) how does age affect drug use? 2) How does gender affect drug use? 3) How does race affect drug use? 4) Which of the three independent variables have greater impact on the risk of drug use among university students?" As you already know, you may state these as hypotheses as well. For example, instead of the question 1) above, you may write, "Hypothesis 1: Age affects the chance of drug use." It is not necessary to use both questions and hypotheses for the same issue you investigated. You can choose either way.

Hypotheses can be phrased in a variety of ways. Generally speaking, your hypotheses should be an assumed relationship between the independent and the dependent variables. While writing a simple research hypothesis, you should name two variables and indicate what type of relationship you expect to find between them (Pyrczak and Bruce 1998). Such a relationship could be positive, negative, or non-directional. For example, if your research tested whether women's contribution to subsistence economy was negatively related to fertility rates, you would write: "It was hypothesized that in societies where women's work is important for household subsistence, they are likely to have fewer children."

Your research hypothesis may be stated as non-directional, meaning only expecting a relationship between two variables without predicting whether it is a positive or a negative relationship. For example, you would write: "It was hypothesized that women's economic contribution is related to fertility rates." You may also state hypotheses predicting a difference or a lack of difference between different groups. For example: "It was hypothesized that fertility rates are lower among women who make significant contributions to the family economy than those who do not"

You may have studied a hypothesis which included several independent variables affecting one dependent variable. For example, your research may have used multiple regressions to find out how family support, parental supervision, and educational inspiration affected children's grades. In this case, you would write: "It was hypothesized that student family support, parental supervision, and educational inspiration are positively related to their grades."

If your research utilized a structural equation model, such as Lisrel or Amos, your research hypothesis may have included multiple independent and dependent variables. If your study examined several relationships among multiple variables, you can write a series of hypothesis. For example, if your research expected that juvenile family attachment, educational commitment, and parental supervision (independent variables) are negatively related to juvenile substance use and deviant behavior (dependent variables), and your research expected that the independent variables are positively correlated to each other, and the dependent variables are also positively related to each other, you may state your hypotheses in three steps. For example, "it was hypothesized that juvenile family attachment, educational commitment, and parental supervision are positively correlated; it was also hypothesized that juvenile family attachment, educational commitment, and parental supervision have a negative impact on their substance use and deviant behavior; it was further hypothesized that juvenile substance use is positively related to their deviant behavior." If your study population is a particular group of people, you should specify the group, and your hypothesis should be specific and clearly stated (Pyrczak and Bruce 1998).

Research Methods

In your final research report or thesis, you need a section to describe in detail how you designed and conducted your research. Your research methods section not only communicates how you collected the data, but also allows your readers to evaluate whether your research was properly carried out to ensure reliable and valid findings. Since you are writing the final report at the point when your research has been completed, you should write this section in the past tense. You need to include details of your research methods. The common recommendation is that you include enough details of your research methods for anyone to replicate your study exactly the way you did. The following information is typically included in the methods section, and you may use subheadings for these items within your method section.

Study Population and Sample
Describe your study population, how you selected your sample (i.e., what sampling technique you used to select your respondents), and what the sample size was. Discuss whether your sample was representative of the study population and whether there was any possible source of sampling bias. In experimental designs, the methods of assignment into the experimental group and the control group should be reported. If the sample was small and/or non-representative in an exploratory study, the limitations of the sample should be discussed. We recommend you to report the basic demographic information of your respondents in this section. For example, report the distribution of gender, race, age, education, income, or any other relevant demographic variables about your sample.

Definition and Measurement of Your Variables
If your study involves abstract concepts, you should specify how you conceptualized and operationalized them. Describe clearly how each abstract concept was measured (i.e., what kinds of question was asked, what level of measurement it was, how it was coded and so on). Make sure you report the measures for all of the independent and the dependent variables in your study. Measurement validity and reliability should also be discussed. If tests of reliability were performed, it should be reported here. If you conducted experimental research, describe the pre-test and post-test measures.

If you modified your variables for the purpose of analysis, the procedures should be described. For example, if you recoded your data or weighted your data, inform your readers how you did it. This section is important for the readers of your paper to evaluate the measurement validity. You should include clear and sufficient details about your measures.

Data Collection Procedures
Tell your readers how you collected your data. If you used surveys to collect data, describe how they were administered (e.g., in-person, online, telephone) and when and where they were distributed, and report the return rate. Evaluate whether the response rate was sufficient and discuss possible biases and limitations if the return rate was low. Discuss ethical concerns and how informed consent was obtained. If you conducted interviews, report when and where you conducted your interviews along with the average length of the interviews. Also report whether the interviews were structured or unstructured, and how probing questions were used. Describe any notable difficulties which may have affected the quality of your data

(e.g., being unable to record the interviews). Experimental research should provide details of the setting, the treatment or independent variable, and any external factors which may have affected the experiment.

Data Processing, Analysis, and Statistical Significance Level
If you used computer data analyses, you should describe what kind of statistical procedures you used in analyzing your data, such as F-test, t-test, or multiple regressions. At the same time, you should report the significance levels of your data analysis. If you developed models for your data analysis, describe how you developed your models, state the equations used, and discuss how well they fit your data.

Findings

It is customary to have separate sections for "findings" and "discussions" in research reports based on quantitative research. Students often ask how these two sections should differ from each other. Before discussing how to write each section, let's think about how the Findings section may be different from the Discussion section in quantitative studies.

In general, the "Findings" section is dedicated to the reports of straightforward statistics and simple answers to research questions and hypotheses (i.e., whether they support or do not support the predictions). The "Discussions" section, on the other hand, involves more in-depth discussions of results in relation to the broader theories and to existing knowledge on this topic, and implications of your results and their applications to the greater society.

Thus, in the "Findings" section, you will report your results that correspond to your research questions or hypotheses. In quantitative studies, the results are likely to be statistics. Some questions can be answered with descriptive statistics, such as percentages, frequencies, and mean/median/mode, which you can present either in text or in graphs and tables. Research questions involving multiple variables will require reports of test statistics from multivariate analyses discussed in Chapter 9. If you proposed hypotheses, you may interpret the test statistics to either reject or confirm your hypotheses. It is important to remember that the findings you report in this section should dovetail the list of hypotheses you listed at the end of the literature review section.

It is usually necessary to report basic statistics about your independent and dependent variables. For example, if you studied the relationship between GPA and marijuana use, you should report the distribution of GPA and the percentage of marijuana use among your respondents. When you report descriptive statistics about your respondents or variables, use percentages followed by frequencies in parenthesis. For example, if you collected data from 552 respondents and 248 students reported using marijuana, state that "45% (248) of the respondents used marijuana." Percentages are not only easier to understand but also make comparison possible, as they are standardized to the total number of cases.

Table 11.1   Things to Include in the Findings Section.

Statistical Procedures Used	Statistical Results Should Be Included in Report
Frequencies	• Percentage and numbers
Descriptive Statistics	• Mean/median/mode, range, and standard deviation
Cross Tabulation	• Frequencies and row and column percentages
If with Chi-square test	• Chi-square value (χ^2) and the significance level of the Chi-square test (p-value)
If association is measured	• Value of phi, Cramer's V, or Gamma, etc. and the significance level of the above measures
Pearson's Correlation	• Value of Pearson's r and the significance level of r
Regression and Multiple Regression Analysis	• R Square (R^2) or adjusted R square
	• F-value, within and between groups, degrees of freedom (df), and the significance level of the F-test statistics
	• Values of β or Beta, and the level of significance
t-test	• Means and standard deviations
	• t value and the significance level
ANOVA	• Means and standard deviations
	• F-value, between and within group degrees of freedom, and the significance level of F statistics
With Post Hoc Tests	• Mean differences and the significance level of the tests for each paired group.

* All data analyses report should include the number of cases being analyzed.

In addition to descriptive statistics, test statistics from multivariate analyses should be reported along with their significance levels. Table 11.1 summarizes what statistics you should report for different types of statistical testing. As shown in the table, if you used Pearson's correlation to study correlations between two variables, use the Pearson's r value to report the relationship between the two variables you studied. You should also report the significance value to show whether the r value is statistically significant. If you performed Chi-square analysis, cite the Chi-square value (with the significance value) when reporting the relationship between the two variables. If you also calculated the strength of the relationship between the two variables, report the strength of the correlations and its significance level.

When you report quantitative data analysis, the statistical results should also be interpreted. For example, if you obtained a Chi-square value of (χ^2) 21.3071 with the significance level of 0.811 for the variables, level of education and smoking, you should report the statistics and also describe what these numbers mean. In this case, the statistics indicate that there is no significant association between level of education and smoking, for the statistical significance level is greater than .05. Try to write in simple plain language and explain technical terms so that people without advanced statistical training would be able to understand your findings. For example, if you report that student GPA is negatively related to their substance use, you may also explain that "negative" relationship means those students who have a higher GPA are less likely to use substances.

It is useful to take advantage of tables, charts, figures, or diagrams to visually present your findings. Charts and tables make comparing data easier. Figures and diagrams may allow readers to visualize correlations or causal relations between independent and dependent variables. Since you are unlikely to include graphs of all variables in your research, consult your faculty mentor about choosing the right visual presentations for the paper. All tables, figures, and charts should be numbered and given titles. We recommend that you include any notes and captions necessary for the readers to understand your tables and figures without having to read the whole results section. In other words, graphs, tables, and figures should be self-explanatory, and they should be understood as stand-alone presentations. In addition, keep in mind that tables and graphs should be used as summary display of all relevant test statistics. Thus, you should avoid directly copying and pasting individual SPSS output files onto your report.

In short, you will provide straightforward answers to your research questions and confirm or reject hypotheses with supportive evidence and statistical data in this section. How these findings relate to the general literature on your research topic should be discussed in the Discussions section.

Discussions

In this section, your discussions may focus on two areas. First, you can discuss your findings in light of previous research, debates, or inconclusiveness on the topic. If your findings support or contradict previous research, point that out and discuss why they do. If your findings confirm or reject your hypotheses, you may also discuss them in relation to the theory tested. Indicate whether your research supports or contradicts the theory and why this is the case. If your findings suggest a need to add more variables or to modify an existing theoretical model, develop an argument for this need in this section. This can show how your work contributes to existing research and to the body of scientific knowledge on your research topic. In this way, you can contribute to the academic field.

Second, your discussions may focus on your understanding of social contexts or application in society. If your findings have specific application to reality, or policy implications, this is the section to discuss them. For example, if your findings indicate that elementary school children's use of smartphones affected their school performance, you may discuss possible implication of the findings to school policies. If your research findings indicate that organizational structure prevents companies from adopting new technology, you may suggest that companies improve their organizational structure so that it will be conducive to the adoption of new technology. Similarly, if your research findings indicate that Asian juveniles are more likely to be influenced by their friends in illegal drug use, you may suggest some programs to isolate drug-using juveniles from other at-risk adolescents and nurture healthy peer associations among non-drug users. In other words, your discussions can include the implication of your research results for the betterment of the society.

Conclusions

The conclusions section includes a few main elements: summaries, conclusions, limitations of your research, and suggestions for future research. Your conclusions begin with a succinct and clear summary of the main findings of your study. Then discuss the implication of your findings for the broader literature on the topic and explain in what way your study contributes to our understanding of this issue. If you conducted an exploratory or qualitative research, develop your theory about the issue you have studied. When you draw conclusions about a social problem or issue of societal concerns, you can make practical or policy suggestions for the betterment of society.

No research is without flaws. Acknowledge weaknesses and limitations of your research; not only is this honest, but also it helps the readers to understand the contexts and conditions under which your conclusions should be interpreted. In addition, point out what future research is needed or what direction future researchers should take. For example, if you used a questionnaire survey to collect data for your research but your sample is not as representative as it should be, point out sample limitations and advise your readers to be cautious when generalizing your research findings to a larger population. If your research has overlooked an important aspect of the issue you studied, you should also acknowledge that.

References

At the end of your paper, you need a complete reference list that includes all the works you cited in the text of your paper, including journal papers, books, and your professors' lectures. Frequently, students ask us how many references they need in the reference list. In fact, how many references you include in your reference list depends on how many you have cited in your report. Whatever you cited in the text of your paper needs to be listed in your references. On the other hand, you should not include any reference which you have not cited in your paper. In other words, the sources that you cited in your text should match the references you listed in your reference list.

Your reference list should be in an appropriate format and the format should be consistent (see Chapter 4 Literature Review, for information about formatting your reference list). In the social sciences, there are several popular formats for referencing and citing; whichever format you use, you should use it consistently. You could use the *Publishing Manual of the American Psychological Association* (6th edition, 2009), for example. It is the reference book for the American Psychological Association's frequently used style, also known as APA style.

How to Write a Report for Qualitative Research

The format and style of a research report based on qualitative research are less well established than the outlines for quantitative research. In fact, there is no fixed structure for a qualitative field research report (Neuman 2011). Qualitative research papers follow a similar format as above in the first few sections, including Introduction, Literature Reviews, and Research Methods. The presentation of findings and results, however, may vary. Qualitative reports typically do not have the Findings and Discussions sections, but, instead, they may have sections based on themes and theoretical claims. Below, we discuss styles and formats of three type of qualitative research: interview-based studies, historical research, and comparative research.

Papers Based on Qualitative Field Research

For a paper based on qualitative field research methods such as in-depth interviews, observations, or focus groups, the overall outlines for the report could be similar to that of a quantitative research project described above. However, there are a few differences to which you may want to pay attention. The title, the abstract, the introduction and the literature reviews can follow the guidelines discussed in the previous section.

Just as you do in quantitative papers, you need to describe your research methods, but there are more details which you would want to include if you conducted a qualitative study. A description of the population and the sampling methods or recruitment procedures are standard items included in the methods section. Qualitative studies are likely to rely on small non-probability samples (such as snowball or availability sampling). If yours is a non-probability sample, especially an availability sample, you need to discuss what efforts you made to obtain a heterogeneous sample, a sample of participants with diverse social characteristics. Limitations of the sample should be acknowledged so that the readers will understand your findings with caution.

Ethical concerns are critical in qualitative data collection, for interviews and observations are usually not anonymous. Participant observations, especially those done without disclosing your identity as a researcher, can involve many ethical problems. Your methods section should report how you have resolved any ethical dilemmas. We highly recommend that you include a clear description of how you obtained informed consent from the participants in qualitative papers. In addition, specify your data collection methods and explain how you recorded and transcribed the data – i.e., whether you tape-recorded the interviews and focus groups, how often you took field notes, what you included in the notes, and so on. Qualitative research may require you to have used some creative ways to collect data, as there is no cookie-cutter formula for qualitative field research. Thus, you need to include enough details of your specific research methods so that others can understand the validity of your research methods.

The golden rule is to give enough information for someone else to be able to replicate your study.

For a qualitative field research report, you may have to write in the first person "I" in many circumstances. For example, when describing how you entered the field, how you talked to people, how you observed things occurring around you, and how you collected data, it is perfectly all right to write in the first person.

Coding procedures should be explained. Describe the technique you used to analyze the qualitative data and your coding schemes in the methods section. You might have used an inductive coding process (such as grounded theory) in your analysis, or used a pre-made coding scheme based on previous studies. While qualitative analyses can be creative and flexible, you still need to demonstrate how you conducted the analysis *systematically* to draw conclusions from your qualitative data.

The sections in which you report your results may be organized differently from one paper to another. The most common way of organizing is to use thematic categories. You may use the broadest categories of themes you found in your data as subheadings, and show how those themes manifested in your data. Quotes from interviews or other text data are most frequently used as evidence to support the themes or the claims you are making. Content analysis of visual data (e.g., photographs and drawings) may include images as illustrations. Even descriptions of what you actually observed, i.e., people's facial expressions, gestures, or actions, and stories you collected can also serve as supportive data for your theoretical claims. When you write qualitative research reports, focus on the information that answers your research questions.

Another way of organizing the analysis section is by the research questions you had set out to answer. In addition, if you had structured interviews, you may choose to summarize your findings according to your pre-determined interview questions. If appropriate, it is okay to quantify your findings and report them accordingly. For example, if you found images of inter-personal violence in 89% of adult video games, you may report this percentage in your findings section and describe even in greater detail the typology of violent images. This is more frequently done in content analysis than other forms of qualitative research. You may also use tables, create figures, or draw diagrams to illustrate the concepts, themes, and their inter-connections, as illustrated in Chapter 10.

What you should avoid is to present simply juxtaposed narratives by different participants. In other words, your findings from qualitative research should not be a list of parallel statements (i.e., Person A said this and Person B said that, etc.). Keep in mind that the findings of qualitative analysis are syntheses of the data collected. Thus, your findings section should report what the overall trends are across the participants, and how the collected narratives and observations as a whole answered your research questions. We recommend organization by themes, by theoretical claims, or by research questions when writing the results section of qualitative research reports.

After the section on the results, the conclusions, reference list, and appendices can be prepared in ways similar to what we described in the previous section on quantitative reports.

Historical Research

For a historical research report, include a title, an abstract, and an introduction that briefly describes the method and data used for your research. Then, the major body of your writing should be a well-organized description of a chronological development of what you selected to study, such as the development of non-governmental groups, a political party, a historical event, or the change of a policy over a period of time. The information/data about the historical development were probably obtained from your reading of books, archival records, documents, or academic research papers. In writing such a paper, you should have a clearly defined theme, well thought out research questions, and an appropriate structure. As you describe the historical development of an organization or policy, you may also analyze, synthesize, and summarize your findings. Simple factual descriptions (i.e., A and B happened, or person A did this) would not qualify as a good research paper; there should be a thematic focus beyond the factual data (e.g., why A and B happened, or why A and B are common in the histories of similar groups). For example, consider Michel Foucault's famous work on the prison system in *Discipline and Punish: The Birth of the Prison (Surveiller et Punir: Naissance de la Prison.* 1975). While he used historical data on the development of the penal system, the aim of his analysis was to develop a theory of power and control, not factual report of the methods of punishment and correction.

Of course, it is not easy to maintain a balance between details and focus, as historical data include complex events and contexts. It may be also difficult to determine which of the many external factors should be considered as relevant to your focus. For example, a topic such as the development of public schools for girls in the United States would involve consideration of many related external factors including the women's movement, class division, tax debates, and development of social service organizations. Depending on what your theoretical focus is in this example (e.g., education for women, debates on tax-supported schools, or the role of charity in the development of education), you should draw the line on the external contexts you want to include and exclude in your final analysis. That means, your analysis should always center on your theoretical focus when you write the report of your historical research.

A report on historical research may identify a few major causes and consequences of the organization or policy studied over a period of time. Such causes and consequences may also have implications or applications which you may want to apply to current situations. Such a discussion would be appropriate for your Conclusions section. At the end of your report, you need to provide a complete reference list.

Comparative Research

A comparative study could be between groups of people, between organizations, or between societies or cultures. Comparative studies can utilize quantitative methods or use secondary data collected by governments or large research institutes. If this is the case, you will follow the standard format of a quantitative research report described above.

A comparative study can be based on qualitative research, too. Although you may make comparisons between several groups, comparisons between two groups might be more manageable for your research project or for your thesis if you have limited time and resources. Your report for comparative research should focus on the same comparable variables. For example, if you compare how a police department developed in two cities, your comparison should always focus on the developments of the police departments. If you compare how political structure, religion, women's status, and education affect economic development in two countries, your comparison should always focus on these variables.

Usually, comparative research focuses on the similarities and differences between the two organizations or groups which you compare. Such comparisons should be done and written systematically. You should systematically describe in what aspects they are similar and in what aspects they are different. When writing a report for comparative research, use numbers, tables, diagrams, or charts to demonstrate either the similarities or differences between the two organizations or two societies that you made comparisons.

In making comparisons, make appropriate comparisons between the two organizations or societies. Similarly, when you write your report, report on those similarities and differences between the two organizations or societies that you compared. After you systematically write your comparisons, report your analysis, summaries, discussions and conclusions.

A Final Check

After you have completed writing your final report or thesis, have a final check before you submit it. Here are some practical suggestions:

1   Never submit your final report immediately after you completed your writing. You should put the completed paper aside at least for a few days. Then, you may reread and revise your final report. In this way, you may be able to recognize the errors or mistakes that you made and make necessary changes or revisions. Generally speaking, when you are writing your final report, everything may sound correct and clear to you. When you leave your completed paper aside for a few days and come back to read it again, however, you are more likely to notice errors or unclear sentences. Another better way to find errors is to ask someone to read it. Another person is much more likely to find errors

in your paper. But more importantly, he/she will be able to view it from a reader's perspective; he/she will be able to tell whether the writing communicates the message you intended and point out unclear sentences. If this person finds unclear sentences or paragraphs, revision is necessary.

2   Editing is always necessary. When you are writing your final report, you pay attention mostly to the content of your writing. Now after you finish your draft or after you correct errors you made before, you need to read your paper again. This time, focus your attention on editing and make sure to correct any spelling errors, erroneous punctuation, incorrect citation formats, or inappropriate expressions. Today, most word processor software has helpful features that check your spelling. You cannot depend on the computer software entirely, for computer software will not alert you to a correctly spelled but inappropriately used word.

3   After your revisions and the final editing, the last thing you need to do is to check the format of your final report. Especially if you have written a Master's thesis or an honors thesis that is to be deposited in your university library, there are specific requirements for the fonts, margins, text alignment, and page numbering formats. It is necessary to make sure that your title page has all the needed information and it is in a neat and appropriate format. Your title page can make the first good or not so good impression of your paper. Similarly, your tables, charts, and citations should be in an appropriate format.

References

American Psychological Association. 2009. *Publishing Manual of the American Psychological Association.* 6th ed. Washington DC: American Psychological Association.

Foucault, Michel. 1975. *Surveiller et punir: naissance de la prison.* Paris, France: Edition Gallimard.

Neuman, W. Lawrence. 2011. *Social Research Methods: Qualitative and Quantitative Approaches.* 7th ed. Boston, MA: Allyn and Bacon.

Pyrczak and Bruce. 1998. *Writing Empirical Research Reports: A Basic Guide for Students of the Social and Behavioral Sciences* 3rd ed., Los Angeles, CA: Pyrczak Publishing.

Further Reading

Becker, Howard S. 2007. *Writing for Social Scientists: How to Start and Finish Your Thesis, Book, or Article.* 2nd ed. Chicago: University of Chicago Press.

Giarrusso, Roseann (ed.). 2008. *A Guide to Writing Sociology Papers.* New York: Worth Publishers.

Lester, James D., and James D. Lester Jr. 2014. *Writing Research Papers: A Complete Guide.* 15th ed. Upper Saddle River, NJ: Pearson-Longman.

Orcher, Lawrence T. 2005. *Conducting Research: Social and Behavioral Science Methods.* Glendale, CA: Pyrczak Publishing.

Sword, Helen. 2012. *Stylish Academic Writing.* Boston, MA: Harvard University Press.

Internet Resources

Online Writing Lab (OWL) at Purdue University. Guides on Research Papers. https://owl.english .purdue.edu/owl/resource/658/01/

Quick Tips for ASA Style. American Sociological Association. http://www.asanet.org/documents/ teaching/pdfs/Quick_Tips_for_ASA_Style.pdf

The Chicago Manual of Style Online. http://www .chicagomanualofstyle.org/home.html

Exercises for Chapter 11

Use Exercise 11.1 to lay out an outline for your final report. Once you complete your final report, evaluate whether your report is sufficient and effective; Exercise 11.2 will help you review each section of your final report.

Exercise 11.1 Writing outlines

Before you start writing your final research paper, you should write an outline first:

1   Title

2   Abstract

3   Introduction

4   Literature Review

5   Research Methods

6 Findings

7 Discussion (for report of quantitative research)

8 Conclusions

9 References

Exercise 11.2 Final Report Self-Check Rubric

Sections of the Final Report	Good (Check mark)	Need More Work (Make a short note of what you need to do)
Title: Is my title direct, descriptive, and concise? Does it capture the contents of my report? Does my title page have all required items?		
Abstract: Does my abstract clearly summarize my topic, research questions, my sample, methods of data collection, and the significance of my study? Is it within the required word count?		
Introduction: Does my introduction include all the elements necessary in an introduction (i.e., a clearly stated research purpose, sufficient background information, significance of the research)?		

(continued)

Sections of the Final Report	Good (Check mark)	Need More Work (Make a short note of what you need to do)
Literature Review: Does my literature review include classic studies on the topic, updated literature, and relevant theories? Is my literature review well-organized and well-structured? Does it present my research questions or hypotheses?		
Methods: Does the methods section include sufficient descriptions of the sample, the measures, data collection methods, and data analysis strategies I used? Does it include demographic characteristics of my sample?		
Findings: *For quantitative research:* Does the section provide all necessary statistics to inform the readers about my findings? Do my findings address all of my research questions or hypotheses? *For qualitative research:* Does the section provide all necessary information that responds to my research questions, or has it summarized my findings? Have I supported my claims with evidence from the data?		
Discussion: What answers do my findings provide to the research questions? Did I make connections between my findings and existing studies and theories? Have I clarified how my findings fill gaps in the existing literature? Have I examined the social and policy implications of my findings (if applicable)?		
Conclusions: Are the summaries succinct and effective? Have I explicitly stated how my study contributes to the field? Have I listed the limitations of my study and suggested future research directions for the readers?		

(continued)

References: Is my reference list complete, and does it conform to an appropriate format? Does the list include all of the studies I cited in the report, and only the ones cited in the report?		
Visual Presentation of the Data (if applicable): Are my charts, tables, diagrams, or figures accurate and effective? Are all tables and figures numbered and have titles?		
Proofreading: Is my report free of spelling and grammatical errors? Does it conform to the formatting requirements for the report?		

Your Project Outcome after Chapter 11

At this point:

- You have a full report including all of the sections described in this chapter.
- You have obtained feedback from your project supervisor or your committee on the complete draft of your final report.
- You have incorporated the feedback from your project supervisor or your committee, and revised the final report accordingly.
- You have thoroughly proofread your completed report, and configured it according to the format requirements for your assignment.
- You are ready to submit your final report.

Index

Student Research and Report Writing: From Topic Selection to the Complete Paper, First Edition. Gabe T.
Wang and Keumjae Park. © and Published 2016 by John Wiley & Sons, Ltd.